Herder and the Poetics of Thought

Herder and the Poetics of Thought

Unity and Diversity in
On Diligence in Several Learned Languages

Michael Morton

The Pennsylvania State University Press
University Park and London

Library of Congress Cataloging-in-Publication Data

Morton, Michael.
  Herder and the poetics of thought : unity and diversity in On diligence in several learned languages / Michael Morton.

          p.   cm.
  Includes Über den Fleiss in mehreren gelehrten Sprachen.
  Bibliography: p.
  Includes index.
  ISBN 0-271-00663-3
  1. Herder, Johann Gottfried, 1744–1803—Philosophy. 2. Herder, Johann Gottfried, 1744–1803—Style. 3. Herder, Johann Gottfried, 1744–1803. Über den Fleiss in mehreren gelehrten Sprachen.
  I. Title.
  PT2354.M65   1989
  838'.609—dc19   88–7697
                                                                   CIP

For Frank Ryder,
and for Danny

The living substance is, further, that being . . . which is in truth actual only insofar as it is the movement of positing itself, or the mediation between a self and its development into something different. . . . only this sameness which reconstitutes itself, or the reflection into itself in being different—not an original unity as such, or an immediate unity as such—is the true. The true is its own becoming, the circle that presupposes its end as its aim and thus has it for a beginning—that which is actual only through its execution and end.

Hegel, Preface to the *Phenomenology of Mind*[1]

Haec omnia inde esse in quibusdam vera, unde in quibusdam falsa sunt . . .

Augustine, *Soliloquies*[2]

πόλλ᾽ οἶδ᾽ ἀλώπηξ,
ἀλλ᾽ ἐχῖνος ἓν μέγα
Archilochos[3]

Contents

Preface

Over the years that it has taken to complete this study, I have bene-
fited in ways too numerous to mention individually from the comments, advice, and support of teachers, colleagues, and friends. I
would like to thank, in particular, Frank Ryder, to whom, along with
my son, the book is dedicated, and to whom, as my dissertation ad-
visor at the University of Virginia, it primarily owes its existence;
Walter Sokel, Benjamin Bennett, David Miles, and Cora Diamond,
who were, along with Professor Ryder, its first readers and critics;
Wulf Koepke, Christoph Schweitzer, and Alice Kuzniar, who gener-
ously gave of their time to read, evaluate, and offer suggestions for
the improvement of later drafts of the manuscript; the members of
the German Department of Harvard University, in particular Karl
Guthke, Dorrit Cohn, Maria Tatar, and Gail Finney, all of whom pa-
tiently endured a lengthy presentation of part of the manuscript and
still found it possible to offer both words of encouragement and some
very constructive advice; and (only chronologically last) my colleagues at Duke University, James Rolleston, Frank Borchardt, Tilo
Alt, Peter Burian, Annabel Wharton, and Herbert Bernstein, in conversations with whom (as well as the occasional—occasionally even
vigorous—disagreement) many of the ideas expressed here were
honed.

A special debt of gratitude is owed to Philip Winsor of the Pennsylvania State University Press, without whose confidence in the
worth of this project it might never have seen the light of day.

Work on this study was supported at different times by very gen-
erous grants from the *Deutscher Akademischer Austauschdienst*, the

program of Mellon Faculty Fellowships in the Humanities at Harvard University, and the American Council of Learned Societies. My thanks to these organizations and to the individuals (many of them unknown to me) who made the actual decisions to extend support.

Many thanks, finally, to Norma Dockery and Teresa Smith, who typed the manuscript in its final form.

Introduction

I

The last ten years have witnessed a considerable renewal of interest in the philosopher and critic Johann Gottfried Herder. Part of an increasingly active engagement with the eighteenth century generally, based in turn on a growing recognition that it is to this period that we need to look if we wish to get at the foundations of the characteristic thought and sensibility of modernity, this new attention to Herder has already done much to reclaim him for contemporary discussions in a number of different fields, from literary theory to philosophy of language, from psychology to philosophy of history, from aesthetics to cultural anthropology, and the list could go on. This is entirely in keeping with the extraordinary range of Herder's interests and with the significance of the contributions he was able to make in such a large number of areas.

Yet it is also, ironically enough, this very protean quality of his genius that, at least until relatively recently, has probably done as much as anything else to block the emergence of a more widespread and informed appreciation, not simply of his importance in a general sense, but of what precisely that importance consists in. Patrick Gardiner notes:

> The great variety of [Herder's] interests—psychological, historical, aesthetic, linguistic, religious, and philosophical—and the originality he displays in his exploration of these diverse fields make him a figure of outstanding interest and significance. At the same time, the very complexity of his achievement renders it difficult to summarize. He cannot be said to

have produced an over-all "system" in the classical manner, nor can his numerous and influential contributions to thought and speculation be appropriately represented as interrelated elements in a single grand design.[1]

The same cast of mind, with the same concomitant danger that it represented for his place in history, had already been noted in 1804, a year after his death, by Herder's younger friend Jean Paul:

> This noble spirit was misunderstood and misjudged from opposite sides and by parties themselves opposed, but not entirely without his own fault. For he had the defect of being not a star of the first or otherwise special magnitude, but rather a group of stars, in which everyone then finds whatever constellation he pleases. . . . Men of many-sided abilities will always be misjudged; those of only one sort, rarely. The former have an effect on all people, those who are like them as well as those who are not; the latter affect only their own kind.[2]

Herder was to assume—indeed, in the last years of his life had already begun to assume—the somewhat singular position in the history of thought that, with relatively few exceptions, has tended to be his lot since: on the one hand, a figure of whom almost everyone has at one time or another heard something—his is easily one of the half-dozen or so best-known names from the eighteenth century in Germany—and on the other hand, a thinker of whose actual writings far fewer have read more than a very little (if anything at all). Hans-Georg Gadamer's assertion of more than forty-five years ago, that of the "greats" of German literature Herder is the only one who is no longer read,[3] though doubtless at least somewhat exaggerated, nonetheless contains, now as then, a fundamental kernel of truth.

Alexander Gillies's explanation of this, on its face, at least slightly paradoxical state of affairs recalls to some extent Jean Paul. "It was Herder's tragedy," he says,

> that the literary movement he set on foot developed in its own way and not in his. He was not born to command, but to inspire and to suggest. . . . His thoughts, lavished in all directions, so original and so stimulating, quickly became the whole world's property; to their author was left only the mortifying spectacle of watching others take possession of the kingdom to

which he had pointed the way, and seeing them rule it in a manner that was not his.[4]

And thus, while "there is [today] hardly a branch of human culture which is not indebted to him, directly or indirectly, . . . few are aware of their ultimate obligation."[5]

Fritz Martini, while echoing Gillies's overall assessment (in part, almost word for word), also adds one further, and pivotally important, clue to an understanding of why the history of the Herder-reception has unfolded as it has:

> . . . he dispensed a lavish abundance of ideas in all directions. He was the greatest inspirer and stimulator in German intellectual history, someone whose influence extended far beyond the borders of the German language. *He nevertheless did not succeed in producing what would have been his definitive work.* However deeply his thought has impressed itself on modern European intellectual life, *none of his books has remained a living, effective part of the canon.* It was his tragedy that others were to impart the shape and direction to what had been his thought and intuition.[6] (emphasis added)

The passages that I have singled out for emphasis here give explicit and concrete expression to the point made in slightly different ways by both Gardiner and Jean Paul. Unlike the overwhelming majority of the other most important and influential thinkers in the tradition, there has never been in the case of Herder a single work (or, if not that, at least a manageably small set of works) that has acquired what might be called epitomal status—no *Critique of Pure Reason,* no Preface to the *Phenomenology of Mind,* no *Beyond Good and Evil* or *Being and Time*—no work, in short, that, like each of these (as well as many others we could name), while it does not exhaust the thought of its author, might nonetheless be taken to *epitomize* it, in the sense that a grasp of that work is understood to be both a necessary and virtually a sufficient condition for grasping the entire body of thought. One reason—perhaps the major reason—that Herder has tended not to be read, his formidable reputation and the universally acknowledged extent of his influence notwithstanding, is, in other words, the deceptively simple one that with him it has historically not been at all obvious where one is to begin.

In my way of formulating the issue of what I am calling an epitomal

work in the case of Herder (or, for that matter, generally), the reader
will perhaps have detected what seems to be a bit of waffling. Do I
mean that there is in fact no such work in the corpus of Herder's
writings, or only that, for whatever reason, none has ever come to be
so regarded? And, if the latter, do I mean to imply that that is a
failure of perception (and thus that if we were to search harder we
would in fact find the work in question where it has been all along,
merely overlooked) or rather one of imagination (and hence that,
given the requisite interpretive energy, such a work could in a literal
sense be brought into being by our own determination to read Herder
in a certain way)? Or do I have in mind a more pragmatic understanding of the notion, to the effect that there has simply never been a
sufficiently large and respected group of readers of Herder inclined
to view any one of his works (and thus, by extension, the body of his
writings at large) in the terms implied by the concept of an epitomal
text? My reason for putting the matter in such a way as to invite
these questions is precisely so as to avoid having to commit myself,
whether explicitly or only by implication, to a definite answer to any
of them. That is, however, not the intellectual cowardice it may initially appear to be, but rather what I hope is a judicious way of accommodating my discussion to the current state of critical theory.
There are some very large issues involved in these questions, issues
that are at the heart of contemporary debates regarding the ontological status of texts and our reception of them. Those debates, in turn,
have fundamental implications for theory of knowledge generally.
These are, however, also—the point of immediate relevance in the
present connection—debates the terms of whose eventual outcomes
are not even remotely in view yet.

   We are still very far from possessing a satisfactory theory of knowledge, chiefly, I believe, because we still understand far too little
about language. An awareness of that fundamental linkage is, not
incidentally, among the most important aspects precisely of the Herderian legacy, and it is a mark of how much further we have to go in
this regard that much of the contemporary discussion of these matters
seems to proceed in what amounts to a pre-Herderian environment.
Not in the sense, of course, that anyone still needs to be alerted to
the ultimate inseparability of epistemological and linguistic concerns
itself; that much has been for some time now virtually a critical com-
monplace. There is, however, very frequently encountered today, in
one form or another, the position that one must either adopt a view
of the world that regards reality as existing independently of and

apart from our perception of it, or, on the other hand, acknowledge that all our apparent judgments of fact are actually only interpretations, deriving from some context, some perspective, or some set of interests in particular, and thus at best relatively (as opposed to objectively) true. That way of posing the alternatives, however (as well as the suggestion that there is no third possibility), is pre-critical through and through. It reenacts in slightly different terms the eighteenth-century opposition between rationalist (or, as Kant termed it, dogmatic) metaphysics and empiricist skepticism, and so locates itself prior to the critical revolution in philosophy undertaken, as we shall see, not only by Kant but, even before him, by Herder himself.

The history of thought testifies to the perennial character of certain issues. The opposition of rationalism and empiricism, which is addressed in their different ways by Kant and Herder, recurs at the turn of the nineteenth to the twentieth century in the clash between, on the one hand, various forms of materialism or positivism broadly construed, and, on the other, the nominalist and sensationalist assaults on such views by Mauthner and Mach. This opposition as well evokes a "critical" response, in the form of Wittgenstein's *Tractatus* (about which there will be more to say in chapters 2 and 4). And so it will in time also be, I am inclined to think, with the analogous opposition in the present day. Both the irreconcilability with one another and the long-run unsustainability of either a naive "metaphysics of presence" or a semantic and conceptual indeterminacy that would dissolve the world into a flux of mere "interpretations" or a play of endless semiosis will, I believe, eventually call forth something that we might envisage as a "critique of interpretive reason." This would take the form of an analysis of discourse and experience in which, once again, as earlier with Herder, Kant, and Wittgenstein, both the stability of signification and the integrity of fact would receive a philosophically adequate foundation.

Exactly how this is to be accomplished is, however, obviously a question for the future (as, of course, is the prior one of whether I am right in supposing that it will be undertaken at all). Even were I capable of carrying out such an analysis myself, this would in any case not be the place for it. Fortunately, however, neither is that necessary. This brief excursus onto the terrain of contemporary theory was prompted by some questions that arose in conjunction with my introduction of the notion of an "epitomal work" and the suggestion of its possible applicability to Herder in particular. In the following chapters, I will discuss one text, the essay *On Diligence in Several Learned Languages* (*Über den Fleiß in mehreren gelehrten Sprachen*), *as if it were,* in at least a number of respects, for him that "epitomal work," in the sense of being both thematically and formally a decisively important key to the character of his thought at large. On the further, and philosophically more fundamental, questions that proceeding in this way ineluctably raises regarding the ultimate status of *On Diligence* in the Herderian oeuvre, I propose, for the reasons I have indicated, to take no position. As I have suggested, I do not believe that I have the answers to these questions; I do not believe that anyone today does. But I do believe that the sort of analysis that I propose to carry out here can nonetheless legitimately be undertaken while we are waiting for those answers to be found.

But, it may well be objected, why specifically *On Diligence?* Would it not make more sense to look, for example, to the *Fragments on Recent German Literature* (*Fragmente über die neuere deutsche Literatur*) or to the *Ideas on the Philosophy of the History of Mankind* (*Ideen zur Philosophie der Geschichte der Menschheit*)? It is true that we tend to think of Herder's career as beginning with his epoch-making collections of *Fragments* in 1766 and 1767; and the *Fragments* are, to be sure, the first work of substantial length that he produces. Almost at a stroke they propel him to the front rank in the increasingly animated discussion of fundamental questions of poetics and aesthetics in Germany in the 1760s. In particular, their reception by younger authors establishes him as a leader of the generation whose writings in the 1770s and 1780s initiate a revolution in German literature, the effects of which continue to be felt throughout Western literature at large to this day. And, if the *Fragments* mark the effective beginning of Herder's career, the *Ideas* have regularly been viewed as its summit, the magnum opus providing a nearly comprehensive statement of his mature views. Their four completed parts appear between 1784 and 1791, with plans and sketches for the unfinished part five, projected as the conclusion of the entire massive work, continuing until 1792.

Both the *Fragments* and the *Ideas* are, however, in a number of respects less-than-ideal candidates for the sort of analysis on which I am intent here. They are both very large works, often diffuse, not to say rambling, in their exposition. They both cover an extremely wide range of topics and issues, not always distinguishing sufficiently (or at all) between what is of genuine and lasting importance and what is either of merely local and transitory interest or downright insignificant. Despite their size, both remained uncompleted (something generally true of Herder's larger projects). And then there is the matter of the language, for which he has become notorious. Gillies maintains, "Few have suffered so much from the lack of sustained clarity and precision in their writing . . ."[7] In sum, the *Fragments* and the *Ideas,* their enormous (and widely acknowledged) importance notwithstanding, exhibit precisely those features that have led to the state of affairs to which I referred in speaking of the absence of an "epitomal work" in the Herderian corpus, a work, again, that is *itself* read as the standard vehicle by which one both acquires an initial familiarity and begins a productive engagement with the thought of its author. Faced with either the *Fragments* or the *Ideas* in their entirety—and much the same could be said of a number of others among Herder's better-known and more influential works, from the *Critical Forests (Kritische Wälder)* to the *Letters for the Advancement of Humanity (Briefe zu Beförderung der Humanität)*—the temptation to rely on the summaries, paraphrases, and commentaries of specialists becomes (understandably) well-nigh irresistible.

Yet that comparative ease of access is bought at a steep price. Two things in particular that tend to be lost thereby are a sense for the way in which Herder could (as he indeed could) devote an entire text to the construction of a single, cohesive argument, and, closely linked to this, a feel for his distinctive rhetorical idiom, with its interweaving of philosophical and poetic strains. There are, however, a good many of his works—all too often, unfortunately, among his lesser known ones—that exhibit both these qualities in striking fashion, and to my mind none more so than the early piece *On Diligence.* Inasmuch as this is, indeed, with the exception of some poems (including an ode in praise of the Russian Czar Peter III[8]), his first published work, in a certain sense it solves the problem of where to begin reading him in the most obvious way possible. It is equally obvious, however, that that consideration by itself would not warrant the attention I propose to give the essay. Such a justification must come from the text itself— both what it *says* and what it actually *does*—not merely from where it happens to fall in the series of his writings.

I believe that that justification is in fact to be found there and that in light of it the position that the piece occupies among Herder's works need not be viewed as merely fortuitous. In taking *On Diligence* as a kind of test case for what I refer to above as his distinctive rhetorical idiom, and in thus attempting to show as comprehensively as possible the structure of a given one of his texts and how that structure functions, I also want to indicate at least some of the extent to which his subsequent work grows out of this one essay. In the terms of one of his favorite images, I want to suggest that *On Diligence* can be seen as the "seed" in which the "organism" of his thought is already largely present in virtual form. Indeed, commentators have from the beginning noted the considerable degree to which the young Herder prefigures all that follows in his career. Recalling their time together in Straßburg in 1770–71, Goethe, for example, notes in his autobiography, "With regard to the fullness of the few weeks that we lived together, I can certainly say that everything that Herder was afterward to work out in gradual stages was already indicated in germinal form. . . ."[9]

The manuscript of the original version of *On Diligence* appears in one of the notebooks, or *Studienhefte,* from his time as a student in Königsberg under the heading *To determine the limits of the diligence that we ought to dedicate to our native language and to learned languages (Die Grenzen des Fleißes zu bestimmen, den wir der Muttersprache und gelehrten Sprachen widmen sollen).* According to Haym, it was composed as a speech and delivered at Easter in 1764 on the occasion of an academic exercise at the Collegium Fridericianum, the school in Königsberg where, at the same time that he pursued his own studies at the university, he was active as a member of the faculty.[10] Gaier, on the other hand, says that he did not present the speech until later in the year, after he had assumed his position at the Cathedral School in Riga.[11] The problem with this view, of course, is that, as Clark points out, Herder did not arrive in Riga until December.[12] In the meantime, however, he had significantly revised the essay and published it in the *Gelehrte Beiträge zu den Rigischen Anzeigen* of October 1764 (Jg. 4, Stück 24, pp. 185–90) under the now definitive title *Über den Fleiß in mehreren gelehrten Sprachen.* It thus becomes difficult to see why he would have delivered an earlier (and, by his own implicit admission, inferior) version of the piece after arriving in Riga. (He could, of course, have presented the later, published version in Riga, but, if so, that would then simply be one more reason to question Gaier's judgment in choosing the first version of the text for his edition of Herder's early writings.[13]) Herder's son Emil included the earlier version in his *Lebensbild* of 1846 under the title *On the Relationship of the Study of Foreign Languages to that of the Native Language (Über das Verhältnis des Studiums der fremden Sprachen zu dem der Muttersprache).*[14] This version also appears, with minor changes in the text but under the title of the published version, at a very late point in the standard Suphan edition of Herder's works.[15] The published version itself, however, which is the one I use here, appears (as I have suggested, appropriately enough) as the first piece in volume one of the Suphan edition.[16]

Although there is in the literature nothing apart from the present study that treats *On Diligence* in its entirety, it is interesting to note some of the connections in which scholars have mentioned or alluded to the essay in the course of their discussions.

Alexander Gillies agrees that "the seeds of [Herder's] later achievement are . . . to be found in his first works,"[17] noting further, "[i]n these early years he . . . conceived the programme of his whole life's work, so that there is scarcely a point of major importance that is not foreshadowed in some way."[18] Gillies does not, however, undertake to trace that foreshadowing to *On Diligence*. He refers to it by name only once, in the context of a discussion dealing with the antecedents of the ideas developed in the *Fragments:*

> Herder saw . . . that literature had a cultural function, and in a short essay, 'Über den Fleiß in mehreren gelehrten Sprachen' (1764), had already raised his voice in favour of literary patriotism, calling for a more balanced attitude in regard to the imitation of other countries, so that the national stock and national originality should be strengthened and not impaired as had hitherto been the case.[19]

Several pages later, Gillies cites a passage from the *Fragments* in which Herder speaks to the question of the proper relationship between native and foreign languages (I, 401). He points to the link between this passage and a corresponding one from *On Diligence* (I, 6; see appendix, 11. 164–72), which he does not, however, identify by name, referring to it simply as Herder's "earliest piece of criticism in 1764."[20] Nor does he note that Herder continues the passage from the *Fragments* to which he calls attention here with lines taken nearly verbatim from the conclusion of *On Diligence*.

On the other hand, his study includes a number of implicit echoes of the early essay, both in the form of passages cited from later works and in his own commentary on these. For example, in his discussion of the *Ideas* he notes that for Herder:

> The whole world is thus a school in which each must learn and cultivate that *Humanität* which is inherent, in embryo, within

> him. . . . The vehicle of education is tradition—the accumu-
> lated and transmitted experience of the race—which is
> brought into contact with the innate powers of the learner.[21]

Precisely the same dialectic of tradition and individual creativity toward the goal of realization of the ideal of humanity is, as we shall
see, already at the heart of the argument of *On Diligence*.

As suggested earlier, however, in the face of Herder's poetically
and rhetorically charged prose style, Gillies simply comes to a halt:

> No major writer was hampered by so unsatisfying a style as
> Herder. He never wrote with precision. He was repetitive, ad-
> monitory, ejaculatory. He indulged in picturesque, telling,
> even extravagant metaphors, but was lacking in adroitness. . . .
> He knew what he wanted to say and that it needed to be said.
> Yet he could not achieve a balanced and coherent form in
> which to say it. Even his syntax breaks down at times. In the
> excitement of his earlier works, anger, bitterness, sarcasm, re-
> proach, exhortation are communicated in the abruptest and
> most confusing manner.[22]

While it may be true that some of Herder's writing fits this description
(or part of it at any rate), it is by no means the case that all of it does.
More troubling in Gillies's indictment, however, is his reluctance to
ask what purpose Herder may have had in writing as he does, even
there, where what results may at first appear to represent merely an
inability to express himself in cogent fashion. To assume, however,
that "precision" is incompatible with, for example, a style that is "re-
petitive, admonitory, [and] ejaculatory" or one characterized by striking metaphors or one that sometimes departs from standard syntax,
is both to construe precision too narrowly and, more important yet,
to measure Herder by the standards of a sort of writing he does not
seek to emulate.

Gillies notes that Herder "was at his best when delivering his message orally, from the pulpit or in conversation,"[23] but does not follow
this up by showing how he seeks to realize the strengths of oral discourse within the framework of written prose. The same "forcefulness
and boldness, the irregularity and figurativeness"[24] that, as Gillies
points out, he finds in the poetic language of early man, or "the boldness and abruptness, the vividness and figurativeness"[25] that are for
him the hallmarks of Ossian, Shakespeare, and Percy's *Reliques*—

these are at once qualities that he is intent on reviving in the literature of his own age and—of critical importance to the attainment of that end—characteristics that he imparts to his own language as a matter of conscious intention. In the first of the *Critical Forests*, as Gillies notes, he identifies the essence of poetry as "energy" (*Energie*), manifested in the poet's linguistic self-expression and the effect of that "power" (*Kraft*) on the "imagination" (*Phantasie*) of the reader or hearer, its "effect on our soul" (III, 157). Precisely this, as the analysis of *On Diligence* will show in detail, is what he seeks to accomplish in his own works, which accordingly, far from being pieces in which "feeling and imagination ran ahead of expression,"[26] display a carefully constructed alignment of expressive form with the specific intellectual and emotional content they are designed to convey. Just as his conception of poetry replaces the traditional Horatian formulation of the possible ends of literature—*aut prodesse aut delectare*—with what will subsequently become, at least for a time, the primary category of *movere*, so he is intent on realizing something analogous to this in his own works of theory and criticism.

Edgar Schick's study of the relationship between Herder's language and his thought also contains a single reference to *On Diligence*. He begins his examination of Herder's "metaphorical organicism" by noting "the symbolization, in his essay *Ueber den Fleiß in mehreren gelehrten Sprachen* (1764), of language as a plant which undergoes natural metamorphoses in the various soils and climates which nourish it."[27] He mentions the essay's "brief sketch of linguistic variation and mutation in different historical periods and geographical regions," and remarks that "already at the age of twenty" Herder "concludes his introduction to his topic, significantly enough, with a vivid 'sinnlich' synthetic vegetable metaphor rather than with analytic deduction . . . : 'So verwandelte sich diese Pflanze nach dem Boden, der sie nährte, und der Himmelsluft, die sie tränkte . . .'"[28] Thus it can be seen that "at the very outset of his literary career, Herder relies on organistic imagery to give emphasis to his exposition, . . . strik(ing) tones of 'organic belonging' to time and place and also of natural, organic growth and flux which will become . . . such a prominent element in his thought."[29] There is, to my mind, no question that this way of reading Herder represents a distinct advance over Gillies's approach. At the same time, however, there is at least some reason to question whether Schick has fully appreciated the implications of the tendency in Herder's writing to which he points. The disjunction between "metaphor" and "analytic deduction" implicit in the phrase "rather than," as well as the characterization of the role of imagery in Herder as merely "to give emphasis" to the exposition, together suggest a still incomplete understanding of the actual relationship between poetic and discursive language in his work.

Schick does say that, in dealing with Herder, "'content' and 'form' usually cannot be fruitfully separated,"[30] and he acknowledges the correctness of Eric Blackall's observation in his seminal article on Herder's language that the poetic quality of his prose is not adventitious, but rather reflects conscious intention and is achieved only as a result of close attention to fine points of composition.[31] He further characterizes Herder as a "*poetic* thinker,"[32] and he criticizes Gillies's negative assessment of that aspect of his way of formulating his views. Referring to the image of the tree, employed in *Another Philosophy of History for the Cultivation of the Human Race (Auch eine Philosophie der Geschichte zur Bildung der Menschheit)* as part of an effort to achieve a dialectical resolution of the apparent antinomy between the ideas of cultural and individual autonomy on the one hand and development toward the realization of universal humanity on the other, Gillies had said that this was merely "a poetic device that cannot replace the logic that is not there."[33] He sees in the duality in question merely a "contradiction," adding the somewhat curious comment that "the dualism of the idea of development and the idea of the individual value of each phenomenon could not be harmonized, until Hegel achieved the solution *at the expense of history*" (emphasis added).[34] In fact, of course, both Hegel, and, as we shall see here, Herder before him, discovered a way of resolving this dilemma precisely *through* their reinterpretation of it in terms of history. To Gillies, Schick responds that "while the image of the tree is indeed poetic, it is not just a device but rather *is* the logic of Herder's exposition and fuses his ideas of the historical process into a concentrated, organized, vivid expression."[35] At the same time, however, he also, for example, cites with approval Bruno Markwardt's description of "an image . . . for Herder" as merely "a resting place (*Erholungsstätte*) for purely conceptual thought," an opportunity for the senses "to revel freely in themselves."[36] Despite the unmistakably positive elements in Schick's approach to Herder's characteristic discourse, it is nonetheless the case, as we shall also see, that agreement with a view such as Markwardt's implies an at best partial sense for the way in which the poetic elements in his writings function as themselves components of the sort of argument his works are designed to achieve.

Joe Fugate, in his study of Herder's aesthetics, also makes one reference to *On Diligence*. This comes in the context of a discussion of his view of the relationship between language and thought and is offered as evidence of the importance that from the beginning he attaches to the unique bond between human beings and their native language. The passage cited runs as follows:

> If, then, every language has its particular national character, it seems that nature lays upon me an obligation only to my native language, because it is more commensurate with my character than any other and coextensive with my distinctive way of thinking. I may perhaps be able to imitate stammeringly the language of foreign nations, without, however, ever penetrating to the core of its uniqueness and beauty (XXX, 8).[37]

This represents, however, only the first stage of the argument of *On Diligence*. The position taken here is, though not abandoned, modified in decisively important respects at a later point in the essay. To cite only this passage is thus to give an incomplete picture of Herder's view of the relationship between native and foreign languages, and so also, as we shall see, to miss something fundamental in his conception of the dialectical movement toward the realization of the ideal of humanity.

In the conclusion of his study, Fugate characterizes Herder's writings as

> organic works of art in which the structuring, the development of certain ideas, the adoption of certain aspects of criticism, the choice and suggestion of examples, etc. reveal definite principles of composition and organization, an inner method of presentation which says much more than mere rational concepts could ever express.[38]

There is here, it seems to me, a genuinely sound insight into what is at work in Herder's most characteristic and innovative mode of expression. It remains necessary, however, to show in concrete detail how what Fugate describes in general terms is realized in an actual text, and to that end an analysis of *On Diligence* proves, as I have suggested, ideally suited.

Although Robert Mayo's study of Herder and the beginnings of comparative literature deals chiefly with anticipations of a certain aspect of his thought on the part of French, English, and German critics and is thus on the whole not immediately connected with the concerns of the present study, he does at one point mention *On Diligence,* and in a way that is of more than passing interest for the discussion here. Referring to the seventh and eighth collections of the *Letters for the Advancement of Humanity,* the texts on which he focuses for the purposes of his argument, he says:

> The seventh and eighth collections do indeed contain all of Herder's essential ideas about comparative literature; ideas which he had put forward in many different works from the earliest essay *Über den Fleiß in mehreren gelehrten Sprachen* (1764) onwards.[39]

Mayo has a clear sense for the essential continuity of Herder's thought throughout his career. He notes that "sometimes the contents of such important works as *Über die Wirkung der Dichtkunst* and *Von Ähnlichkeit der mittleren englischen und deutschen Dichtkunst* are repeated almost word for word"[40] in the *Letters.* Incorporation of elements from earlier texts in later works with little or no change is in fact a highly characteristic aspect of Herder's method of composition generally. We shall see several examples of it in the course of the discussion of *On Diligence* as we come to say something about its relationship to some of the later and better-known works, from the *Fragments* to the *Ideas.*

Robert Clark's large study, *Herder: His Life and Thought,* remains, after more than a generation, among the most highly regarded and frequently consulted overviews of Herder's work. As the subtitle suggests, Clark's goal is to provide a comprehensive intellectual biography of his subject. He does not, accordingly, merely mention *On Diligence* in passing but rather devotes a part of his discussion specifically to it, with the aim of at least summarizing the argument that it advances and indicating what Herder's purpose was in presenting it. I do not wish to appear unduly harsh in my assessment of this attempt. The plain fact is, however, that Clark's comments indicate that he simply has no idea of what the essay is about. His gloss of the text betrays no inkling either of the real problem that Herder confronts here or of the means by which he proposes to come to grips with it. *On Diligence* is, in his view, "merely an exercise in the use of Rationalistic style. . . . obviously a naive, formal essay, without importance for [Herder's] later thinking."[41] As Clark sees it, all that the argument of the essay comes to is, in the end, to urge that "both kinds [of language], the native and the foreign, must be studied."[42] The possibility that, in view of the relationship that Herder sees between national language and national character, as well as between forms of language and basic structures of consciousness, there might be for him something more that would have to be said here; that, indeed, the question of the relationship between native and foreign languages might have far-reaching implications for the development of both the individual and the human race at large; and that, accordingly, the way in which Herder approaches that question in *On Diligence* might be of some importance for an understanding of his work generally—these are all questions that Clark either does not address at all or simply dismisses.

He has, in particular, no use for the suggestion that there might be some significant connection between the ideas developed in *On Diligence* and those expressed in Herder's later writings. He twice notes that Haym takes precisely this position in his biography of Herder and twice himself rejects it.[43] Haym, however, like Suphan, who in the introduction to volume one of his edition speaks of *On Diligence* (along with Herder's other contributions to the *Rigische Anzeigen*) as "the first efforts in the direction of that 'human philosophy' (*menschliche Philosophie*) . . . on which, from early on, he had set his sights" (I, xvii), sees matters in what seems to me a much clearer light. Of *On Diligence* he says:

> We encounter here so many a turn of phrase that will soon recur in Herder's first larger works; there is, indeed, not a single thought here that is not taken up and developed further there. So early were certain basic views firmly established in him . . . [44]

For example, he notes:

> The chosen theme [of the essay] already points to what would form the foundation of his subsequent discussions of literature, the relationship of language and thought . . . [45]

The relationship between language and thought is, in turn, the central theme of the *Treatise on the Origin of Language (Abhandlung über den Ursprung der Sprache)* of 1770, and, as Haym notes, "in this treatise was the whole Herder."[46] As I hope to show here, what Haym sees in the *Origin of Language* can also be seen to a very large extent, if in much more condensed and latent form, in Herder's first critical essay. In *On Diligence* we have, to borrow a phrase used in another connection by Hamann, Herder *in nuce*.

(There is one other commentator in particular who has indicated a strong sense for the importance of *On Diligence* to an understanding of Herder at large. That is Hans Dietrich Irmscher, to whom I will be referring in a number of connections in the discussion of the text to follow.)

II

The immediate question that Herder addresses in *On Diligence* is one of language study: should students be instructed only in their native language, or should they learn foreign languages as well? While this is certainly a question of some moment (today no less than two centuries ago) and obviously one with respect to which many people have some strong convictions, it is nonetheless perhaps not quite the sort of question from which we would expect an essay to begin whose ramifications are as extensive and as weighty as we shall see those of *On Diligence* to be. Characteristically, however, Herder finds it impossible to pursue his subject without at once locating it in a context of larger issues pertaining to the overall nature and development both of individuals and of civilization as a whole. These include questions of the origin of language itself and of the relationship of linguistic structures to forms of thought, as well as of the function of a national language in founding a culture and shaping its history, and of the role in turn played by culture in determining at any point in its history what can (and so ought to) be accomplished by its members.

Not only does Herder's native intellectual temperament incline him to this sort of reflection; in the case at hand, the nature of the topic itself tends in the same direction. The question of proper ordering of the curriculum has implications for a general theory of education; and for Herder and his contemporaries theory of education is in turn only one aspect, though an especially crucial one, of a still larger field of issues regarding the status of human beings viewed both as individuals and as members of the several collective bodies—society, nation, culture—to which they belong. In this respect at least, Herder is very much at one with the broad tenor of his age. Questions pertaining to education function as one of the major centers of gravity for the thought of the eighteenth century generally, and nowhere is that more the case than in Germany. They are a central concern of virtually every leading thinker and artist of the period, whatever the particular field of endeavor, providing a point of orientation for intellectual and artistic efforts at the same time that the concept of education itself emerges and assumes concrete shape in the constellation of works intended as contributions to it. Such linkage of immediate and ultimate aims appears regularly in Herder's writings. It reflects one aspect of what we can call (borrowing from Schick) his metaphysical organicism. For him, there are no absolutely discrete phenomena; everything is eventually related to everything else. Thus, whatever the particular topic taken as a point of departure—and it is also characteristic of him to begin, as he does in *On Diligence,* at the level of something (apparently) quite specific and delimited—a proper consideration of it will, in the end, with a certain latent inevitability raise fundamental questions of the nature and purpose of human existence at large.

Though organically conceived, reality is for Herder nonetheless not a seamless whole, but rather a fabric manifesting at once continuity and disjunction. This aspect as well of his worldview is reflected at the level of the larger questions to which the initial concern of *On Diligence* gives rise. For it soon becomes apparent that the several answers to these questions, while each apparently necessary in its own right, cannot readily be accommodated to each other. That difficulty, moreover, far from being a problem to be resolved simply by weighing and reconciling different priorities, stems from a basic tension within the structure of human nature itself between, on the one hand, the *foundations* of our identity, necessarily specific to some nation and some culture in particular, and, on the other, the *fulfillment* of that identity in the ideal of universal humanity. It appears, that is, that the same linguistic-cultural determinants that form the *basis* of our existence threaten at the same time to impede permanently our *growth* by confining us within the intellectual and cultural limits of the one society into which we are born (and the same holds true *mutatis mutandis* for the society itself). If it is true—as for Herder it is—that human existence must always be *situated,* that in order to be anything at all a person must be something in particular, linguistically and culturally, it is in his view no less the case that human existence worthy of the name requires *development*. And development in this sense means not merely experiencing new and different things but rather extending one's *capacity* for experience beyond the structures given in one's native situation—not merely quantitative, but qualitative growth. And yet, if we take as seriously as Herder evidently means that we should the role of these givens in constituting our *identities* in the first place, it becomes difficult to see how the latter requirement, the *realization* of ourselves as properly human, can be met without doing fundamental damage to the very foundation on which that development toward self-realization has to begin, if indeed a goal thus conceived can be achieved at all.

The general problem to which this conflict points remains a central preoccupation of Herder's *menschliche Philosophie* in all the myriad forms that it assumes throughout his work. In the case at hand, how can the individual or the nation remain firmly grounded in its own native foundations (the minimally necessary condition of personal or national identity) and at the same time so extend its horizons as to absorb the thought and works of other individuals in other cultures, without which there can be no possibility of a full human existence? In the concrete terms in which he will confront the problem in *On Diligence*, how is one to reconcile, both for oneself and for one's *Volk*, the competing demands of nationality and *Weltbürgertum?* How can a person be, for example, both specifically and uniquely German and at the same time in some sense a citizen of the world, at home in all times and places wherever human beings are found? In this early piece, Herder already sounds the twin themes of *particularism* and *cosmopolitanism*, with which in a variety of forms he will wrestle all his life. We see here as well the first of several points that we shall have occasion to note on which his outlook differs in important respects from the one broadly characteristic of the Enlightenment. For him, the ultimate aims of our existence do not constitute an unproblematically harmonious totality, to be realized as the culmination of an essentially smooth and continuous process of development; rather they appear, at least as initially conceived, as deeply at odds with one another. In consequence, the realization of human potential, which, if it is to occur at all, must in some way take account of that basic element of contrariety in our very being, becomes for him a significantly more difficult matter, both conceptually and practically, than it tends to be for the *Aufklärer* among his contemporaries.[47]

Fundamentally the same problem arises, moreover, not simply at any given time but also over time. For Herder, both the characteristic strengths or virtues and the weaknesses or incapacities of an epoch, a culture, or a people are all manifestations of its distinctive finitude, its unique fulfillment of a—necessarily limited—set of possibilities out of the full, infinite range of human possibility at large. He insists on doing justice to that uniqueness, which for him means apprehending it on its own terms. One must attempt to see the distinguishing features of a culture as if one were oneself a part of it, to feel one's way into the particular form of life that it represents and experience it, as it were, from the inside out. Apart from the question of how precisely that sort of sympathetic identification is to be achieved (assuming it to be possible at all), there is the further problem—a logical as much as a pragmatic one—that apprehending a given culture in this way would appear, at least initially, to preclude regarding it at the same time from the outside in, that is, in relation to other cultures as part of the overall movement of history.

The evident difficulties in reconciling with a theory of progress, or even of development, the demand that forms of human life be apprehended as unique and autonomous, plus Herder's unmistakable and repeated insistence on the latter and his corresponding denunciations of attempts to evaluate other cultures in terms alien to them, have, taken together, led even as acute a commentator as Isaiah Berlin to conclude that in fact he had no theory of progress, or that at most it remained both inchoate and peripheral to the dominant current in his thought. This, Berlin maintains, is fundamentally pluralistic and relativistic, placing its emphasis in the end squarely on the ultimate incommensurability of different cultures.[48] Yet it is difficult to see how this conclusion can be sustained. The role played, both conceptually and structurally, by the theme of development and progress in all Herder's major works, from the *Fragments* to the *Ideas* and beyond, is surely too prominent and important not to be accounted for in its own right.

There remains nonetheless the problem of accommodating to each other points of view that, on their face, appear decidedly incompatible. Like Berlin, Arthur Lovejoy, for example, sees here only contradiction. He differs from Berlin merely in what he takes to be the alternative for which Herder in the end opts. For him, this is the "idea of cultural progress" rather than that of an irreducible relativism among individual centers of culture.[49] Later in his essay, however, Lovejoy returns again to the question, and he is this time apparently content to leave the issue undecided:

> ... there was a latent incongruity between this preaching of the wisdom and duty of being content with the characteristics of your own age and national culture, and the idea of progress. ... Herder was not, I think, very sensible of this incongruity ... [50]

In fact, as I hope at least to suggest here, there is no problem of which he was more sensible, and none to whose solution his entire career was more dedicated. Herder's situation, contemplating the manifold forms of human life, both in the present and over time, is similar to that of a physicist studying the nature of light. For certain purposes it is necessary to regard light as a wave phenomenon; for others, it is no less necessary to say that it consists of particles. Each of these perspectives appears to exclude the other, and yet the nature of the phenomenon itself is such that neither is dispensable. Herder is no less aware of the difficulties involved in his position than is the physicist, and just as the latter will not rest content with a disjoint account of a natural phenomenon but will rather bend every effort to reconcile the two descriptions with one another, so he will seek to do the same for the two moments of cultural autonomy and historical progress.

Both these dilemmas—that of particularism and cosmopolitanism, and that of autonomy and progress—are in turn simply specific manifestations of Herder's reinterpretation of a problem that stands at the beginning of Western philosophy generally, that of the One and the Many.[51] It is fair to say, indeed, that this is the master problem of his entire career. In *On Diligence,* for the first but far from the last time, he sets himself the twofold task of both *delineating* the problem, which for him means stating the opposition between the poles of the universal and the particular in the strongest terms possible, expressing the competing demands associated with them in such a way that each appears definitively to exclude the other; and yet nonetheless also finding a way to *unite* these two poles, in a synthesis, however, that does not go back on the initial formulation of the problem but rather preserves the element of opposition between them.

Though his roots are, of course, in the eighteenth century, Herder's thought is thus also linked to a much older tradition, that of the *coincidentia oppositorum*. The attempt to realize a true coincidence of opposites in the sense not merely of a harmonizing of originally opposed poles, but rather of a synthesis that both unites and yet at the same time preserves opposition, ranks among the perennial concerns of philosophers (though, obviously, not in every case under precisely that name). It engages thinkers in antiquity and the Middle Ages no less than in the eighteenth century, and it assumes, from the medieval period on, an especially prominent and important place in the German intellectual tradition. After Herder, and certainly in large part as a result of his influence, it becomes, in particular, a central element of the sensibility of Romanticism both in Germany and elsewhere.

The figure with whom the expression *coincidentia oppositorum* is probably most frequently associated is the fifteenth-century philosopher and theologian Nicholas of Cusa.[52] For the initial source of the idea (and ideal) of a coincidence of opposites, at least in Western thought, however, we need to look to the writings of the pre-Socratic Ionian philosopher Heraclitus.[53] Though neither Charles Kahn, in his commentary on Heraclitus's fragments, nor M. F. Burnyeat, in his deservedly appreciative review of this work, makes explicit reference to Herder, both indicate to the reader familiar with his writings a quite remarkable degree of similarity between his approach to the problem of achieving a genuine coincidence of opposites and the one adopted by Heraclitus. As we shall have ample occasion to see in the course of this study, much of what Burnyeat, for example, says of Heraclitus and of the sense for the nature of Heraclitean thought conveyed by Kahn could equally well be applied to Herder. Kahn's work, says Burnyeat, "is the first authentic study of Heraclitus since antiquity.

> For it is the first and only full-scale treatment to be based throughout on the principle that nearly every aphorism is a condensation of many meanings. This principle is the proper and necessary tribute to the deliberate difficulty of the language. There is no one answer to the question of what a Heraclitean saying means. It generates several meanings within itself and yet more meanings in resonance with other sayings. It follows that the approach to Heraclitus' thought must be through his art; the philosophy will emerge only by the use of

literary techniques appropriate to the *logos* in which it is embodied.[54]

For example, with respect to the first of the Heraclitean aphorisms— "Although this *logos* is so always men fail to comprehend, both before hearing it and once they have heard," he notes:

> . . . the syntactic ambiguity of "always" forces us to recognize, right from its first appearance, the semantic richness of the key word "*logos*." Nothing could be more inappropriate than the attempts scholars have made to fix a single "most appropriate" translation of "*logos*." That one word encapsulates a whole philosophy of difference in sameness and sameness in difference: the content of the *logos* is paradigmatically exemplified in the word "*logos*" itself.[55]

Similar considerations hold, as we shall see in case after case, for the key terms in Herder's exposition, and thus also for the overall structure of his argument.

Herder's characteristic way of attempting to realize a coincidence of opposites thus associates him as well with another important strain in the tradition, that of the interweaving of philosophy and literature. Like the notion of the *coincidentia oppositorum* itself, this is something that appears especially frequently in the works of German, or German-speaking, authors. The German tradition of philosophy-as-literature receives one of its earliest, and still most powerful, expressions in the writings of religious mystics such as Meister Eckhart and others in the thirteenth and fourteenth centuries and Jakob Böhme at the turn of the sixteenth to the seventeenth century. Common to the work of these authors is the use of a wide array of techniques of suggestion and evocation in order to impart to the reader a doctrine, a conception, or (perhaps most characteristically) an experience, the substance of which exceeds what can be accommodated to the canons of conventional rational-logical discourse, governed, for example, by the Aristotelian principles of identity, non-contradiction, and excluded middle.

Herder, as we are already beginning to see, faces an analogous difficulty. The sort of synthesis that he has in view does not involve merely finding a way to resolve what appear to be some very fundamental contradictions; he must also preserve within that synthesis precisely the element of tension between contraries that it at the same time overcomes. The means to accomplish this do not, however, lie within the range of standard propositional logic. Faced with that situation, there are basically two possible responses. At least one philosophical tradition, the Anglo-American, is inclined to say, in effect, so much the worse for the point of view that generates such impossible tasks. The principal strain of German-speaking philosophy, however, throughout most of its history says, on the other hand, so much the worse for ordinary propositional logic, if it is unable to meet the challenges put to it by the nature of things themselves. This latter response, it is important to note, does not (or not typically, at any rate, and certainly not for Herder) entail an outright rejection of traditional or conventional forms of reasoning. It does not, that is, amount to a programmatic irrationalism. The aim is rather to assimilate rational modes of conceptualization and argumentation to a broader and more manifold form of discourse and, in so doing, to undertake (implicitly, if not always expressly) a critique and reanalysis of reason itself.

The distinctive form of discourse that Herder develops to this end is, again, of considerable importance for the poets and philosophers (or, as in many cases, poet-philosophers) of his own and subsequent generations, and for none more so than for the Romantics. In order to achieve the sort of coincidence of opposites that he sees dictated by the nature of the phenomena themselves, he constructs his exposition on two levels simultaneously. These levels correspond to two modes of organizing and conveying meaning, which I shall call respectively the *discursive* and the *gestural*. By the former I mean simply the system of ordinary language, within the framework of which there unfolds a straightforward line of argument, apprehensible in the way that one grasps any piece of expository prose. The latter refers to the use of various formal techniques to structure the exposition, in much the way a literary text is composed. These include exploitation of multiple connotations of key terms and contrasting evaluations of the concepts they express; sudden shifts in voice and abrupt changes in the direction of the argument; and the use of figurative language, ranging in scope from individual metaphors to extended images composed in turn of a variety of interactive elements. The relationship between these levels of exposition is itself multiple, consisting variously of mutual reinforcement but also opposition, harmony but also a kind of counterpoint (or, perhaps better, productive dissonance). The overall structure of the text thus becomes in its own right, in exemplary fashion, a principal bearer of the argument, embodying in itself the sort of coincidence of opposites that is its object. It becomes, that is, an implicit representation of the paradoxical dialectic that is, for Herder, both the structure of reality generally and, specifically, his image of human nature.

III

The distinction between discursive and gestural modes of exposition obviously requires some further explanation, part of which I can at least suggest here, the bulk of which, however, would call for a very different sort of study (not to speak of a much longer one) from the one I propose to undertake. The view has taken hold in recent years among some critics that there is, after all, no ultimate distinction to be drawn between natural language generally and the particular uses to which it is put in poetic or literary contexts. That view, it seems to me, is at variance with both common usage and common experience. We mean, and have always meant, different things by 'ordinary language' and 'poetry.' That has, in fact, always been one of the principal interests and attractions that poetry has held for us—that it is precisely *not* the language of every day, but rather a way of *using* that language so as, among other things, to call our attention to what is really at work in the forms and structures of the language that we use unreflectively all the time and to explore the wealth of signification and expression latent in that common fabric of discourse.

It is, I think, worth noting, moreover, that the view that ordinary and poetic language cannot in any ultimate sense be distinguished is one that, in the very act of being expressed, unavoidably undercuts itself. For in order to take that position at all, it is obviously necessary that it be possible to assert at least one fact in unambiguous fashion, namely that there is no ultimate difference between ordinary and poetic language. But if that claim can be made in such a way that it even could be a fact, that is, as something that could in principle be *either true or false* (quite apart from which it might in the end turn out to be), then there is clearly of necessity already a distinction between the two modes of discourse. And, again, the point can be reaffirmed by reference to ordinary linguistic experience. No one who is inclined to deny that there is a significant difference between ordinary and poetic language finds it either necessary or appropriate, in advancing that position, to add that what he or she has just said is itself merely a figure of speech. On the contrary, those who share this view believe that, in asserting it, they are describing a literally true state of affairs. The problem with this particular assertion, however—and it is a problem that in one form or another seems eventually to haunt all versions of relativism and perspectivism—is that, in order for it to be made at all, it must exempt itself from the very limitations that it wants to say are inherent in all uses of language. It must place itself outside the same linguistic field that it wants to maintain is all-encompassing. Derrida is famous for asserting, *il n'y a pas de hors-texte,* although to do so he must overlook (at least) the one proposition itself that says so.

From the fact of a legitimate distinction between ordinary and poetic language, however, it does not follow that the line between the two is an absolutely sharp one, permitting, in the case of any particular utterance, definite assignment to one realm or the other. In the first place, these are not the only types of language use that exist. More important, it is a fundamental mistake to suppose that, in order for a concept to be well-defined, it must be possible to specify clearly and in advance (for example, through a statement of necessary and sufficient conditions) all and only those things to which it properly refers. That is certainly true of some concepts, particularly those of mathematics and many of those of natural science as well. But that it is not true of all, and especially not of those that tend to occur most frequently in everyday discourse, can be seen at once through any number of examples (many of which are now widely familiar by virtue of having been used by thinkers from Wittgenstein to John Ellis). What, for example, is a game? How do we know when someone has learned to read, or to play the piano, or to speak French? What is the difference between a tree and a bush, a flower and a weed, a soup and a stew, and so on? From the fact that we are unable to respond to these questions by giving absolute definitions, it clearly does not follow that we do not know what the concepts in question mean or how to employ them correctly. And analogous considerations hold for the distinction between ordinary and poetic language. It is part of what it means to be able to speak English that, in most cases, we can say fairly unequivocally which is which, and that, where we have a borderline case or a gray area, we can say that, too. Former Supreme Court justice Potter Stewart was much ridiculed in some circles, undeservedly, for saying that, although he could not define pornography, he knew it when he saw it. One might rather hope that a philosophy of language thus attuned to reality would always inform the deliberations of the nation's highest court.

Neither is it the case that ordinary language has for its exclusive province the realm of truth, or fact, and poetic language only that of imagination. As we shall see in the analysis of *On Diligence*, in the interplay there of discursive and gestural modes, it is possible to use the very tension between the two for the purpose of establishing—in the double sense of demonstrating and realizing—a particular sort of truth. This quality of the text is the principal consideration dictating the method of analysis that I have adopted here. Only by working in very small steps through the essay, sentence by sentence and sometimes even word by word, is it possible, it seems to me, to gain a sense for the way in which Herder unfolds his argument on two levels at once and so sustains in it the finely tuned balance of opposites that he seeks. Were one to attempt instead, for example, to proceed in some sense "thematically," abstracting out the "main points" of the essay and treating them as headings under which other, subsidiary points could then be grouped, it is hard to see how the text could then fail to appear as simply a static structure of concepts and theses, and one, moreover, that, in view of the flat self-contradictions that, seen from this perspective, it would manifest, would appear to more than justify the opinion of Herder held by some (see, for example, the earlier discussion of Gillies's study) that, other merits notwithstanding, he is in the end a hopelessly confused, or at least undisciplined, thinker. The reading that I propose, on the other hand, is both comprehensive and one that enables us to view the essay as a coherent whole. Without such a reading, one must account in some other way first, for the striking structural patterns in the text and second, for the manifest logical difficulties (in the conventional sense of the term) with the argument that Herder presents. That is, failing some such interpretation as the one I suggest, it seems to me that one is left confronting, on the one hand, a text filled with an extraordinary (indeed, for a piece of fewer than two thousand words, virtually incredible) number of coincidences and, on the other, an image of the author as a man oblivious to the most elementary requirements of sound reasoning. And these are surely conclusions of a sort to be adopted only when all else has failed.

There is a kind of distant resemblance between the approach I take to *On Diligence* and the one made famous by Roland Barthes in his enormously influential reading of Balzac's novella *Sarrasine, S/Z*. Like Barthes, I undertake to bring to light the manifold workings of a single, relatively brief text. Like Barthes, in order to do so I focus in succession on the particular elements (sometimes very minute elements), ranging from the macro-structural to the phonemic, of which it is constituted. Like Barthes, I use that basic sequential reading as a springboard from which to then show how the text in fact works by moving both forward and backward within itself and at various (and variously intersecting) tangents to the nominal, surface line of exposition. (Like Barthes, I even include what he calls the "tutor text"[56] in an appendix to the analysis.) Unlike Barthes, I do not point to five "codes" at work in the text, but instead to three; and rather than speak of them as "codes" at all, I prefer to think of them as *functions,* that is, as dimensions of the *rhetorical* enterprise in which Herder is here, as always, in the first intance engaged. The first of these functions, which in a way also embraces the other two, is the combination, already alluded to, of discursive and gestural elements in the exposition. The second is what we shall see to be the injection of a historical (or historicizing) dimension into the structure of the argument itself. And the third is what might be called the pragmatic dimension of the text, the way in which the argument is constructed so that its very meaning comes into being, ultimately, only by being instantiated in the receptive experience of the audience that assimilates it.

Herder himself, we may note, left us a clue to the importance of *On Diligence* for his work at large. In his treatise *On Knowing and Feeling in the Human Soul (Vom Erkennen und Empfinden der menschlichen Seele)* of 1778, he says:

> The first, open and ingenuous, work of an author is . . . usually the best: he has just begun to blossom, his soul is still dawning. . . . We always love the half more than the whole, morning with its promise more than noon with the sun at its zenith. (VIII, 209)

1

Language, Culture, and *Denkungsart*

The exposition of *On Diligence* unfolds in three stages, corresponding broadly to the pattern of thesis-antithesis-synthesis that, a generation later, becomes the characteristic framework, not merely of the Hegelian system, nor even solely of German Idealism, but of Romantic thought and sensibility generally. In the first part of the essay, Herder develops an argument for confining oneself to the study of one's native language; in the second, he presents a counter-argument, introducing a set of reasons for learning the languages of other peoples; and, in part three, he reasserts the position of part one, now transformed, however, in light of the considerations introduced in part two, to the end of determining the nature of the relationship between the two sorts of language and thus the terms that must govern the study of each. In addition, each section of the text is dominated by a particular temporal dimension: part one by the past; part two, the present; and part three, the future. Central to the overall argument of *On Diligence* is that its several stages are cast in the form of an historical overview of the development of the human race. Establishment of this sort of historical perspective is a key element of Herder's procedure throughout his career. Resolving contradiction, in whatever particular form it is encountered (as here, between native and foreign languages), requires, for him, seeing the opposition not in static but in dynamic terms, not as a fixed antinomy but as one moment in a progressive dialectic.

This way of apprehending phenomena is reflected as well in his penchant for genetic explanations. The surest and most complete grasp of any object of investigation stems, in his view, from an account of its origin and growth. In order to understand what something is, he consistently urges, study how it came to be. Part one of *On Diligence* opens in this way, offering a capsule history of the rise of the myriad languages of mankind. If he is to explain why one should pay particular attention to one's native language, Herder feels, he must first show how there came to be a plurality of human languages at all. For it was not always so; originally, in the Golden Age that was the childhood of the human race, all people were united by a common language. But, he says, beginning the essay:

Part I, § 1

> That time of flourishing is gone in which the small circle of our earliest forefathers dwelt with the patriarchs, like children around their parents; that age in which, according to the simple, sublime word of Scripture, all the world was of one language and one speech. There prevailed then, instead of the burdens of our learning and the masks of our virtue, rough, simple contentment. But why do I depict a lost portrait of irreplaceable charms? It is no more, this Golden Age.

The essay opens on a note of what has been lost in the movement from the earliest stages of human history down to the present day. Haym speaks of "a mention, reminiscent of Rousseau, of the age of the patriarchs"[1] at the outset of the piece, and Herder does indeed appear, at least at first glance, to imply that our history has been merely a process of decline from our beginnings and to express a corresponding nostalgia for that original state. In addition to the dominant Rousseauian tone, however, it is possible to discern in this passage anticipations of a counterargument of a sort not found in Rousseau (or, at any rate, not the Rousseau of the *Discourse on the Arts and Sciences,* the great expression of pessimism regarding the value of culture and civilization on which his reputation and influence were initially founded).[2]

While it is necessary to point out here the principal elements of the opening paragraph that lay the groundwork for that counterargument, it is also the case that their full significance can become clear only a good deal later, after we have traversed nearly the entire length of the essay. That state of affairs, though giving rise to a certain difficulty in the mechanics of organizing the explication of the work, is at the same time a point of structural significance central to its interpretation. As we shall see, the development of the human race that Herder contemplates here involves a kind of circular movement in which the conclusion returns to the beginning, rendering it for the first time fully intelligible. Reaching the end of the chain of exposition presupposes having started back where one did and having covered all the ground in between; at the same time, the beginning is fully illuminated only in light of the end and in that sense becomes possible only when the end has been reached.[3]

Let us then examine more closely the composition of the opening paragraph:

1. "That time of flourishing is gone . . ."—With his use of the demonstrative "that" (*jene*), rather than the definite article, Herder points implicitly to an important feature of the Golden Age to which he does not otherwise call special attention, namely its specificity. The emphasis here is not simply on the attribute of the period—"that time *of flourishing*"—but also on its delimitation: "*that* time of flourishing," that is, that one in particular, a unique state at the beginning of our history but not necessarily the only "flourishing time" there has ever been or ever will be. The word that I render here by 'flourishing,' *blühend*, is moreover a term that occurs frequently in Herder, and it is characteristic of his technique that such recurring terms provide important clues to the gestural dimension of his arguments. In particular, *blühend*, in its various applications, will prove to be among the two or three most important words in the entire exposition of *On Diligence*.

2. " . . . the small circle of our earliest forefathers . . . with the patriarchs, like children around their parents . . ."—Important here is the association of the earliest stage of the development of the race with the period of childhood in the life of the individual human being. The biological (as distinguished from the more metaphysical) principle of palingenesis, according to which ontogeny recapitulates phylogeny,[4] is a key element of Herder's thought. Sometimes in straightforward fashion, and, if anything more often, in inverted form as here (with the emphasis on the development of the whole following the pattern of the individual entity), it provides the structure for a number of the best-known passages in his work, for example, the section "On the Ages in the Life of a Language" ("Von den Lebensaltern einer Sprache") in the first collection of *Fragments* (I, 151–55).[5] The point of particular significance for the argument in the present connection is that the early stage of human history, like childhood, is not

only not the end of our development, it is also in an important sense inferior to subsequent stages, precisely by virtue of being less developed. This is not to say that childhood does not also have certain advantages over later periods of life, qualities that are lost as we grow older, and that Herder sums up in the characterization "rough, simple contentment." The contentment of childhood is, however, just that—"simple" (*einfältig*). It is harmonious and integral, but also naive and unarticulated, and insofar a privative rather than a substantive condition.[6]

A sense for the ambivalent virtues of childhood, or childlike states of being, forms a prominent part of what we regard as the characteristic outlook of Romanticism, and not only in Germany. Rousseau's first *Discourse* had constituted an initial assault on the Enlightenment assumption that growing older is inherently a progressive movement, or at least the necessary condition of progress, both for the individual and for the race at large. Among the English Romantics, Wordsworth in particular develops a vision, strongly colored by Neoplatonism, of the child's special proximity to the divine source, and thus of our lives as a falling away from that original blessed state (a loss that may, however, at least be tempered by the capacity of art, especially poetry, to recall traces of what one once was).[7] The German counterpart of this is a body of thought that is both theory and program, at once philosophical and poetic in character, which has as its goal the regaining of the positive aspects of our original condition. That aim does not, however, entail an attempt to turn back the clock and undo the effects of all that has happened since (which, it is recognized, is not possible in any case, even supposing it to be desirable). Rather we are to proceed toward our goal precisely (if paradoxically) by continuing in the direction on which we are already embarked. Thus, when that goal of reestablished unity and harmony is finally attained, it will also reflect the development that has been required to achieve it and will accordingly be experienced not as a privative but rather an articulated unity. It is not the concern of the present study to pursue the various particular forms that this program assumes in the work of, for example, Schiller, Kleist, Novalis, and the Schlegels, as well as in that of the post-Kantian Idealists, from Fichte through Schelling to Hegel. Most of that story is, in any case, familiar. The concern is rather to show how Herder stands at the beginning of this movement in German thought and how he does so, moreover, from the beginning of his own career.

3. ". . . the burdens of our learning . . . the masks of our virtue

. . ."—Both the notion of learning, or scholarship, and that of con-
cealment will recur in the essay in altered form and with new evaluations. That will not, however, cancel the senses and evaluations they
have here. Again, the point has significance beyond the immediate
context. The reader of Herder must always be on guard against supposing that, for him, things must be *either* one way *or* the other,
either x or not-x (*tertium non datur*). That assumption, laid down
originally by Aristotle as one of the three key postulates of sound
logic, had for centuries functioned as a fundamental principle of
Western thought; but it is an assumption that Herder is intent on
challenging. I suggested in the Introduction here that one way of
characterizing the method of argumentation that he develops in *On
Diligence* and applies in subsequent works is, indeed, precisely as a
vehicle for extending the limits of intelligibility itself beyond those
set by Aristotle. Thus, *both* argument *and* counter argument remain
in force, for the overall import of the exposition depends on the possibility of sustaining a particular sort of equilibrium between the two.

4. "But why do I depict a lost portrait . . ."—With this paralepsis
Herder brings the opening paragraph full circle, concluding it on the
same note on which it began—and yet, not exactly the same note.
For what at first appears to be a merely rhetorical question has in fact
received at least the beginnings of an answer in the very paragraph
it concludes. While overtly emphasizing, on the discursive level, both
the gulf between humanity's beginnings and its present state and also
the irrevocability of the loss of those things that characterized the
former, Herder has at the same time implicitly, on the gestural level,
begun to locate that original state in the context of a great process of
development. The foundation is being laid for enabling the audience
not merely to see *that* something that once was is no more, but also
to understand *what* exactly that something was and, most important,
in what relationship it and the present stand to each other. The initially bare notion of the loss of the Golden Age expressed in the opening sentence has accordingly undergone a development in its own
right. The first paragraph thus presents in brief compass an example
of the sort of circular movement alluded to above, from the privative
to the articulated and differentiated, that it is the concern of what
follows to elaborate on the scale of human history at large.

In posing the question that concludes the essay's opening paragraph, Herder also shifts for the first time to the first-person singular.
What has been presented thus far, we are to understand, is not
merely a matter of independently existing historical fact, taken di-

rectly from the "simple, sublime word of Scripture" and passed on to the audience without further ado. It is also, and in equal measure, a product of the workings of an individual intellect operating in the present day. This consideration may also help to explain the use of what appears initially to be a somewhat curious locution, "lost portrait" (*verlornes Porträt*), rather than, for example, the more natural "portrait of a lost age." The portrait itself is, of course, not lost, for we have it in front of us both in Scripture and in Herder's own words. What it portrays is, on the other hand, both gone forever and yet at the same time, *precisely as portrayed* (though only so), still present. The expression "lost portrait" compresses these several senses or aspects of the point into a single formulation, but without obscuring the necessary distinctions between them. The best evidence that the distinctions are preserved is simply that the expression catches our attention; were it conceptually, so to speak, a seamless whole, we would pass over it without special notice. As the grammatical object of "I depict" (*ich schildre*), the word "portrait," moreover, calls additional attention to the central role of the implied speaker in constituting the entire complex of relationships in the first place. Later in the essay Herder will again switch to the first-person singular in order to emphasize further this same constitutive function. At the heart of his purpose in this work is, as we shall see, an understanding of the mind as above all mental activity, specifically—anticipating Kant, Coleridge, and others—an activity of productive synthesis.

Part I, §2

He now turns to the moment that marked the end of the Golden Age and the beginning of the next great epoch of human history. Just as the leading characteristic of that age was the linguistic unity of the human race—this was the time when "all the world was of one language and one speech"—so it ends with the shattering of that unity at the Tower of Babel:

> As the children of dust undertook that edifice that threatened the clouds, there the cup of confusion was poured out over them. Their families and dialects were transplanted to all points of the compass, and there were created thousands of languages according to the different environments and mores of thousands of nations.

Herder emphasizes that the different languages of man are, initially, the result of an enormous catastrophe, a kind of second fall of mankind from grace. He thus carries forward and at the same time elaborates the theme of loss introduced in the opening paragraph. He also repeats the characterization of our earliest ancestors as children. Here, however, that designation faces in two directions at once. In reinforcing a point made in the opening paragraph, it also prepares us, precisely by keeping the concept of childhood before our attention, for a variation on that theme at the conclusion of the essay where certain characteristics of "children" will be given a fresh application to the people of the present age as well.

With respect to the origin of languages, the events of the Tower of Babel constitute a case of what we can call *negative causation* in both senses of the word 'negative'—factual and evaluative. As to the former, the confusion and dispersal of the human race at the Tower does not itself directly engender new languages; rather it functions negatively, removing something else (the single language common to all people up till that time) that had prevented their emergence, and creates thereby the conditions under which they can (indeed, must) develop. Once that process is underway, other factors begin to assume a prominent role in it. The as yet inchoate languages are "transplanted" into different regions throughout the world, where, in accordance with the particular characteristics of different environments and cultures, they grow into national languages properly so called.[8]

The concept of negative causation remains, in later works, a key element of Herder's thought. In the *Treatise on the Origin of Language,* for example, it is a form of negative causation grounded in the constitution of human nature itself that provides him with a crucial piece to the puzzle of how language arose. Here the problem is how to both do justice to the difference between the rational and sensual dimensions of human existence and at the same time avoid opening an unbridgeable gulf between the two. The principle of negative causation affords a means of accomplishing that twofold task, permitting the establishment of a simultaneous continuity and yet complete qualitative difference between the two aspects of our being. In Herder's view, the mind is neither something that is simply added on to the senses, while belonging itself to a fundamentally different ontological order (in its essentials, the Cartesian position, which in one form or another continued to hold considerable sway during the Enlightenment), nor yet something that emerges out of the senses themselves by a process of gradual refinement or spiritualization (a position reflected, for example, in Condillac). The one theory acknowledges the difference between the two sides of human nature, but at the price of being ever thereafter unable to establish a real connection between them; the other guarantees the unity of the human being, but at the price of blurring real distinctions.

For Herder, as noted earlier, the mind is fundamentally and essentially productive mental activity, and it arises, he says in the *Origin of Language,* through a *negative* characteristic of the human sensory apparatus—namely its lack (in contrast to animals) of an instinctually determined specific focus. Thus he can say that man and animal are qualitatively different sorts of beings but at the same time that that difference issues from and reflects precisely the nature of what they have in common (V, 27). The distinction consists "in an entirely different unfolding and direction of all powers (*Kräfte*)" (V, 29) in man. Where man's senses are weaker than the animal's in respect of particular concentration, "in just this way they acquire the advantage of freedom; . . . thus [man] becomes a free-standing being, is able to seek out a sphere of reflection, can reflect himself in himself" (V, 28). In this inherent *incompleteness* of man, in the sense of an absence of determination in advance of the nature and course of his existence, there originates the peculiarly human capacity for reflection and with it the vocation of each person to determine his own being—in a pivotally important formulation for Herder's thought generally, and one to which we shall have occasion to refer again later in this study, to be "the purpose and goal of his own cultivation" (V, 28)—above all through the linguistic construction of the world.[9]

In light of Herder's rejection in the *Treatise* of Süßmilch's theory of the divine origin of language, his implicit characterization in *On Diligence* of the specific nature of God's action in initiating the process by which languages come into being is all the more significant. In showing the flaw in Süßmilch's theory in particular, he did not, of course, commit himself to the position that there is no sense at all in which God is to be regarded as the ultimate originator of language. Nonetheless, the argument of the *Origin of Language* did strike at least one of his contemporaries, Hamann, as in fact tantamount to a rejection of the view that God had anything essential whatever to do with the emergence of language. That reading—for Hamann obviously a decisive point against the treatise—seems to have puzzled Herder. Responding to Hamann's negative assessment of his theory (expressed in a piece with the, for Hamann, characteristically cryptic title of *The Last Will and Testament of the Knight of the Rose Cross*

Regarding the Divine and Human Origin of Language), Herder writes to him, "Yet I still do not understand how, speaking scholastically and in terms of book understanding, your gift of language [that is, Hamann's conception of language as ultimately a gift from God to man] differs from mine" (Herder to Hamann, August, 1772).[10] Clark maintains that, by answering Hamann in this way, Herder "merely shows that he has not understood the *Rose Cross*."[11] In fact, however, any misunderstanding seems rather to have been Hamann's of the *Origin of Language*.

Herder's position, while subtle, is nevertheless, I think, clear. As the exposition of *On Diligence* already enables us to see, in order to regard God as the originator of something (for example, language), it is in his view not necessary to regard him as the proximate cause of that thing in its present form. It is entirely sufficient that he be acknowledged as the source of the process by which it comes into being. Secondly, and more important, it is not necessary to suppose that God functions solely as the positive cause of things, that is, that they must emerge either as direct products of acts of creative will or not at all. God is no less the cause of something if he works negatively, in the way that he is represented as doing in his response to man's attempt to construct the Tower of Babel.

Neither, moreover, is the emergence of language to be interpreted as merely a matter of environmental determinism. Herder twice has recourse in the passage at hand from *On Diligence* to the ability of German to express a passive idea by means of a verb in the active voice used reflexively: the original dialects *verpflanzten sich*—literally, "transplanted themselves"—and *es schufen sich*—"there created themselves"—multitudes of languages. On the one hand, he thus stops short of attributing to languages qualities of personal agency, yet at the same time he avoids having to say that they then arise simply as a result of the application of external forces to a given, in itself inert, material. The suggestion is rather that languages possess an internal principle of development, a kind of organic entelechy, that impels their emergence. Through a combination of discursive and gestural exposition, he is thus able, again, to stake out a middle position in what appears initially to be an ineluctably "either/or" situation, a position that at once partakes of and distinguishes itself from what at first seem to be the only available alternatives.

Languages and the people that speak them develop in concert with one another. As "dialects" become "languages," so "families" grow into "nations." In the *Fragments*, this principle is reasserted as part of the notion of a common law of development governing all phenomena (which is there characterized as "the circular course of all things" [I, 152]). The stages of growth and development of a language and those of a civilization are the same. At no point in his career does Herder suppose that each nation first arose in its native "environment" and with its characteristic "mores," and that its people then, so to speak, got together and worked out a language. Though somewhat crudely stated, this is, in its essentials, the conventionalist theory of the origin of language, versions of which were advanced by various Enlightenment thinkers. The assumption implicit in this view, that there could at some time have been human beings completely formed in all respects, including capacities of mind, but not yet possessed of language, reflects, for Herder, a profound misunderstanding of both language and human nature.

Like the creationist theory, the conventionalist view is also analyzed and its flaws exposed in the *Origin of Language*. Herder shows without much difficulty that both Süßmilch's creationism and Enlightenment conventionalism, other differences between them notwithstanding, are equally inadequate as explanations of the origin of human language. For whether one supposes that language must have been developed in its entirety by God, who then imparted it to man, or that language took its start from groups of people agreeing among themselves on how to refer to things, one has in either case already implicitly assumed a prior existence of language, either in the very possibility of man's comprehending the divine instruction or in the ability of the supposed original founders of language to communicate with one another. The originality and boldness of the *Origin of Language* lies to a large extent in Herder's taking these two positions, which had till that point seemed to many to exhaust between them the field of possible explanations, and saying, in effect, that each is partly right but by the same token also wholly wrong—not simply because each takes part of the answer for the whole explanation, but because, in so doing, it forms a mistaken notion even of that part of the whole on which it fastens. In developing his own theory, Herder at once incorporates and transforms these positions and so is able to represent them as aspects of a unified and coherent statement.

That move is, interestingly, precisely analogous to one that Kant makes in the *Critique of Pure Reason,* a decade after the *Origin of Language,* in order to resolve a problem with which he had been trying to come to terms since his Inaugural Dissertation of 1770, *On the form and principles of the sensible and intelligible world.* Kant recognizes that neither rationalism nor empiricism affords an adequate foundation for explaining reality and our knowledge of it. The one leads in the end merely to what he calls dogmatism—as exemplified in the systems of the Continental rationalists from Descartes to Leibniz—the other to a radical skepticism of the sort to be found in Hume. And yet, at least at first glance, there seems to be no third possibility. Kant's solution, like Herder's, proceeds from a thorough reanalysis and reformulation of the terms of the problem on the basis of a conception of the mind as constitutive mental activity. On that foundation he is then able to develop an epistemology that combines elements from both sides of the apparent rationalist-empiricist antinomy, now, however, reinterpreted in such a way that each appears in its proper form and thereby in its true relationship to the other.

Most important to note in the present connection with respect to *On Diligence*, however, is the introduction of the image of transplanting. *Verpflanzen*, "to transplant," is another of the key terms that will recur in the essay, assuming as it does several different ranges of application and receiving new evaluations. Here, in its first appearance in the piece, it characterizes the initial stage in the growth of national languages. As that process continues, we see coming into play as well the second, evaluative aspect of the notion of negative causation mentioned a moment ago, to which we can refer (borrowing a phrase from Walter Sokel) as the phenomenon of "the positivity of the negative." Though it was, in itself, as we have noted, a catastrophe that occasioned the transplanting of families and dialects, yet Herder goes on to describe the results of that forced uprooting and resettling in substantially positive terms.

The notion of the positivity of the negative remains one of the leading ideas in all of Herder's work. Late in his career, in the twenty-fifth of the *Letters for the Advancement of Humanity* (1793), he asserts, "No ill that mankind encounters can be or should be anything other than beneficial for it" (XVII, 122). In this respect as well he anticipates a pivotal element in the outlook of much of German Romanticism. Reflexes of this structure are manifest throughout both the literature and the philosophy of the period. To mention but one especially prominent instance, it is announced as, in a way, the central theme of Goethe's *Faust* in the juxtaposition of two things the Lord tells Mephistopheles in the "Prologue in Heaven." On the one hand, "Man ever errs the while he strives" (v. 317); but nonetheless, "A worthy soul through the dark urge within it / Is well aware of the appointed course" (vv. 328–29).[12] This general way of looking at things is, indeed, in my view, the single most characteristic and pervasive feature of the complex of thought and temperament comprehended in the idea of German sensibility. It is reflected no less in the form of the heroic ethos peculiar to the *Nibelungenlied* and in the "negative dialectics" of Theodor Adorno and others of the Frankfurt School than in the Romantic period, where it is, I think, all but impossible to overlook. Herder's originality in this regard is thus not absolute, but relative to his time (a way of assessing the matter in its own right, of course, entirely Herderian in spirit). Though the idea itself of the positivity of the negative is not his invention, it is to a considerable extent his work that both ensures the central position of that idea in the thought of the *Goethezeit* and, in so doing, also contributes significantly to determining the particular forms it assumes there.

In the immediate context of *On Diligence,* the vehicle of its presentation is a series of brief characterizations of the languages of a number of different peoples, both ancient and modern. Of particular interest in this connection is what is said about the Greeks (to whom more space is devoted than to any other nation):

> There the Greek appears, like a plant opening, in the most blissful and mildest of climes. His body is, in the words of Pindar, bathed in gracefulness; his veins pulse with a soft fire; his limbs are pure sensitivity; his vocal instruments exquisite; and thus there arose among them that exquisite Attic language, the embodiment of gracefulness among its sister tongues.

At the same time that it brought to an end "that time of flourishing" (*jene blühende Zeit*) that was the childhood of the human race, the collapse of the project at Babel was the necessary condition of a new, but analogous, flourishing—Herder's verb here is *aufblühen*—that of the Greeks. Having had the "cup of confusion poured out (*ausgegossen*) over" it, mankind, or at least a part of it, is able to realize itself in a way that is "bathed (*übergossen*) in gracefulness." In being dispersed linguistically, culturally, and geographically, humanity has also taken a step from "rough, simple contentment" to highly developed civilization.

The parallel between the first and second "flourishings" of humankind is emphasized further in the way that Herder grounds what he says about the Greeks. Just as the "portrait" of the Golden Age in the opening paragraph was drawn "according to the simple, sublime word of Scripture," so the Greeks are now characterized "in the words of Pindar." And just as that Biblical account had something essential in common with its object—both it and the "contentment" characteristic of the Golden Age were spoken of as *einfältig*—so Herder here twice uses the word "gracefulness" (*Grazie*), referring first to what Pindar says about the Greeks and then to the language in which he says it.[13] The very fact of Pindar's poetry itself testifies implicitly to the heights that man's fall from his original state has enabled him to reach. The echo of *jene blühende Zeit* in the *Aufblühen* of Greek civilization, and the reinforcement of that echo in the structural analogy between the references to the Bible and to Pindar, together suggest a theory of historical cycles in which at each stage the new and unprecedented, notwithstanding its uniqueness, nonetheless also recalls, and in a sense even reenacts, what has gone before.

Part I, 83

There follows a quick review of the languages of several other peoples, each linked to prominent features of national character and environment. "The Romans, the sons of Mars," says Herder, "spoke more strongly, and drew above all on Greece for flowers of speech with which to embellish their native dialect." He thus touches for the first time on the phenomenon of cultural interchange and introduces thereby the possibility that a language, in addition to simply growing in accordance with its internal power of development, may also be cultivated as a matter of (more or less) conscious intent. Specifically, the rough and earthy qualities of a language may be complemented, and the whole language thus refined, by grafting on to it more "gracious" elements of another tongue. The sentence immediately following begins, "The warlike German speaks in still more manly fashion . . ." This parallels the first half of the sentence on the Romans, "the sons of Mars." Rather than complete the parallel, however, Herder goes on to mention the French, the Spanish, and the rest. In thus leaving, as it were, a blank space in his exposition, he suggests implicitly that there exists a possibility for cultivating German analogous to the cultivation by the Romans of their own language, that is, through a judicious use of the resources of foreign languages. The suggestion is reinforced by a switch in verb tense, from the preterite in connection with the Romans ("spoke," "drew") to the present for the Germans. At a point in his argument where he is on the verge of insisting most strongly on the study by Germans of German, to the virtual exclusion of all other languages, he has also planted in his audience's mind the beginnings of a suggestion tending in the opposite direction. The seed of that counterstrain in his own argument will then germinate in its own right at a later stage in the exposition.

For the moment, however, he declares, summing up, "Thus this plant was transformed according to the soil that nourished it and the sky from which it drank. It became a Proteus among the nations." The figure of Proteus is an image of unity-in-diversity that occurs frequently in Herder's writings. There is, moreover, an interesting secondary connotation to its use in the present connection. The name Proteus is so firmly associated simply with the *ability* to change shape that we do not always think to recall Proteus' *motive* for undergoing metamorphoses of all sorts. The story is in Book IV of the *Odyssey,* vv. 351–570 (especially vv. 384–424 and 454–63). Proteus is described as possessing considerable knowledge, but also as being loath to divulge it; it is by changing shapes that he seeks to compel interrogators to release him and thereby avoid having to answer questions. If, however, one holds on firmly, following him through all the changes he can muster, one will in the end be able to extract from him the answers one seeks. In light of the way in which Herder, later in the essay, will characterize the proper relationship to languages other than one's own—as one of active appropriation—his use here of the image of Proteus functions not only as part of the summing-up of the exposition to this point but also as an anticipation of what is to come. The thematic anticipation is, moreover, at the same time a clue as to how the text has to be read. As will become more apparent as we make our way into part two of the essay, fidelity to its material requires that the argument itself undergo a number of transformations. Nonetheless, it remains, like Proteus, a single entity and will in the end, if the audience has (so to speak) held on, yield an answer.

In addition to Proteus, the sentence last cited contains another image of unity-in-diversity, one that may at first glance appear too obvious (especially in a piece by Herder) to require much comment. He speaks of "this plant" being transformed in accordance with different environments (or rather, transforming itself—the verb here is *verwandelte sich,* which in turn recalls the earlier constructions *verpflanzten sich* and *schufen sich* and so carries forward the theme of organic entelechy noted earlier in connection with those verb forms). No reader of Herder is surprised to encounter at an important juncture in the argument an image drawn from the organic realm. That very familiarity can obscure as well as illuminate, however, if because of it we neglect to ask what specifically the image means and how it functions in the context at hand.

There is in particular the question of why he uses the grammatical singular. Where, that is, in all the foregoing is there something onto-logically singular to which the image might be understood to corre-spond? The image of the plant clearly has to do with the several languages he has been discussing, but, precisely in virtue of that fact, the referent cannot very well be any one of them in particular. The reference is rather to *all* of them, which is to say, to a *plurality* of entities. Notwithstanding the emphasis on the diversity and particu-larity of languages and peoples that is the dominant strain in the argument at this point, the very expression of that fact thus also con-tains an implicit suggestion that human language, and, by extension, the human race at large, is in some ultimate sense a unitary phenom-enon. This is, again, as with the implied possibility of a development of German analogous to that of classical languages, the seed of an argument counter to the overt line of part one that will come to frui-tion in its own right later in the essay. Herder introduces that theme, however, in gestural fashion, and thus avoids undoing the genuine distinctions among languages that he has drawn explicitly in the two paragraphs preceding. Once again, as in the essay's opening para-graph, the exposition has completed a kind of circle, now from the undifferentiated unity of the Golden Age, to fragmentation after the Tower of Babel, to the prospect of an articulated, differentiated unity embodied in the organism of human linguistic activity.

Part I, §4

With the image of "this plant" Herder adumbrates gesturally a num-ber of related themes that, later in the essay, he will recall and elab-orate in both discursive and gestural fashion. Insofar as the implica-tions of that image tend toward an ultimate unity of languages, however, they constitute a counterstrain to his explicit line of argu-ment in part one. In the last principal paragraph of this section, he draws the conclusion toward which the first part of the exposition has been overtly moving, namely that there exists a unique relationship between each people and its language by virtue of the common cir-cumstances of their evolution:

If, therefore, each language has its particular national character, it seems then that nature lays upon us an obligation only
to our native language, since this is perhaps more commensurate with our character than any other and coextensive with our
distinctive way of thinking (*Denkungsart*).

He here enunciates explicitly for the first time in his career a
theme that will become one of the pillars of his philosophy—the fundamental link between language and thought, or rather, between particular language and particular mode of thought. *Denkungsart* ranks
among the most characteristic terms in Herder's lexicon, and it reflects an especially important point of disagreement between his outlook and what is on the whole the dominant one of the Enlightenment. He rejects the view, held by most thinkers at least since the
time of Descartes (and one that may, in fact, be as old as philosophy
itself), that the constitution of the human intellect is in its essentials
the same in all times and places. For him, as we see, language and
intellect develop together, and thus the "minds" of mankind are as
various and as irreducibly distinct as its languages. His position here
anticipates views that will be propounded a generation later in Germany by Wilhelm von Humboldt (with his notion of a distinctive
Weltanschauung embodied in the form and "spirit" of each language),
and almost two centuries later in America by Benjamin Lee Whorf
and others. And it is this side of his thought that may at first glance
appear to set him in stark opposition in his own day, for example, to
his teacher Kant and in our century to Noam Chomsky and his followers.

The intellectual and cultural relativism implied in the notion of
Denkungsart does not, however, represent his last word on the nature
of the human mind, but rather leads us by another route into his
distinctive version of the problem of the One and the Many. Herder's
thought, as noted, seeks to move in a kind of sustained tension between the poles of the universal and the particular. At this point in
the exposition, to be sure, he emphasizes the aspect of relativism, but
that is part of his method. The genuine equilibrium between the One
and the Many can be sustained only if the uniquely individual character of each of the elements of the Many is developed in a way that
appears to render impossible their ultimate assimilation into a single,
all-embracing One. For if they are not so described, the side of the
Many loses its cofundamental status; plurality becomes merely ap-

parent (as, in different ways, it does, for example, in Plato and Spinoza) as against the real unity of the One. That result, however, tips the balance to one side in a way that Herder is not prepared to admit. At a later stage in the exposition he will come to speak of synthesis, but it is in the nature of the case that that discussion can emerge only out of the present consideration of particularity.

The bond between national language and particular *Denkungsart* has consequences for language pedagogy:

> I may perhaps be able to imitate stammeringly the languages of foreign nations, without, however, penetrating to the core of their uniqueness. I may perhaps, with much exertion, learn the words of dead languages from the monuments they have left, but their spirit has vanished for me.

The overt point is clear enough. Since by virtue of my own national and cultural heritage I cannot be a genuine member of another culture, I can never fully and truly grasp a language other than my own native tongue. And from that seeming impossibility Herder appears to conclude that the study of foreign languages has no place in the curriculum. He continues, the scornful tone in his voice (at least on the surface) clearly audible: "And it is to these foreign languages that we must sacrifice the days of our most vigorous flourishing, our liveliest memory, the freshest fire of our youth . . ." At the same time, however, in view of what we have already seen of the essay, we will not be surprised to find here as well an implicit counterstrain in the argument.

With respect to the first of the passages just cited, we note that for the second time in the essay Herder speaks in the first-person singular, and here as well in what might be called a negative connection (cf. "But why do I depict a lost portrait . . ." in the opening paragraph). It will turn out, however, that the verb used to express that negative point (that is, the inability to do more than "imitate stammeringly," in the manner of a child, the sounds of a foreign language), *nachlallen*, is also preparing us for a variation on the theme of language as spoken by children at a later point in the exposition. Specifically, the verb *lallen* will occur again, near the end of the essay, in conjunction with a characterization of our initial acquisition of our native language, a discussion, however, that at the same time also has important implications for our prospects of actually being able to assimilate foreign languages.

In the second of the two passages last cited, we encounter for the third time in the essay the word "flourishing" (*blühend*). Its use here, however, also involves a shift from one level of development to another, from that of the human race at large to that of the individual human being, and thereby implicitly underscores, through the use of a term common to both, the fundamental analogy between the two. "The days of our most vigorous flourishing" are (as the term *Jugend-feuer* here also makes clear) the days of our youth, and the tone of the sentence in which these expressions occur suggests, at least on first reading, the same thought that would be conveyed explicitly were it introduced with the words, "Is it not a terrible shame and disgrace that . . . ," namely that we must "sacrifice" our youth in a (necessarily futile) effort to learn other languages. We must, however, recall the terms in which other periods characterized as *blühend* have been spoken of earlier. In particular, the *Aufblühen* of Greek civilization could occur only when *jene blühende Zeit* of the original Golden Age had passed. The possibility of the one depended on the other—its virtues no less than its shortcomings—being "sacrificed." Analogously, then, we might suppose that, in order to move on to a later stage of "flourishing" in our own lives, it will be necessary to "sacrifice" much of what is most characteristic, indeed best, in our own youth. Thus it is possible to hear in the sentence in question a second tone of voice, or undertone, to the effect of "Yet it is in the nature of things and in the long run for the best that . . . ," namely that something be sacrificed now for the sake of something else later on, analogous to it, but of a higher order. Herder is far from insensitive to the loss that is entailed thereby, but for him there is simply no alternative (or at least none compatible with growth and development). Central to his outlook, as we have suggested, is the twofold conviction that, although from losses there often come gains, every gain on one front is paid for with a loss somewhere else.[14]

Part I, §5

The space I have devoted to developing the gestural implications of several key terms and other elements in the first section of the essay must not, however, cause us to forget their status in the exposition at large. They express undertones, counterstrains in the argument, laying the foundation for what will later be made explicit. But neither they nor what will come after annuls what has been said explicitly here on the discursive level. The argument for exclusive attention to one's native language remains in force—as far as it goes. And we learn at once precisely how far that is. The brief paragraph marking the transition from the first to the second part of the essay opens, "All these objections against the expenditure of our effort on other languages (*Alle diese Einwürfe wider die Sprachen unseres Fleißes*) do appear to have nature very much on their side . . ." This echoes the earlier assertion that it is *nature* that appears to charge us with an obligation only to our native language. Were we still, in some sense, in a "state of nature," that, to be sure, would be sufficient, and the essay could end here. The second part of the sentence just cited, however, explains why it does not and cannot do so:

> . . . because, however, the contemporary state of culture (*die heutige Beschaffenheit der Kunst*) is very far indeed from nature, it is accordingly almost the central concern of our sciences of pedagogy to determine the respective limits of that effort (*die Grenzen des Fleißes*) on which foreign languages and our native language have a claim.[15]

Kunst is here, as frequently in Herder, a shorthand term for modern culture and civilization generally. The present state of humanity is in a sense a "fallen" one, in that direct contact with *Natur* has been lost and there has arisen in its place the web of institutions and conventions that determine our lives today. That state of affairs may strike us as dispiriting, until we notice that the transition from part one to part two of the essay is in fact isomorphic with the one between the first two subsections of part one, from the Golden Age to post-Babel man. And as was the case there, so also, as we shall see with the passage from *Natur* to *Kunst*—here as well something is lost, but something more gained.[16] The overall structure of part one thus appears to afford us in its own right a guide to the reading of the essay at large, and that impression will be borne out as we proceed. As the second subsection of part one dealt with the rise of a plurality of national languages, so part two will return to that theme, now viewed from the perspective of the present day. Given a state of affairs in which such a plurality has arisen, the question becomes: what are the implications of that situation for the present and future conduct of our lives?

2

On the Advantage and Disadvantage of Multiplicity

The second principal section of *On Diligence*, like the first, consists of three subsections. In part two, each of these manifests fundamentally the same rhetorical structure. In each case, the opening of the subsection is dominated by a form of the subjunctive, and in each case that mode is countered by an abrupt shift to the indicative, an abruptness underscored at each point by the use of *aber* (which I render, according to the context, as "but" or "however") in the sentence marking the transition. The component sections of part two thus also constitute a threefold repetition of the structure of the transition paragraph between the first and second parts of the essay: "All these objections . . . because, however, the contemporary state of culture . . ." In addition, the movement in that transition paragraph from "appear" (*scheinen*) to verbs of definite assertion—"is very far" (*sich entfernt*), "is" (*ist*), "determine" (*bestimmen*), and "have" (*haben*)—is continued in part two in the three shifts from the hypothetical to the real mode.

It is, on the other hand, of course, not to be expected that in part two Herder would merely echo what he has already done in part one. Rather, like a composer who has begun by introducing a particular theme, he now returns to it in order to articulate aspects and qualities latent in it. This technique is another side of his overall method of moving from an undifferentiated (and thus, in the perspective of the whole, privative) unity to a developed state of unity-in-difference. The principal vehicle for carrying forward that movement in the section now to be considered will be the development of a notion already touched on in part one—that of the multivalence of phenomena, their simultaneously positive and negative character.

The course of the exposition in the first two subsections of part two can be represented schematically in this way:

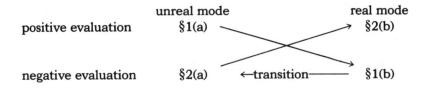

	unreal mode		real mode
positive evaluation	§1(a)		§2(b)
negative evaluation	§2(a)	←transition——	§1(b)

With the passage to the third subsection, the situation becomes somewhat more complex, as we shall see. For the present, the task is to explicate in detail the structure indicated by the above diagram.

Part II, §1 (a)

The second section of *On Diligence* begins:

> Were every nation, enclosed within its borders and bound to the soil of its own country, to enjoy the gifts of nature from the womb of the earth, without illicitly demanding a tribute of wealth from other peoples, perhaps no one would find himself exchanging the patrimony of his fatherland for foreign allures. I would not need to ape the gallant speech and equivocal civilities of others, and no city would become a hodgepodge of ten languages of commerce.

The counterfactual form of the opening verb tells us at once that the state of affairs about to be described does not actually exist, and it appears to suggest as well the speaker's opinion that that is unfortunate. The echo of the essay's opening paragraph (*Jene blühende Zeit ist dahin . . .*), or at least of what we saw was the overt sentiment of that paragraph, is clear. That echo, however, also alerts us to another aspect of the passage at hand, one that might otherwise be easy to overlook. We have seen that the passing of the Golden Age, while undeniably a loss, was also the price of still greater gains, and there is an undertone to the counterfactual construction here that tends in the same direction. The concept of enjoyment expressed by the verb *genießen* has, in addition to its basic meaning, at least in a context

such as the present one the connotation of contentment, of being sufficiently pleased with the current state of affairs that one does not
care to change it for anything different (the same feeling, for example, of which Faust speaks in concluding the pact with Mephistopheles [vv. 1692–1711]). The price of that, however, as in *Faust*,
is in turn stasis, the end of development, the prospect of which is, if
anything, still more abhorrent to Herder than to Goethe.[1]

With the passage to part two of the essay, Herder continues the
mode of exposition seen in its opening section: explicit presentation
of one line of argument, so framed, however, that it contains at the
same time the implicit suggestion of a counterstrain (which will then
receive its own development at a later stage in the overall presentation). The use here of the word "nature" contributes to the same twofold effect. At the level of overt argument, it expresses the keynote of
the hypothetical state of affairs sketched in the antecedent of the first
sentence ("Were every nation . . . to enjoy . . . without illicitly de-
manding . . ."). There is evoked here the image of a number of simple
agrarian societies, each self-sufficient and content, and the tone of
the two sentences suggesting what a world so constituted would be
like (by contrasting it with the world as it is) strikes us, at least initially, as strongly approving. It is, after all, contemporary society that
acts "illicitly," that induces its members to "exchange" (*vertauschen*)
their birthright for a latter-day mess of pottage in the form of the
gallantries and "equivocal civilities" of other nations,[2] and that makes
of the modern city "a hodgepodge of ten languages of commerce." By
contrast, the image of the nation as rural community may well seem
distinctly appealing.

At the same time, however, precisely the emphasis on the "naturalness" of this way of life recalls the contrast drawn between *Natur*
and *Kunst* in the transition paragraph from part one to part two, and
in the last chapter we saw something of the implications of that opposition. To return to nature, in the sense of the sort of life envisaged
in the first half of the opening sentence of part two, would be just
that—a return. Each nation would in fact reenact, on a small scale,
the way of life of the Golden Age. Such a retracing of steps on the
part of humankind is, however, as noted earlier, for Herder precisely
the opposite of what we ought to wish for ourselves, even supposing
that it were possible.

In this light, moreover, other elements of the predominantly negative characterization of contemporary society in the passage at hand
reveal a second aspect. The "hodgepodge" (*Gemisch*) of languages in

modern commercial centers recalls the "confusion" (*Verwirrung*) at the Tower of Babel, something that, as we have seen, represented a catastrophe and yet at the same time, in the long run, an event necessary and even salutary in its consequences. The expression "enclosed within its borders" (*in ihre Grenzen eingeschlossen*) appears initially innocent and straightforward enough, contributing to the image of the national agrarian community a quality of solid security, as when beyond the reach of threats from the larger world outside. In addition to this role in its immediate context, however, the expression also functions as an element in the overall development of the argument, and in so doing its meaning also assumes new dimensions. It echoes the concluding phrase of the paragraph immediately preceding ("to determine the respective limits of that effort on which foreign languages and our native language have a claim") and thereby, in effect, responds to the formulation of a problem to be resolved by suggesting a possible solution to it. For if one interprets the "limits" (*Grenzen*) of the effort appropriately applied to native and foreign languages as the "borders" (*Grenzen*) of one's own nation, and if that nation is entirely "enclosed" within those borders, then the problem is dealt with automatically. This, however, amounts less to a solution than to a dissolution of it. There ceases to be any situation in which the question of "foreign" as opposed to "native language" can even arise, and one is thereby spared the burden of reflecting on how to come to grips with it.[3]

That is in fact precisely the state of affairs sketched in prospect in the opening sentences of part two. To see this, however, is also to see at once that, no matter how attractive that way of life may appear (especially by contrast with contemporary conditions), it cannot constitute a genuine response to the problem. It does, to be sure, ensure a dominant position for the native language—and for Herder, the great champion of attention by Germans to things German, that is indeed something devoutly to be wished for—but it does so in a fundamentally illegitimate way, by, as it were, changing the rules of the game to exclude competitors. Its concept, as noted, is that of the linguistic unity of the Golden Age, which was, as we have also seen, an essentially privative state. It moreover compounds the fault by being thoroughly artificial (ironically enough, in view of its ostensible foundation in "nature"), inasmuch as the actual time when "all the world was of one language and one speech" in fact lies in an irrecoverably distant past. The expression *in ihre Grenzen eingeschlossen*, however, in addition to recalling and at the same time working a variation on something from earlier in the text, also looks ahead in the essay, and in a correspondingly twofold fashion. Both its principal terms, *Grenzen* and *eingeschlossen*, will appear again, but either in entirely new senses or in significantly different connections. In particular, the former, transposed from the sphere of literal reference to that of image, will introduce the final section of the essay, in which Herder will present his program for resolving the problem of native and foreign languages in a way that does justice to both.

As a final note to the opening passage of part two, I want to suggest one way of thinking about the use here of the verb *vertauschen*, which I render above as "exchange." We have seen (for example, in connection with the concept of negative causation) something of the paramount importance for Herder of recognizing and doing justice to what I have called the multivalent character of phenomena. In this, he is the direct ancestor of such thinkers as Hegel and Nietzsche, and he also anticipates the technique, variously employed by both of them, of accomplishing that task not merely (or perhaps even primarily) in discursive terms, but rather, as far as possible, gesturally, by exploiting the manifold connotations within the range of expression of single terms. Nietzsche's writings, of course, include numerous instances of such terms; it is a characteristic of his style that has done much to give rise to the charges of inconsistency and self-contradiction that have always been brought against him. In the case of Hegel, there is one term in particular that needs to be mentioned in this regard, *aufheben* (often rendered as "sublate"), the pivotal position of which in his system can scarcely be overstated and about which there will be more to say in a moment.

It happens that there exists naturally in German a set of words that might almost be thought of as made to order for the task in question, namely those with the prefix *ver-*. The range of meanings expressible by *ver-* is considerable, and, what is of particular interest here, those meanings often tend to cluster at opposite poles from one another. It can be used, for example, to express both an action brought to completion and one that is not only not completed but in fact botched. *Vertauschen* provides an especially good illustration of this semantic multiplicity. It is today most commonly used to indicate a mistaken exchange (a well-known literary example is the title of Thomas Mann's story *Die vertauschten Köpfe*), and it seems clear that that is the primary sense intended by Herder in the present context. Nonetheless, the word also means simply *austauschen* or *auswechseln* (these are, in fact, the first definitions given for it in the *Wahrig*

Deutsches Wörterbuch), which carry no negative connotations whatever; and from the vantage point of a later stage in the essay, it is no less clear that he is interested in this latter sense of the word as well. That is, precisely at a point at which he is most concerned to show what can go wrong in exchanges between different cultures, especially if the members of one simply abandon their own heritage in favor of foreign ways, he at the same time lays the groundwork for a later argument that such exchange, correctly undertaken, may prove to be both beneficial and indeed, in the long run, positively necessary.[4]

It is, of course, not every word in *ver-* whose meaning can move in this way from one end of the semantic spectrum to the other. The point is rather that a single linguistic element has the potential, depending on the context, to express entirely opposite notions, and that that feature of language, properly exploited, can in turn be used by a writer like Herder to weave into the very fabric of his exposition one of his most fundamental convictions as to the nature of reality itself. Let us consider, by way of comparison, Hegel's use of probably his best-known (and, arguably, his most important) term. One definition of it runs as follows:

> *aufheben:* in the Hegelian dialectic (in accordance with the multiple signification of the term), to elevate, as well as to preserve, as well as to destroy (negate). That which is posited in the thesis is *aufgehoben*, i.e., negated, in the antithesis, and then through negation of the negation posited anew, now, however, at a higher level, elevated above the starting point of the dialectical movement. This yields the synthesis, which preserves in itself the thesis in a higher form . . . [5]

The definition indicates clearly the three senses of the term *aufheben* and the ways in which it functions in the unfolding of Hegel's dialectic. Equally important, it also makes clear that, at any given moment in the system, not all three senses are operative simultaneously, but rather that, from one moment to the next, one sense or another becomes the dominant one. That does not mean, however, that for the duration of that moment the other two senses become irrelevant. If that were so, there would have been no philosophical point in the use, specifically, of *aufheben*, for as the definition shows, it is quite as easy to render the three senses of that term through expressions that themselves stand to each other in no special relationship whatever. The point, of course, is that Hegel is intent on describing a single process (the unfolding of reality as the development of Absolute Spirit to self-conscious self-realization), but one that manifests different aspects at different moments, and it is a cardinal principle of his method that the form of the exposition (because itself implicated in that process of development) must in its own right display the structure of that which it describes.

Thus, H. B. Acton's comment that "because of the happy circumstance that in German *aufheben* means both 'to cancel' and 'to preserve'—its literal meaning is 'to lift up'—Hegel was able to express . . . with brevity and acuity" the requirement that the dialectical "method of pressing and accentuating contradictions . . . discard error but also . . . preserve truth"[6] misses what is really the heart of the matter. For Hegel, the issue is not one of mere convenience, or of felicitous style (perhaps not the first thing that comes to mind in connection with Hegel in any case), but rather one of accuracy, of the exposition's fidelity to the form of truth. And so it is as well with Herder. As we have already seen to some extent, and as will become still more evident in what follows, the integral relationship of form and substance of the exposition is, for him, no less a requirement than it is for Hegel, and for essentially the same reason, that is, because of the central role that the exposition is itself obliged to play in the developmental process that it is describing.[7]

Part II, §1(b)

Herder now makes the first of the shifts mentioned above from the subjunctive to the indicative: "But how much do our glittering needs of today not require that we move in both sorts of world?" The rhetorical question contains a clear (almost heavy-handedly sarcastic) note of disdain for contemporary society. The reference to "glittering needs" (*glänzende Bedürfnisse*) carries forward the theme sounded with the expression "equivocal civilities" and is in turn carried forward and rendered concrete in the next sentence, where he speaks of "the gold on the royal diadems, the delicacies of our tables, all the appurtenances of splendor and luxury, which one disguises with the mask of convenience." The "mask" recalls the "masks of our virtue" referred to at the outset, and, as mentioned there, a variation on that motif will appear later in the essay for the purpose of making a very different sort of point. The notion of *Glanz*, seen here in the expression *glänzende Bedürfnisse,* will recur as well in that same connection later in the piece, correspondingly reinterpreted and reapplied.

All these trappings of "splendor and luxury" are merely "loot plundered from distant worlds." Herder thus makes explicit an element of his criticism of contemporary society alluded to in the earlier reference to a "tribute of wealth" extorted from other peoples. And he continues, expanding on the theme, but at the same time introducing a new element: "The more sought after the booty, the more its value increases; and thus the political wisdom of commerce learns languages, so that other nations might at least be cheated in their own tongues." The pattern of genetic explanation begun in part one of the essay is continued in part two. As its first section was concerned with how there *came to be* a plurality of languages, so the second section undertakes to explain how anyone ever *came to learn* any but his or her native language (and thus also to account for the state of affairs in which the questions addressed in *On Diligence* can arise at all).

The two cases are in an important respect analogous. Each stems from a phenomenon negative in itself, but one that is also the source of an overall, long-run advance. The first of these, as we have seen, was the Tower of Babel. In the second case, what Herder finds to be the initial impetus to the learning of other languages is, interestingly enough, simply greed (and its consequence, economic imperialism). In order most expeditiously to separate other peoples from those of their goods that we covet, it proves useful to know their languages. This opening of linguistic frontiers does bring the hitherto separated peoples of the earth together, but, at least initially, in a condition of enforced bondage: "Thus the politics of the state forges from the different languages a single great chain (*Kette*) . . ." On this basis, however, there then occurs something not originally envisaged by those who created that chain. The sentence just cited continues: " . . . and in just this way those languages come to form a great bond (*Band*) of learning."[8] The range of connotations of the two key terms here, *Kette* and *Band,* make it possible to express in gestural fashion the indissolubility of the link between the negative and positive aspects of this development.[9]

Having reintroduced the notion of learning, or scholarship, he now draws the first important conclusion of the second part of the exposition. So long as it remains impossible to accord any one language pride of place before all the others as the single medium of scholarly activity, and so long as plans for a universal language remain among "the empty projects and journeys to the moon," then "so long will a multitude of languages remain a necessary evil, and thus almost an actual good." This is Herder's most explicit statement in the essay of the principle of negative causation, and it expresses both senses, the factual and the evaluative, in which he intends that it be understood. Somewhat surprisingly perhaps, in view of the pivotal importance of that principle for his thought generally, he does not, however, seem to assert it in entirely unqualified fashion. Both the tone of the implied contrast between "the scattered host of scholars" and the prospect of unifying them through imposition of a single language, and especially the use of the word "almost" (*beinahe*), might well be taken as expressing a note of uncertainty (at least), as if he wished to leave open the possibility that the introduction of a single, universal language might indeed be a desirable step, if only it were a practicable one. He is in fact, of course, not in the least uncertain on this score. We have only to recall what we already know of his conception of the problem of the One and the Many and how it is to be dealt with to see at once that such a program could never command his assent (and the subsequent course of the exposition will establish that point more unequivocally still). Why, then, if that is so, does he appear, for a moment at any rate, to leave the matter at least somewhat in doubt?

The key to an answer lies, first of all, in noting that we are dealing here not with an isolated case, but rather with one part of a larger pattern running through the text. Earlier we saw expressed tentatively a position that is also later asserted categorically (and one that represents, if anything, a still more basic element of Herder's thought than the matter under discussion here). This was in the statement that "our native language . . . is perhaps (*vielleicht*) more commensurate" with our character and mode of thought than any other. Herder, of course, does not think that this is merely "perhaps" the case, and he will say as much in part three of the essay, where he speaks of an "exact bond" between language and mind. Each of the three sentences following the one just mentioned is also qualified by "perhaps." They thus reinforce, at the same time that they continue to work variations on, this structure of apparent tentativeness and ambivalence, to be followed later by definite assertion:

> I may *perhaps* be able to imitate stammeringly the languages of foreign nations. . . . I may *perhaps* . . . learn the words of dead languages. . . . Fortunate it is that the peoples whose lan-

guages they were have passed away; otherwise who knows how much ignorance, coarseness and violence to the original they would *perhaps* accuse me of.

We have already had something to say about the interplay of overt point and implicit counterstrain built into the first part of this passage. Similar considerations hold for its continuation, and in all three cases, as with that of our "obligation" to our native language and its relationship to our *Denkungsart,* part three will provide the perspective from which what is initially only a tentative statement can be transformed into something definite. (That transformation, however, as we shall also see, will depend significantly on a corresponding transformation in the interpretation and evaluation of the notions themselves that are involved here.)

There is one other point in the essay thus far at which an assertion was qualified with "perhaps," and that is in the second half of the opening sentence of part two: " . . . *perhaps* no one would find himself exchanging the patrimony of his fatherland for foreign allures." Here again, we have already discussed, with emphasis on the use of *vertauschen,* the twofold import of the sentence. The inclusion of *vielleicht* reinforces that quality of manifold signification from another direction. We find ourselves obliged to ask, that is, whether the fact that, under the hypothetical conditions of the nation as agrarian community, "perhaps" no such exchange as the one indicated would, or could, take place is a prospect that should gratify or dismay. In the immediate context, as seen, the answer is apparently the former. But as we have also noted, once the notion of "exchange" has itself undergone the requisite development and been given a new interpretation (or rather, once a sense latent in that notion from the beginning has come fully into its own), the question of its appropriateness will call for a correspondingly transformed response.

Finally in this vein, in the transition paragraph between parts one and two, we saw the need to resolve the initial question of *On Diligence* characterized as "*almost* the central concern of our sciences of pedagogy." But the entire burden of the essay is to demonstrate that, in view of the larger implications of that question, implications that extend well beyond immediate considerations of curriculum, finding an appropriate answer to it is in fact *absolutely* the central issue of education.

The pattern, then, is clear. In the course of the exposition, Herder moves from a more or less tentative statement of his position to a firm assertion of it. Theses central to the argument do not simply appear, as if sprung full-blown from the mind of the author; rather they gradually emerge, take shape, and come eventually to fruition as the argument proceeds. They, as it were, *become* true, and they do so, moreover, precisely as they contribute to the unfolding of the argument that in the end, in turn, serves to validate them. Later stages of the exposition both depend on earlier ones and yet also, in a fundamental (if paradoxical) sense, create them. They *establish* them, in the twofold sense of rendering them for the first time fully intelligible and thereby also grounding in reality (by moving to bring into being) the truth they express. (Thus far we have had occasion to refer only to the first of these senses. The second will come increasingly to occupy our attention as we move further into the essay.) In keeping with his understanding of reality generally, which sees *development* as the primary phenomenon, Herder is intent here on finding ways, not simply to assert, but to express formally by exemplifying in the structure of the text itself, his conception of the *historicity of truth,* a point of view according to which the truth does not simply subsist but rather comes about, [10] and does so specifically in the process by which what was potential becomes actual.

For Herder, attainment of a genuinely historical perspective is not a matter of merely paying more attention to the past. Simply doing, in this sense, more and better history may still be entirely compatible with what might be called an apodictic conception of truth. It is, however, precisely that conception, which assumes that the facts are simply there, that there are things true of phenomena and things not, and that each such truth constitutes a complete and self-sufficient whole, that he sees as in need of fundamental revision. That does not mean jettisoning the older view outright (rarely an approach favored by Herder), but rather calls for assimilating it into a larger context. Apodictic statements of truth are not so much false as incomplete, like individual frames in a motion-picture film. Error does not attach to what is depicted in the frame itself, but it can arise through misinterpretation stemming from the mistaken belief that what appears there may be regarded in static isolation. When Leland Stanford arranged to have a series of photographs taken of a galloping horse in such a way as to show whether or not there is a moment at which all four hooves are off the ground at once, the crucial frame revealed that that is indeed the case. It (obviously) did not show that horses can fly. Similarly, for Herder, determination of the truth of things depends essentially on locating the "facts" in relation to each other in an overall process of development. Both the One and the Many, in all the various concrete forms in which these notions present themselves to us, are, in this sense, "facts"; but they are also contradictory, and hence incomplete, facts. They must therefore each find a place in a larger structure, the terms of which will in some way provide for their reconciliation. History, as a process of development from potentiality to actuality, thus has a *projective* character, in the sense not merely of being pointed in a particular direction but of having a task, or mission, to fulfill. The *idea* of synthesis envisaged here assumes at the same time the quality of an *ideal*.

Part II, 82(a)

For the moment, however, the primary concern is to develop the implications of the passage from "necessary evil" to "actual good," which also marks the transition to the second subsection of part two. Here again, as in the first subsection, the exposition opens in the subjunctive: "How little progress would we have made if every nation, enclosed within the narrow sphere of its language, worked alone for the advancement of learning?" Unlike the preceding subsection, however, this is past, rather than present, subjunctive. There is thus evoked the prospect of something negative—an absence of progress—which has, however, not actually been the case. The negative past-time subjunctive expresses obliquely the point that progress has in fact been achieved precisely because nations have *not* remained bound within the "narrow sphere" of their respective languages. A key term from the first sentence of subsection one, "enclosed" (*eingeschlossen*), recurs here, now, however, with a clearly negative evaluation. At the same time, the notion of "learning" (*Gelehrsamkeit*) assumes an increasingly positive status, a tendency that will become still more pronounced in what follows. Herder has worked his way around to the other side of a phenomenon to which he alluded initially, in the opening paragraph of the piece, with a reference to "the burdens of our learning." Learning, and specifically the ability to use different languages, is coming to be associated ever more closely with progress, indeed, to be represented as a principal key to it. Human resources are limited, however, and progress depends on their being used as efficiently as possible. There is no sense, for example, in a second Newton, in Germany, expending his efforts on discoveries already made by the "English Newton." Yet the danger of that sort of duplication of effort remains always present so long as nations are unable to communicate with one another.

Part II, §2(b)

"Now, however,"—again a shift from subjunctive to indicative to characterize the present state of affairs, a present, however, that in contrast to the first subsection now appears in overwhelmingly positive terms—"what a treasury of discoveries is every language of learning!"

> Secrets disclosed by the midnight lamp of the ancients appear now in the sunlight of midday. Treasures that the sweat of a foreign nation mined from deeply buried veins are shared as booty among other peoples through that nation's language.

What perhaps strikes us first in this passage is the recurrence of the word "booty" (*Beute*), now with a positive evaluation. Used earlier as a term to denote what commercial interests of a nation rob from others in order to cater to the wants of their fellow citizens, it now refers to advances in knowledge achieved in one nation and communicated to all others.

Again, however, as with other such uses of key terms, the later sense (and evaluation) does not cancel the earlier one; both remain operative. By employing a common term in these two, at first glance, apparently quite different connections, Herder not only reminds us that the ability to use languages other than one's native tongue is the key to both operations, but also, equally important, implicitly underscores the point that we are not likely to get the one without the other. If the ability to deal in more than one language enables nations to contribute to each other's advancement, it also at the same time gives them a way to steal from each other. Indeed, it was the latter that made the former possible at all. The recognition of the inevitable costs of progress, alluded to above in the discussion of part one, distinguishes Herder's outlook as sharply as any other single thing from the sort of optimism that largely informs the sensibility of the Enlightenment. That, of course, does not mean that for him the gains do not sufficiently compensate for the cost of achieving them. We have already seen something of how, in his view, they can. But there is a world of difference between a view of history that acknowledges and attempts to account for that possibility and one that supposes that there are no (or no truly serious) costs at all.

Herder rejects the view that the development of the human race represents a uniform, cumulative process of improvement, and he is not reluctant to censure what seems to him the uncritical acceptance of that view by many of his contemporaries. For him the perspective of the Enlightenment is in the main fundamentally unhistorical (in a sense somewhat different from, though related to, the one in which an apodictic conception of truth, as discussed earlier, is unhistorical). In its tendency to interpret the relationship of the past to the present as simply a matter of the former preparing the way for the latter, it misapprehends both present and past. It both assesses itself too highly in comparison with earlier periods and renders impossible an interpretation and evaluation of the past on its own terms. It represents human history, in graphic terms, as an overall steadily rising curve, with each age seen as building directly on the ones preceding and so in each case constituting a distinct advance over them; and it locates itself on that line at, or at least very near, the peak. For Herder, on the other hand, history moves not in unbroken ascent, but rather at once by advances and declines. Thus a properly plotted historical graph will show not a uniformly rising curve, but rather a manifold pattern of peaks and valleys, in which, moreover—the point of greatest importance for the overall conception—the latter are no less essential to the shape and direction of the *whole* movement than are the former. In *Another Philosophy of History,* for example, he expresses the same point: "Precisely the mechanism that made possible the expansion of vice was also that which elevated virtue to such a height and extended its efficacy over such a wide range. . . . the summit borders directly on the valley" (V, 508; see also V, 505–07 and 526–27).

Fundamentally the same pattern that informs the movement of history at large is also discernible at the level of the individual components of that movement. As noted earlier, for Herder the characteristics of any historical moment that constitute its virtues represent at the same time its limitations. Its strengths and its shortcomings have a common source; in the perspective of the whole, they are, indeed, identical. In the eighty-seventh of the *Letters for the Advancement of Humanity* (1796), he makes the point explicit: "Their excellences and their faults come from a single source, from which, with both, with faults and virtues, their language and poetry flowed as well" (XVIII, 56). This dialectic of strength and weakness is, in his view, in one form or another determinative of the character of every historical epoch—including, of particular significance, his own. Some of the best-known passages in his writings are denunciations of the eighteenth century as a time of decline and decay. Yet precisely that state of affairs also contains—in light of his view of the overall movement of history, must contain—the potential for the beginning of a new ascent, and the bulk of his work, beginning with *On Diligence,* is devoted in large part to working out concretely and specifically how that upturn might be brought about.

We recall that, in the overall structure of *On Diligence,* the function of its second part is to establish the need to study more than one's native language. It therefore emphasizes all the possibilities for dissemination of knowledge among different peoples that such study opens up. In so doing, moreover, it introduces, so unobtrusively that we are perhaps not immediately cognizant of it, a new element in the exposition. Knowledge of foreign languages makes possible contact and exchange between peoples not only at any given time—for example, the present, which has been the principal focus thus far of part two—but also over time. Only in this way can a link be established between the present age and the peoples of antiquity. Secrets discovered by the "midnight lamp" of the ancients are now brought forward, through the medium of languages mutually understood, into the light of "midday."

The historical dimension thus introduced into part two also links this section to part one, and the continuation of the exposition develops further that association. At the same time, it expands on the theme just introduced, that it is to a large extent—perhaps primarily—through *linguistic* connections that the development of the human race as a whole has been (and, by implication, will continue to be) accomplished:

> Thus the seeds that were germinated in Asia sprouted among the Egyptians; Greece's sun unfolded these buds fully; and Rome ripened the Greek flower into fruit. Through its colonies, Rome in turn raised this to a tree, in whose shade the nations planted the seeds of their literature. In the same way, the people of today can build on the foundation of the ancients, until at last a happier posterity crowns the work of so many hands with the wreath of perfection.

The list of nations and cultures here corresponds closely to the one introduced in part one in connection with the theme of the development of national languages. The ways in which the two groups are presented, however, differs significantly. Their enumeration in part one, as here, involved a kind of organic image, but there it was the image of transplanting. The dialects brought into being at the Tower of Babel *verpflanzten sich* throughout the world and so grew into national languages. The dominant tone was one of dispersal into separate entities. Each language, and thus each culture, appeared as a distinct organism, related to the others only by way of a single common ancestor. That was, of course, in keeping with the overall purpose of the first section, which was to establish an argument for concentration on one's native language.

Part two, on the other hand, has been developing a case for study of foreign languages, and part of its argument entails recasting the relationship among the various nations so as to shift the emphasis from the aspect of cultural autonomy to that of a unified and progressive historical development. Cultures that in part one appeared as separate entities now assume the status of stages in the growth of a single organism. The themes of cultural autonomy and historical progress, and the tension between them, as we have noted, represent a particularly important manifestation of the fundamental polarity in Herder's thought at large. The relationship between the passage at hand and its counterpart in part one marks a key step in his attempt to deal with that polarity in the context of *On Diligence,* and thereby also introduces a mode of argumentation that will later become a hallmark of his work generally.

The two sections of the essay, and thus the two poles or themes in question, are linked by a common image—that of organic growth and development. At the same time, the conceptual range of that single image is broad enough to suggest two quite different (indeed, strictly incommensurable) things, and, as we see, that is precisely what Herder does. By means of it, he presents the various cultures and their languages as, from one point of view, separate organisms and, from another, stages in the growth of the same organism. In this way, something that is itself a prime image of unity-in-difference—the process of organic growth—assumes, through the multiple use that he makes of it, the function of *constituting* a unity-in-difference in the very structure of the exposition. In constructing the extended organic image here as he does, moreover, Herder draws on two elements, both present in part one of the essay but as rhetorically separate (though related) entities—the catalogue of cultures and languages on the one hand and the notion of "this plant" (*diese Pflanze*) on the other—and articulates them together. In so doing, he also draws together the dominant temporal references of the two parts, the past in part one and the present in part two. He has thus managed to pass, virtually without a seam, from speaking of the contemporary value of a knowledge of foreign languages to describing the historical development of human culture at large as a product of the contributions of myriad peoples and their languages. The passage is, indeed, temporally three-dimensional, for at the same time that it binds together past and present, it uses that synthesis as the basis for a reference to the future (the temporal category, again, that will dominate the perspective of part three). The development of the race will continue—"In the same way, the people of today can build on the foundation of the ancients . . ."—until at last, at an indefinitely distant point in the future, "a happier posterity crowns the work of so many hands with the wreath of perfection."

In part one we saw introduced in gestural fashion the suggestion that history moves in a series of cycles, not identical, but analogous to each other, and the passage at hand presents a variation on that theme. Particularly interesting is the way Herder, so to speak, switches metaphorical horses in midstream in order to do so. It was noted earlier that his preferred images, while entirely effective at one stage of a given argument, can, if pressed too far, become a problem for him at a later stage of the same argument. The present context provides an example both of that circumstance and of one technique for dealing with it. Organic imagery of the sort that he employs is particularly well-suited to expressing a complete cycle of growth, flourish, decline, and eventual dying out. At this point in *On Diligence* he does want to emphasize the aspects of growth and flourish. Instead of passing from there to the period of decline, however, he wants to move directly to a new beginning of the process of growth. Thus he leaves the "tree" of the Roman Empire, omitting any reference to its decline and fall, and guides our attention to the "seeds" planted beneath it. From a single tree there comes in the course of time what we are evidently meant to think of as a kind of orchard, as the former Roman "colonies" grow into distinct "nations."[11]

Having varied his organic image slightly so as to pass directly to a renewal of growth, Herder has also moved from speaking of a single organism to a plurality of organisms engendered from it. In so doing, however, he is in some danger of shifting his emphasis too much to the side of the Many. In order to draw the moment of the One back into the picture, he introduces a second variation on the image, this time a more pronounced one, from the organic realm to the sphere of communal work on a single construction project. The moment of plurality is retained in the expressions "the people of today," "the ancients," and "so many hands," but that plurality is at the same time integrated in the single "work"—in fact, a structure, *Gebäude*—that is the common object of their manifold efforts. (Precisely the same conception, expressed in terms of similar imagery, stands at the heart of his characterization, years later, of his own enterprise in the *Ideas* [XIII, 6]). The image of the "wreath of perfection" then provides the exactly appropriate concluding note to the passage. In reinforcing the idea of the One, it also underscores the element of historicity that is essential to the conception of that idea here, representing it implicitly as something whose real existence depends on being created over time. In addition, the image of the "wreath" (*Kranz*) retains the moment of plurality and multiplicity, expressing the ideal of unity, again implicitly, as both a unity-in-diversity and as a synthesis of nature (the organic realm) and art (human construction).[12]

The passage under discussion also includes for the first time in the exposition an explicit mention of the theme of "literature." (References to works of literature of course played a key role in the argument of part one, with its allusions both to the Bible, which is for Herder no less poetry for being divine revelation,[13] and to Pindar.) The context in which this occurs suggests that each individual national literature, notwithstanding its particularity, has at the same time a heritage extending back through other languages and cultures, and, moreover, that that heritage is the same for all. Again it is a matter of preserving the balance of the One and the Many. Precisely at the point at which the text refers to national, and thus, implicitly, distinct, literatures, the placement of that reference evokes as well a sense for the continuity, and thus the fundamental unity, of human literature at large. Placement is important here in at least one additional respect. "Literature" is the final thing mentioned in the sentence immediately preceding the one that begins, "In the same way, the people of today can build on the foundation of the ancients . . ." The suggestion accordingly seems clear that there will fall specifically to literature, among all the manifold forms of human linguistic activity, a central role in the realization of the comprehensive cultural ideal envisaged in the concluding words of this paragraph.[14]

Part II, §3

We come now to the next intermediate conclusion of part two. Referring to the common activity represented by the image of "the work
of so many hands," Herder asks rhetorically, "And yet, are we to suppose them building together without being able to understand each
other, so that each language remains for the others a collection of
empty sounds? Their efforts would then be just as futile as those of
the workers on the Tower of Babel in their confusion." The argument
of part two thus yields a position directly contrary to the concluding
thesis of part one ("If, therefore, each language has its particular national character, it seems then that nature lays upon us an obligation
only to our native language . . ."). The connection between the two
sections of the essay is reinforced, and at the same time the distinction between them underscored, through the explicit recollection of a
key motif from part one, the Tower of Babel, and its simultaneous
redirection in accordance with the perspective of part two. In part
one it was dispersal that was necessary in order that the human race
develop. The fragmentation of the original, universal language,
though a catastrophe from the point of view of what was lost thereby,
constituted at the same time, from the point of view of what it made
possible, the first step in an enormous advance. Out of the confusion
and dispersal of the human race came a wealth of distinct languages
and cultures, each one realizing concretely a particular set of possibilities from among those given as potential in the original (infinite)
human endowment.

But what if the people at Babel had not responded to their inability to understand each other by dispersing, but had rather tried to
continue work on the tower in spite of mutual incomprehension?
Clearly, the development of the race would have come to a halt.
There would have been neither a completed tower nor the rise of a
multitude of separate nations. Now that the latter has in fact occurred, we can, however, ask a second question, analogous to the first:
What if no effort were now made to overcome linguistic barriers? And
the answer is, of course, that we would see fundamentally the same
thing as would have occurred had work continued on the tower.
Again, development would simply cease. The fabric of human life
would remain diverse, but without coherence. All prospect of achieving a balance of the One and the Many would collapse, and in time
the race would inevitably stagnate. It was necessary that humanity

be differentiated, but it is no less necessary that it now move back toward unity. That unity, however, must not annul the diversity achieved in the process of differentiation. Thus the movement "back" to unity proceeds forward, and the task will presently be to chart the path to be followed toward that synthesis.

Part II, §4

Rather than embark at once on a statement of that program, however, the text continues its tendency to proceed obliquely, again abruptly shifting course. The third subsection of part two opens, "But an objection, and its refutation, will provide still more support for our argument in favor of learning several languages." This rhetorical strategy is among the most characteristic features of Herder's work throughout his career. He is often at his best when refuting someone else. In a kind of variation on the medieval scholastic *via negativa*, the task of demonstrating what he takes to be the errors of others tends at the same time to promote the substantive development of his own theories. A version of what we have seen to be his centrally important notion of negative causation is thus, appropriately enough, reflected in the composition of many of his own works. Examples (with the names of those against whom he is principally arguing) include all four of the *Critical Forests* (Lessing, Klotz, Klotz again, and Riedel) and the *Treatise on the Origin of Language* (chiefly Süßmilch, but also Condillac and Rousseau). In addition to stimulating the development of his own ideas, moreover, this practice has an especially salutary effect on his writing. Given a cast of mind that perceives connections and analogies everywhere and that is always seeking the most comprehensive statement of them possible, he need never fear that his material will give out. If there is a danger that he faces, it is rather that precisely the drive to say everything (indeed, to the extent possible, everything at once) will render his work diffuse. He has more than enough inspiration. The persistent need is rather for organization, and one particularly good source of this turns out to be the (in his view) mistaken theories of others.[15]

The objection that he anticipates at this point in *On Diligence* would concede much of the argument of part two thus far but would nevertheless seek to limit its consequences. It proposes that communication among different nations and cultures might be accomplished just as well through the use of translations as through people becoming acquainted with those different languages themselves: " 'Granted,' one might say, 'that every language is a key to many treasure-vaults . . .' "—the examples mentioned are English science, French *belles lettres,* and Italian painting, sculpture, and music—" 'granted all this,' one might say, 'is not the path of translation shorter than reading each of these works in its own language? Cannot a few take this burden on themselves, in order to free thousands from it?' "[16] Again, as throughout part two, this third subsection falls into two parts, with the first dominated by a nonindicative mode of expression. Instead of the counterfactual structures employed in the first two subsections, however, with both antecedent and consequent in a conditional form of the subjunctive, we this time see something more complex. At the same time, the interplay of negative and positive evaluation, which we saw to be a relatively straightforward matter in the first two subsections, also becomes more intricate.

The whole "objection" is itself hypothetical, and, within that implicitly subjunctive context, recourse is had to two different nonindicative modes, first, a kind of concessive—"granted that . . ." (*es sei, daß . . .*)—and, second, an interrogative. The objection acknowledges the positive value of contact between cultures but sees this as threatening to bring with it a negative consequence in the form of the requirement that everyone assume the "burden" of learning as many foreign languages as possible. Herder's response is twofold. First, switching to the indicative, he will take the supposed negative consequence and show that the proposed alternative to it, the use of translations of foreign works, fails to consider a point of crucial significance introduced earlier in the text. From here he will then move to transform that negative evaluation itself into a positive one. By the end of this section of the text, he will have developed an argument urging that the rewards of a knowledge of foreign languages are such as to make the task of learning them not a burden at all but rather something to be pursued eagerly.

Part II, §5

He begins his response to the hypothetical objection by agreeing with its premise that the use of translations is indeed quicker than actually learning other languages. The price of achieving that saving of time is, however, unacceptably high: "To be sure, this path is shorter, but unfortunately unreliable; it is too short to reach the goal that it seeks."

The reason this is so is because of the assumption implicit in that approach that the content of a text is independent of, and hence separable from, the specific linguistic form in which it is expressed. Given such a view, what we might for any given text think of as a single set of units of meaning, themselves unchanging, could, as it were, be housed within the various frameworks of different languages with a perfect fit every time. It was, however, the burden of the argument of part one to show the untenability of precisely that assumption. Each language embodies a unique *Denkungsart,* which is of necessity reflected in every instance of its use. The notion of a separation of linguistic form and content, such that the former might be removed, leaving the latter free for relocation, contains, for Herder, as fundamental a misunderstanding as there could be of the nature of language itself. The attempt to remove a text from the distinctive linguistic environment in which alone it exists results not in an extra-linguistic "content" capable of being inserted into a different language, but rather simply in the annihilation of the original:

> There will always be things of beauty that shine through the veil of language with double appeal; if one tears away the veil, they fall to dust. There are rosebuds interwoven with thorns; blossoms that one destroys if one unfolds them. Those holy reliques of poetry and eloquence among the Romans, the Greeks, and especially in Scripture lose the core of their strength, their distinctive coloring, the brilliance of their simplicity, their ringing rhythm; these flowers of gracefulness lose everything when I transplant them against their nature.

This passage involves a particularly concentrated use of imagery in order both to recall and transform elements from earlier in the exposition and to express in brief compass several aspects of the general theme of the unity of thought and expression.

The image of the "veil" calls to mind that of the "mask," used twice now, each time to make an overtly negative comment on the character of contemporary society. In part one, the "masks of our virtue" were opposed to the "rough, simple contentment" of the Golden Age; and earlier in part two, the "mask of convenience" was similarly set against the simple enjoyment of "the gifts of nature from the womb of the earth." In each case the initial force of the image was to underscore the artificiality—indeed, the mendacity—of contemporary life and to contrast that condition with the uncomplicated integrity of an earlier era. Had Herder said no more on the matter than this, we might well have taken him to be recommending simply that his contemporaries, as it were, remove their masks and return to an honest and open way of life. As other parts of the exposition have made clear, however, the matter is not, and cannot be, nearly so simple. Notwithstanding his heartfelt and outspoken dislike for many aspects of his own culture, some of his own most fundamental views, as we have seen, forbid an unqualified condemnation of it. If *die heutige Beschaffenheit der Kunst* is a "necessary evil," it is also, at least potentially, an "actual good." As the image of the "veil of language" works a transformation on the earlier image of the "mask," so it also helps to ground that thesis in the nature of *homo loquens* generally.

A veil is, in a sense, a kind of mask, but there is also an important difference between the two. Where a mask only conceals, a veil both conceals and discloses. In so doing, it creates from those opposed elements, at the point of contact between them, an *appearance*. Such an appearance is artificial in the sense of being a human artifact, but it is no less a real phenomenon for being so, and one that ceases to exist with the removal of one of its constituent elements, the veil. Linguistic structures, as we will later see still more clearly, have for Herder a constitutive function analogous to Kant's categories of the understanding. It is important to note this here in order to forestall a possible misreading of the passage at hand. The reference to the distinctive effect of each particular "veil of language" is not tantamount to opposing an artificial appearance to a "reality" behind it, as if one could choose now the one, now the other, depending, say, on whether one's interest at a given moment happened to be more aesthetic or more cognitive. The appearance constituted by the particular linguistic form *is the reality,* a reality all of whose qualities (whether these be thought of more in cognitive or more in aesthetic or in some other terms) are constituted at the same time, in a single operation, and so are ultimately inseparable.

It might be objected, of course, that such appearances correspond merely to phenomena as we happen to have them, and that is certainly true. The point, however, is that this is not, as it were, an inferior substitute for the real thing, in some sense "less real" than something else that is in fact there but merely, as a matter of unhappy chance, beyond our reach. As Kant will point out in a similar connection in the *Critique of Pure Reason*, phenomena-as-we-have-them is what the term 'reality' means. To insist that there must nevertheless be a level of existence underlying this that is the "truly" real or objective one is, he goes on to note, simply to have fallen prey to a kind of grammatically generated confusion. His analysis of the structure of knowledge leads to a characterization of the stuff of experience as "appearances" (*Erscheinungen*). An "appearance," however, seems to entail the existence of something else behind it, something that does the appearing. And that state of affairs, in turn, gives rise to the need in the Kantian system for the "thing in itself" (*Ding an sich*). The "thing in itself" is a notion (or better, simply an expression) that Kant feels constrained to include in his epistemology, even though he is at the same time fully aware that it is a term to which, by hypothesis, no concept can correspond—since concepts correspond only to "appearances"—and therefore one that is, strictly speaking, unintelligible.[17]

Similar considerations hold for Herder's "veil of language." Formulation of the theory generates a kind of empty space that at once demands to be filled and yet cannot be. If the veil gives us an appearance, then it seems that there must be something "real" behind it. If we remove the veil, however, what we are taking away is in fact language itself, which means that that "something" can never be an object of discourse. And that means, in turn, that we can never form a coherent notion of it. It can never make sense even to say of it that it exists (or, for that matter, that it does not exist). It simply does not fall within the range of what can intelligibly be said (and yet paradoxically, as we see, precisely the nature of what does constitute the sayable precludes its vanishing entirely).

The model of language implicit in Herder's image of the "veil of language" recurs in the work of a twentieth-century philosopher with whom he has not been much associated. In the *Tractatus*, Wittgenstein offers the following way of looking at the constitutive quality of language in relation to phenomena:

> Newtonian mechanics, for example, imposes a unified form on the description of the world. Let us imagine a white surface with irregular black spots on it. We then say that whatever kind of picture these make, I can always approximate as closely as I wish to the description of it by covering the surface with a sufficiently fine square mesh, and then saying of every square whether it is black or white. In this way I shall have imposed a unified form on the description of the surface. The form is optional, since I could have achieved the same result by using a net with a triangular or hexagonal mesh. . . . The

> different nets correspond to different systems for describing the world. Mechanics determines one form of description of the world by saying that all propositions used in the description of the world must be obtained in a given way from a given set of propositions—the axioms of mechanics. It thus supplies the bricks for building the edifice of science, and it says, 'Any building that you want to erect, whatever it may be, must somehow be constructed with these bricks, and with these alone.'[18]

Wittgenstein's formulation of the matter makes clear that there are two different sorts of limiting conditions involved here. The immediate limit is the specific character of that grid (the "net" or "veil") that has in fact come to be used by, for example, the culture or the society of which one happens to be a member. For Herder, as he will make explicit in part three, this is one's native language. The general limit, however, is not a contingent matter but rather a logical one. The existence of any world of human experience (or of human discourse—for Wittgenstein, as for Herder, ultimately the same thing) depends on the use of some such gridwork as the ones that both of them have in view. No one image of the world, or *Weltbild*, is logically privileged; what is logically necessary is that one have some *Weltbild* or other, the specific characteristics of which are then reflected in the unique structure of the gridwork that determines it.

The passage from *On Diligence* that we have been considering calls attention in particular to the aesthetic aspect of the qualities peculiar to (because constituted by) different languages. Beyond alluding in general terms to the "things of beauty" specific to each "veil of language," reference is also made in the space of a few lines to "poetry" and "eloquence" and to the "core of their strength, their distinctive coloring, the brilliance of their simplicity,[19] [and] their ringing rhythm." The note sounded earlier with the brief mention of "literature" and carried forward in the passing reference to French *belles lettres* is gradually assuming an ever-larger place in the exposition, and it will continue to do so, to the extent that, by the end of the essay, we will see "poetry," "learning," and the cultivation of a multitude of languages being spoken of all in the same breath.

As noted, Herder does not contemplate a true or ultimate separation of the aesthetic and the cognitive. In this respect his view does differ from Wittgenstein's (or, at any rate, the Wittgenstein of the *Tractatus*). In the *Tractatus*, Wittgenstein distinguishes fundamentally between the realm of fact (the world properly so called), the boundaries of which are the limits of the sayable, and that of value (including the ethical as well as the aesthetic), which falls beyond the scope of legitimate discourse:

> The sense of the world must lie outside the world. In the world everything is as it is, and everything happens as it does happen: *in* it no value exists . . . (6.41)
> So too it is impossible for there to be propositions of ethics. Propositions can express nothing that is higher. (6.42)
> It is clear that ethics cannot be put into words. Ethics is transcendental. (Ethics and aesthetics are one and the same.) (6.421)

This sort of distinction is foreign to Herder's sensibility. Just as there can be no absolute division of the human being into separate faculties, for example, the senses, the will, and the understanding, so for the same reasons the world of human experience is ultimately indivisible.[20]

If this were not the case, that is, if the nature of reality did require a strict separation of, for example, factual and literary discourse, there would indeed be no possibility of constructing the sort of exposition that we see *On Diligence* to be—a theoretical argument cast in large measure in poetic terms. If, on the other hand, there were no difference whatever between the rational-theoretic mode and the poetic-expressive one, then again *On Diligence* would not be possible, for there would be, so to speak, no logical space in which to develop the double-tiered structure of the exposition, with its constant interplay of overt argument and counterstrain. Thus there is no objection to emphasizing the one aspect or the other in a given connection, so long as one does not lose sight of their fundamental unity.

Thus far we have considered what we might call the synchronic side of the argument against substituting translations of foreign languages for actual mastery of them. The argument implicit in the image of the "veil of language" applies to languages generally, apart from any consideration of their respective historical positions and relationships to each other. There is, however, a diachronic side to the argument as well. The passage we have been discussing continues, "There are rosebuds interwoven with thorns; blossoms that one destroys if one unfolds them." Both the key terms here, "buds" (*Knospen*) and "blossoms" (*Blüten*), are familiar from earlier in the text, in particular from the extended organic image at the conclusion of the second subsection of part two. There they were used to refer to stages in the growth and expansion of human culture, each stage associated with a particular people or civilization. The passage at hand articulates certain implications of that association, with reference specifically to the relationship of different languages to each other. The attempt to render one language into another will, in many cases at least, entail moving the original to a different stage (typically a later one) in the overall development. Such a transposition, however, must inevitably destroy the distinctive character of that original. A *Blüte* must remain a *Blüte*. If one attempts to "unfold" it, that is, to render it into a language whose place is further along in the larger progression, that is tantamount to trying to turn a blossom, say, into a tree. In the end one will have neither tree nor blossom. The somewhat cryptic reference in this passage to "rosebuds" intertwined with "thorns" appears to have the same point in view, and, in addition, carries a kind of secondary suggestion of penalties that attach to meddling with languages in their natural state.

There is one further observation to make before we come to the conclusion that Herder draws from his "refutation" of the "objection" regarding the use of translations. We noted earlier that, for him, the Bible represents literature quite as much as does any secular writing, and in the passage at hand we see him expressly including "Scripture" together with works of the Greeks and Romans among the "holy reliques of poetry and eloquence." At the same time that he points out how much is lost in translating such works, however, we recall that in the first paragraph of part one he employed just such a translation as part of his own characterization of the Golden Age. The reference to the age in which "all the world was of one language and one speech" comes directly from the opening words of Genesis 11. The passage currently under discussion throws some further light on the conclusion of that opening paragraph, a conclusion that, as we noted at the time, included what seemed a somewhat curious formulation: "But why do I depict a lost portrait? . . ." In rendering the language of Genesis into German, as he well realizes, he is depicting directly, not an actual state of affairs, but rather the original depiction of that state of affairs—thus a portrait of a portrait. That there are inevitable drawbacks to that procedure the present passage makes clear. Nonetheless, it would not be correct to conclude that, in that earlier passage, he simply granted himself a privilege he is now unwilling to extend to others. We must not overlook the force of the first-person singular pronoun in the question ("But why do *I* depict . . ."). Herder, that is, is not dependent on a German translation of the Bible. He is able to read the original text, and that ability places him in a position, not of passive reception, but of active appropriation and transformation of the original.

In the *Fragments* he will develop explicitly the position implicit here in *On Diligence*. He will point to translation of foreign texts as one important way to expand and enrich the expressive resources of German, but he will also stipulate that the translator must himself be a "creative genius" (I, 178), and not merely, as it were, a neutral medium, in order to realize that goal. Nothing, of course, could be further from his intention than to impede access to the riches of other cultures. But he is adamant that those riches do not, and cannot, exist for us as mere museum pieces to be viewed from a distance. If we wish genuinely to make them our own, he insists, we must ourselves recreate them. In the same spirit as that of Faust's exhortation, "What you received but as your father's heir, / Make it your own to gain possession of it" (vv. 682–83), he will assert in the *Travel Journal from the Year 1769*, "Every man must actually invent his language for himself and understand every concept in every word as if he had invented it" (IV, 451; see also IV, 349).

The characterization of this process in *On Diligence* involves in its own right a transformation of a notion that has already played an important role in the exposition, that of transplanting. We recall that languages and nations arose as the earliest dialects and families *verpflanzten sich* throughout the world, and we have also seen that that movement, though in the short run a disruption of harmony, was in the long run the necessary first step toward realization of a harmony of a higher order. But, says Herder, summing up his rejection of the proposal that we rely for access to foreign languages and cultures on translations done by others, " . . . these flowers of gracefulness lose everything when I transplant them against their nature." It was in accordance with the nature of things that from the original common human language there should arise a plurality of national languages. What would be against nature would be the attempt, in effect, to reverse that flow and to funnel all those various languages back into a single one (one, moreover, selected from out of that plurality and hence without even the capacity in principle of the original mother tongue to absorb them). But that is precisely what a program of rendering foreign languages into (for example) German would amount to.

Even in the present era of *Kunst* the arguments of *Natur* retain their force. Any "transplanting" will accordingly have to proceed in a direction opposite to that of the hypothetical translation project, and that means, in turn, *parallel* to the movement of the origin of languages themselves. This is the course for which Herder argues. He asks, rhetorically, if the great poets of the past are to remain the possessions exclusively of their own eras:

> And does not that Maeonic[21] singer deserve to be heard himself, instead of merely having dismembered pieces of his work read! Did he sing for his poor marketplace alone? Was it for his century alone that Pindar transplanted[22] the Olympic crowns of victory among the stars? Shall Augustus alone have the royal pleasure of hearing Horaces and Virgils?

The answer (to all but the first of these questions) is, of course, no. And the question then becomes how, specifically, that contact is to be established. The answer, and the paragraph immediately following, in which the implications of that answer are developed, together culminate the argument of the essay to this point. The way in which they do so, moreover, which we shall presently examine in some detail, affords at least as good a view as any other point in the essay, and perhaps better, of the extent to which the mature Herder is already present *in potentia* in his first work.

There is, first, the immediate response to the rhetorical question:

> No, Emperor! you animated them through your Maecenas; I enjoy them! You, Louis, created through your Colbert the golden century of science and learning; I transplant myself into it. Two or three languages learned, and I hear every great mind speaking in his own tongue.[23]

The grammar of "I transplant myself" (*ich verpflanze mich*) echoes that of *ihre Familien und Dialekte verpflanzten sich* in part one. Herder's program for *learning* foreign languages is based ultimately in a recapitulation in microcosm of the process by which languages *originated*. He envisages a reenactment of the original workings of *nature*, but one now undertaken intentionally and self-consciously, and thus at the same time an effort wholly *artificial* in character and so reflecting, as it must, the quality of the present age. The structure that we see taking shape here is, in its essentials, that of the distinctive Herderian synthesis of art and nature, a synthesis that, as we by now expect from him, both unites and yet also preserves fundamental difference. The same structure is discernible throughout his subsequent work in conjunction with a wide variety of particular issues and concerns. One of these is the question of how a genuinely vital literature is to be created in the rationalist climate of the eighteenth century. The way in which, in the third collection of *Fragments*, he speaks to the contemporary poet in this regard (employing, interestingly enough, a number of the same terms to characterize the native linguistic resources of German that we have seen in *On Diligence* in connection with the works of Greek, Roman, and Hebrew authors) reflects the same simultaneity of convergence and differentiation of the two moments:

> You must represent artificially (*künstlich*) the natural expression of feeling . . . you must have the simplicity and the richness, the strength and the distinctive coloring, of the language so in your power that through these you can bring about what you would achieve through the language of tone and gesture . . . (I, 395)

Part II, §6

The act of "self-transplanting" involves the individual consciousness in a movement of expansion and differentiation analogous to the one that led initially to a multitude of national languages. The passage last cited continues, "At once I raise myself to them and extend my soul to the limit of every environment." In fact, as the text goes on to make explicit (thereby also developing what we saw to be an important implication of the extended organic image at the conclusion of the second subsection of part two), such extention of oneself has long been a decisive factor in the achievement of progress of all sorts:

> Thus did Cicero become an orator through the writings of Demosthenes; thus Alexander wept at the grave of Achilles for the glory of the conqueror; with the image of Alexander before him, Caesar made himself a hero; and Peter, in like manner with the figure of Richelieu, the creator of Russia. Just so, says Plato, just as through contact the magnet imparts its own

power to countless bodies at once, so geniuses inspire new geniuses with continual wonders.

In part one, the process of "self-transplanting" (*sich verpflanzen*)
was closely linked with another, that of self-creation (*sich schaffen*).
Families and dialects *verpflanzten sich* throughout the world, and *es
schufen sich* thereby their languages in accordance with environment
and national character. And just as the former notion recurs in the
present section in the expression *ich verpflanze mich*, so also the latter, in a relationship to "self-transplanting," moreover, analogous to
that of part one: " . . . with the image of Alexander before him, Caesar made himself (*schuf sich*) a hero." The force of the reflexive, however, is clearly not confined to the single case of Caesar, but rather
extends as well to the immediately following clause, where we are
told that, as Caesar drew inspiration from the "image"of Alexander
the Great, so, analogously, Peter the Great, inspired by the model of
Cardinal Richelieu and his efforts to establish a strong French nation,
"[made himself] the creator of Russia." In fact, it is evident that a
single analogical structure governs the entire passage, including, of
particular importance, the sentence that introduces it, "At once I
raise myself to them . . ." Thus the chain of first-person singular reflexive constructions, though partly explicit and partly implicit, is
clear: "I transplant myself," "I raise myself," "I create myself."

The question then arises with respect to Herder in particular: to
what end? What is the specific result that he envisages in his own
case from this activity of self-creation? Let us look again at the series
of analogies in the passage last cited. It would be surprising, in light
of the attention to detail that we have seen manifested thus far, if the
figures to be mentioned at this point had been chosen more or less at
random, merely as examples of a particular phenomenon but without
special significance in their own right for the unfolding of the argument. The terms "orator," "conqueror," "hero," and "creator" constitute what may strike us initially as a somewhat curious list. Connect-
ing the last three with each other presents, to be sure, no particular
difficulty, especially in view of the names associated with them—Alexander the Great, Julius Caesar, and Peter the Great of Russia. It is
not immediately clear, however, what the first term, "orator," is doing
in this company.

On the other hand, this is the only one of the four with an obvious
link to Herder's own situation in his capacity as the speaker of *On
Diligence*.[24] And in that fact we have a first key to the passage. Just

as Ciceronian oratory was schooled on that of Demosthenes,[25] so Herder, able to "transplant" himself into the world of both those "holy reliques . . . of eloquence," means to realize in his own work not an imitation of the Greek and Roman masters, but rather an analogy to their works. His aim is not (indeed, in accordance with his own most fundamental principles, cannot be) to produce a mere copy of the achievements of the past. The goal must rather be something that will be for his own time and people what Demosthenes' or Cicero's speeches were for theirs. In the *Fragments,* he makes the point in explicit terms:

> . . . it is thus not absolutely high praise to say: this poet sings as did Horace, that orator speaks like Cicero, this philosophical poet is another Lucretius, this historian is a second Livy. I say: not absolutely! But it is a great, a rare, and an enviable praise when it can be said: thus would Horace, Cicero, Lucretius, and Livy have written, if they had written about this incident, on this level of culture, at this time, for this purpose, for the mode of thought (*Denkart*) of this people, and in this language. (I, 383)

It remains then to determine the particulars of the analogy that he seeks to establish between his work and that of his great forebears. Central to that analogy is the relationship between the orators Cicero and Demosthenes on the one hand and the conquerors, heroes, and creators that he mentions in the same breath with them. And, on closer examination, it appears that there is in fact not the pronounced difference between the two sets of figures that we seemed to find initially. For neither Demosthenes nor Cicero was merely an orator; each was at the same time a statesman. In both cases, moreover, their best-known oratory is a response to what they perceive to be mortal threats to their countries, democratic Athens and republican Rome, and an attempt to rouse the citizenry to defend itself and its way of life. As Demosthenes' *Philippics* urged the Athenians "to awake from their slothful apathy," appealing to "the public spirit that animated the State in former days,"[26] so Cicero's orations against Catiline and his own *Philippics* against Marc Antony sought to move his countrymen to take the steps necessary to preserve the Roman commonwealth in the face of assaults on its liberty. Cicero's contemporary, Cato, we are told, "saluted [him] as 'father of his country.'"[27] Here, then, is the link between the orators and the political and military figures mentioned with them. Each of these—Alexander, Caesar, Richelieu, and Peter—was also, in his way, a kind of "father of his country."

The implications of all this for Herder are far-reaching indeed. By "transplanting" himself into other languages and cultures, he seeks to acquire the ability, comparable to that of great figures of the past, to "create himself" in the act of becoming the "creator" of his own nation. It is a work to which the exposition of *On Diligence*, precisely through its development of a program of *sich verpflanzen* and *sich schaffen*, is intended to make the first major contribution. Herder's optimism and self-confidence are here, at age twenty, nearly boundless, and he will continue to be borne by that wave for some time. The *Travel Journal* of 1769, for example, five years after *On Diligence*, is full of sketches for such grand projects as the one adumbrated here (see, for example, IV, 362–64 and 401–05). And, as Hans Dietrich Irmscher observes:

> The distinctive element of these plans for political reform lies in the fact that their execution is always viewed as the task of an individual who, with this deed, at the same time brings himself into being. In Herder's opinion it is only the great individual who is in this way capable of feeling the essential nature of a whole province or people, of knowing it from the inside, and of mastering it like his own body: as objective reality and yet also the product of his own power (*Kraft*), so that, in the other, he yet remains with himself, indeed here for the first time finds his own identity.[28]

When Herder speaks of creating a society (or a nation, or a culture), he has in view the totality of aspects of human life that go to make up the entity in question. Like the individual human being, a people, or *Volk*, constitutes, for him, a differentiated, but ultimately indivisible, organism. Throughout the present section of *On Diligence*, the exposition has, in fact, been calling attention implicitly to that fundamental quality of human groups. In the hypothetical argument for the use of translations at the beginning of this section, reference was made to three different sorts of cultural activity. Only two of these, however—the work of English natural scientists and philosophers and that of French men of letters—involve any use of language, at least in the ordinary sense, and thus may have appeared to be the only ones to which a discussion of the use of translations versus that of original texts would be at all relevant. It will turn out, however, that that issue has a direct bearing on appreciation of the fine arts as well, and hence that there was a substantive point to including in that passage, in addition, a reference to the sculpture, music, and painting of Italy.

The paragraph immediately following, which provided the response to the argument for translations, also included references both to poetry and oratory and to science and learning. In addition, a point was made of calling attention to the roles played by rulers and patrons in providing, both through material assistance and, as important, in the overall tone and direction that they impart to their societies, a foundation and context for cultural activity of all sorts: " . . . you [Augustus] animated them [Horace and Virgil] through your Maecenas. . . . You, Louis, created through your Colbert the golden century of science and learning . . ." This reference recalled a point introduced implicitly in the first two subsections of part two, namely the extent to which cultural development depends on material conditions. And just as the text at that point exploited variations in grammar and syntax to indicate the positive consequence of phenomena largely negative in themselves, so something similar now occurs here, with the earlier "gold on the royal diadems" echoed and at the same time transformed in "the golden century" created by Louis XIV and his ministers.

This linkage of the opening and closing sections of part two also recalls the depiction of the "Golden Age" with which the essay opened and thereby fulfills the promise, implicit, as we saw, in part one, that the original Golden Age would not prove to be the only one the world would ever see. It does so, moreover, in accordance with the overall positive-negative-new positive pattern ("Golden Age"— "gold on the royal diadems"—"the golden century") that has been at the heart of the exposition throughout.[29] And finally, the earlier reference to the creative role of national rulers also foreshadowed the direction taken in the paragraph now under discussion (the concluding paragraph of part two), in which, building on the response to the hypothetical translation alternative, the initial assertion of the constitutive role of the "veil of language" has begun to be expanded into the outlines of a comprehensive program of cultural and national renewal.

The care with which the cast of characters has been assembled in the analogical structure governing what we have seen thus far of this

paragraph becomes ever more manifest. We have noted the dual status of Cicero and Demosthenes. Each holds an important place both
in the history of letters and in that of his nation, and in each case the
latter distinction was attained to a large extent by virtue of achievements in the former sphere of activity. A comparable dual status is
apparent in the figures of Alexander, Caesar, and Peter the Great,
but with the causal nexus reversed. Alexander was, of course, himself
exclusively a conqueror and head of state; precisely in that capacity,
however, his role in the history of culture was enormous. Significantly, it is that aspect that is emphasized in one standard overview
and assessment of his accomplishments:

> We owe to Alexander, a man of genius at the head of a military
> monarchy, what no Greek city-state would have been able to
> achieve, the extension of Greek civilization over the East. . . .
> Hellenic civilization, as it extended to new regions, became
> exposed to new influences, and the Hellenistic Age . . . came
> into being.[30]

Alexander did not merely conquer new domains; he inaugurated a
new era of civilization.[31] And the same is true of Caesar and Peter
the Great. The one was the major figure in Rome's transition from
Republic to Empire, and thus to the period of high culture under
Augustus to which allusion has already been made.[32] The other was
the first Tsar to assume the title of Russian Emperor (in 1721) and
also the first ruler of that land to seek to elevate its culture by opening
it to influences from Western Europe.

At the same time, moreover, that Herder has taken care to select
as his models figures whose impact on the world was both cultural
and political, further reflection on these choices reveals yet another
consideration that guided him in making them. His purpose at the
present stage of the exposition requires not only that he be able to
cite individuals the nature and effect of whose actions were of a certain sort. The several developments of those figures, the ways in
which they became the men they were, also manifest a particular
feature in common. Each was able to extend himself beyond his native cultural foundations and draw inspiration and power from a foreign model. That inspiration, moreover, was in each case mediated in
the form of art, either linguistic or plastic. The first instance of that
mediation—significantly first, in view of its special relevance, as

seen, to Herder's own immediate situation—is Cicero's use of Demosthenes' "writings" on oratory. Alexander "at the grave of Achilles" may not at first appear conformable to the pattern, but that is because the reference itself involves the use of an image to evoke the productive effect on Alexander of a work of literature. Achilles is not an historical figure but rather one of legend and myth. His mode of existence is poetic rather than real, chiefly in the verses of Homer, and these we know Alexander read enthusiastically, even carrying a copy of the *Iliad* with him on his campaigns.[33] In the cases of Caesar and Peter the Great, the pattern itself is clear—the "image" of Alexander and the "figure" (*Säule*) of Richelieu[34] are products of art— here again, however, the cultural links go beyond the bounds of strictly literary or linguistic phenomena.

The concluding section of part two has passed easily from one to another of virtually all the things that we understand by the term 'culture,' including not only intellectual and artistic activities of all sorts but also the political and societal conditions that tend to promote such endeavors. In so doing, however, it has at the same time maintained its principal focus on the express purpose of *On Diligence*, the resolution of certain questions pertaining to the study of languages. Since any culture represents an organic unity, any particular product of that culture, whether literature or philosophy or science or art, is ultimately an expression of the whole. The manifest differences between them notwithstanding, these are therefore all of a piece in the sense that, if one is able to apprehend any one of them fully, one is thereby able to apprehend them all. At the same time, those forms of expression that rely essentially on language have a kind of semi-privileged or first-among-equals position. For language, by virtue of its integral relationship to "national character" and "mode of thought," is the direct embodiment of that cultural whole of which, for example, science and art and the rest are all, in variously more mediate or indirect fashion, expressions as well.

This consideration also affords some further insight into the reasons why the structure of the extended analogy among historical figures is as it is. As we have seen, the orators Demosthenes and Cicero are not merely included along with the "conquerors," "heroes," and "creators." They head the list. If it is above all in language that civilization and culture are founded and embodied, it is in the first instance the rhetoricians—for Herder, the practitioners of a kind of publicly directed and activist poetry—who create and develop language. Again, he returns to the point in the *Letters for the Advancement of Humanity* (88th Letter, 1796):

> . . . to lay hold of, and to compel to speak, that Proteus that we customarily call national character and which certainly expresses itself no less in the writings than in the customs and the actions of a nation—this is the work of a high and distinguished philosophy. It is exercised most reliably through study of works of poetry, i.e., of the imagination and the feelings, for in these the entire soul of the nation reveals itself most freely. (XVIII, 58)

In learning the language of another culture one gains access to everything that that culture produces. And conversely, failing that linguistic competence, one must remain forever barred from developing a full sense for any of its manifestations. Hence the suggestion that, in resorting to translations of foreign works, one would lose access, not only to English thought and French literature, but also to Italian fine art. Without having "transplanted" oneself into the other culture by learning its language, one would inevitably lack the comprehensive foundation essential to a genuine grasp of any of those works. Similarly, it made no difference that Cicero's contact with Demosthenes, and Alexander's with Achilles-Homer, occurred directly through language, while in the case of Caesar with Alexander and Peter with Richelieu it was by way of works of plastic art. The crucial factor in each case was the ability to extend oneself into another culture, embodied in a single individual in the capacity of cultural and national creator, and so to develop the capacity to create oneself in the same way.

The image of the magnet, borrowed from Plato to sum up this extended analogy, implicitly underscores the special position of language, and especially literary or poetic langue, in the overall vision of culture and cultural advancement being developed here. The image is from the *Ion*, where Socrates employs it to characterize at once the force of inspiration that the poet receives from the Muse and the effect, in turn, of the poet's work on those who hear it: "This stone does not simply attract the iron rings, just by themselves; it also imparts to the rings a force enabling them to do the same thing as the stone itself, that is, to attract another ring, so that sometimes a chain is formed . . ."[35] At any point in the chain, a ring, as it were, faces in

two directions at once, drawing power from those before it and, at the
same time, imparting that force to those that come after. And it is in
just this way that "geniuses inspire new geniuses with continual wonders." Herder has recourse to this same image later in his career in a
similar connection. In his treatise *On the Effect of Poetry on the
Mores of the Peoples in Ancient and Modern Times (Über die Wirkung der Dichtkunst auf die Sitten der Völker in alten und neuen
Zeiten)* of 1778, he writes:

> A poet is the creator of a people around him; he gives them a
> world to see and has their souls in his hand to lead them to
> it. . . . Like the magnet with the iron, he is able to draw hearts
> to him, and as the spark of electricity penetrates everywhere,
> making its way irresistibly, so also his lightning strikes the soul
> wherever he will. (VIII, 433–34)

The *Sketch for a Memorial to Baumgarten, Heilmann, and Abbt
(Entwurf zu einer Denkschrift auf A. G. Baumgarten, J. D. Heilmann und Th. Abbt)* similarly makes use of the image, here in language directly reminiscent of *On Diligence:* "Souls, says Plato, have
this in common with the magnet, that they communicate their power
to each other and so animate each other with a continual series of
wonders" (XXXII, 176).[36]

We are now in a position to draw together the several threads of
the present section and so to represent the stage to which the argument of *On Diligence* has been brought. The structure of the analogy
developed in the final paragraph of section two looks like this:

$$I \text{ (i.e., Herder)} : x :: \text{Cicero} : \text{Demosthenes} ::$$
$$\text{Alexander} : \text{Achilles} :: \text{Caesar} : \text{Alexander} ::$$
$$\text{Peter} : \text{Richelieu}$$

The question, then is: What is the value of *x* in this expression? It is,
in fact, nothing less than the entirety of human history, as embodied
both in the great individuals (the cultural and national heroes) of each
people and in the distinctive character or spirit that informs each
culture and constitutes it in its uniqueness: "At once I raise myself to
[*every* great mind] and extend my soul to the limit of *every* environment." Through the process expressed in the notion of *sich verpflanz-
en,* which is accomplished concretely in the act of learning other languages, Herder means to elevate and expand himself so as to become

one with the development of the human race at large in each of its particular stages.

But a virtually infinite expansion of this sort requires a countervailing moment, lest it lead to a dissolution of individual identity. There must be a movement of contraction as well, in the sense of a focusing of oneself, and this occurs in the activity expressed by *sich schaffen*, accomplished, as the extended analogy has indicated, in the act of creating at once a nation and a culture. This twofold movement has, indeed, been built directly into the overall structure of the third subsection of part two. Its first two paragraphs emphasized linguistic (and thus cultural) multiplicity and differentiation. The final paragraph has focused on the activity of great individuals. And at the point of transition between the two, bridging the penultimate and the concluding paragraphs, stands Herder himself—"At once *I* raise myself . . ."—like the ring in Plato's image facing both ways at once, at once receiving and transmitting inspiration. In his *On Knowing and Feeling, the Two Principal Powers of the Human Soul (Vom Erkennen und Empfinden den zwo Hauptkräften der menschlichen Seele)* of 1775, he writes:

> In everything that is power, interiority and expansion can be distinguished, and so also in the cognitive, governing power of the soul. . . . This profound power requires expansion, in order that it not be consumed by itself; and it requires interiority, in order that it not dissolve into airy nothingness. (VIII, 309)

Essentially the same polarity, with the two movements variously dominated as, for example, *Konzentration* and *Expansion,* or *Sich-Verselbsten* and *Sich-Entselbstigen,* is, of course, also one of the key elements at once of Goethe's metaphysics generally, and specifically of his image of human nature (see, for example, *Dichtung und Wahrheit,* Part II, Book 8).[37]

The closing words of the second section of *On Diligence* make explicit the moment of creative activity:

> With German diligence I seek to combine the solid English humor, the wit of the French, and the radiance of Italy. I gather the spirit of every people into my soul! Reward enough, I should think, to animate our diligence in the acquisition of many languages.

The allusions in the first paragraph of this section to characteristic products of English, French, and Italian culture are here replaced by references to the distinguishing marks of the "spirit" (*Geist*) of those cultures (that is, to the respective sources of those products), to which access is to be had by way of their languages. And it turns out that the German national character, and hence the German language, does after all have a kind of privileged position—not as a language into which others may be translated, but rather by virtue of its unique capacity for *synthesis,* characterized here by means of the notion of "diligence" (*Fleiß*).[38] The German language appears in a similar light in the *Fragments.* There Herder speaks of his language's potential for accomplishing a twofold cultivation of itself, by moving simultaneously in what he has up to that point in the text characterized as contrary directions, at once toward "poetry" and "philosophy" (I, 158). German, he maintains, possesses a singular capacity for combining the two in a "prose of good common sense and philosophical poetry" (I, 217).

The synthesis in question in *On Diligence* is initially the work of an individual, who functions in this capacity as a kind of vehicle or active embodiment of the national soul. Thus we hear first, "With German diligence *I* seek . . ." That individual's task is then to effect the synthesis on the level of the entire nation, and the passage accordingly concludes with " . . . to animate *our* diligence in the acquisition of many languages." The nation will in this way take the next step forward in its own development and at the same time, by virtue of all that (as we shall presently see) is entailed in that movement, contribute in decisive fashion to the development of humanity at large. The individual "creates himself" through becoming "creator" of his country, that is, by moving it to realize itself as a nation; and the nation, in turn, "creates itself" by becoming, at this point in history, "creator" of the human race as a whole.

The outline and basic structure of Herder's program for achieving a genuine *coincidentia oppositorum* of the One and the Many are now largely clear. A plurality of national languages arose as emanations from an original, undifferentiated unity. The return to unity, now, however, differentiated and articulated, is the work of an actively synthesizing intellect, which reenacts in microcosm that movement of expansion and return. That this operation is possible at all is itself a consequence of the initial disruption of unity. It depends decisively, that is, on there having arisen a separate, distinctive German language, the medium through which that synthesis will be undertaken. Thus unity restores itself, paradoxically, by means of its own disruption. Differentiation must be sustained as the ground of unity; unity remains the ideal end of differentiation. Part three of the exposition will elaborate in more detail both the means for carrying out this program and the wider implications of accomplishing it.

3

Synthesis and the
Ideal of Humanity

In its third and final section, the character of the exposition in *On Diligence* undergoes a fundamental change, one that, in retrospect, we can see was anticipated implicitly near the end of part two. In shifting to the grammatical first-person singular at the point of transition between the penultimate and concluding paragraphs of that section, Herder was, in effect, as we noted, like the ring in Plato's image, facing in two directions at once. He had (to vary the metaphor) located himself on a road under construction, a path beginning in the past, running up to its point of partial completion in the present, and pointing from there out toward the future. That position, in which he was for the moment the *object* of his own exposition, corresponds to the one he now occupies in the capacity of its *subject*, between parts one and two on the one hand and part three on the other.

One way of appreciating the significance of this position is to contrast Herder's standpoint here with that of a philosopher to whom he is in a number of other respects, as suggested earlier, closely linked—Hegel. (In drawing that contrast, moreover, a further and perhaps unsuspected affinity between Herder's thought and that of yet another thinker comes to light.) The Hegelian system describes a vast, all-embracing circle, one that is closed with finality in and by the system itself. What begins as bare, undifferentiated Being culminates in the articulated totality of self-knowing absolute Spirit, realized epitomally in the very system that has described that development (and thus, by a short step, in the concrete universal of the individual mind whose creation the system is). Notoriously, Hegel had hardly completed his grand edifice before the questions began to be raised: what did he think would happen next? and how would it (whatever it might be) be accommodated to the system? Ironically, the very comprehensiveness of that system soon came to appear to many as the principal mark of its incompleteness. For, unless history actually does come to an end, there must presently arise circumstances that lie outside the closed circle. Controversy between opposing camps of Hegel's followers was not long in developing, with consequences, perhaps most obviously in the form of Marxism, for our own time.

Marx's initial move in appropriating Hegel's idealism for his own purposes was, as he said, to "invert" it—in a famous remark, he speaks of "standing Hegel on his head." In the dialectical materialism that results from that inversion, he gets things (as he sees it) for the first time, so to speak, right side up, with the sphere of objective phenomena and that of mind or spirit now conceived in proper relationship to each other. By itself, however, that move would not have sufficed to avoid the specific problem with the Hegelian system just noted. That problem stems, as seen, from the system's claim to be a comprehensive *description* of reality. Marxism, on the other hand, is part description and part *program*. Marx locates his system, not at the end of history, but rather (as he appears to have believed) very near the end, and he covers the intervening distance not with a description of an actual state of affairs but with a call for revolutionary action. Where the Hegelian system, that is, *represents* a circular development, Marxism *envisions* one. For the ultimate goal of the revolution, the classless society, is seen as reinstating on a higher level the essence of the "primitive communism" that, according to the theory, was humanity's earliest form of social organization. But the circle remains open. The communist millennium must still be realized in fact.

In this respect Herder looks ahead to Marx rather than to Hegel. We have noted that in *On Diligence* he is intent in his own right on representing the development of the human race as a great circle, from an original state of unity, through disruption of that unity, to its restoration in a higher synthesis. That movement, however, is still underway. Parts one and two have traced as much of the development as has occurred in fact, bringing it up to the moment at which the essay is composed and presented to its audience. In part three the text must therefore, in a sense, go beyond itself. It must obviously remain situated in the present. Yet the specific character of that situation, the nature of the historical juncture at which it finds itself, requires that it reach at the same time into the future. In his capacity as author and speaker of the piece, Herder is at once object and subject of the development it describes, both part of the flow of history and the agent of its further advance. The historicity of his own position means that he cannot himself close the circle. He cannot present in its entirety a synthesis that has not yet occurred (but that will fall rather, as he has said, to "a happier posterity" to complete). At the same time, however, the nature of that position obliges him to assume an active role in history by working to bring about the closing of the circle. Part three of the essay therefore adumbrates as project the direction to be taken to that end. The aspect of program, which has provided a kind of unifying undercurrent to the exposition throughout, now becomes almost completely dominant. Both Herder, the principal forerunner of Romanticism,[1] and Marx, in some respects at least perhaps its most tangibly influential heir, are thus to this extent more "romantic" in outlook than is the greatest purely philosophical voice of the period, Hegel. For Goethe, Schiller, Friedrich Schlegel, Novalis, Kleist, and others of the period in whose works the model or image of circular development plays an important role, the circle also typically remains open. The path toward completion of the journey may be suggested in some way, but (for reasons that we will see in *On Diligence* as well) not followed all the way to the end.

The same conclusion emerges from another sort of consideration of the difference between parts one and two on the one hand and part three on the other. The first two sections of the essay, the differences between them notwithstanding, manifest fundamentally the same logic of exposition. In each case, there is presented first a statement of fact, and from it there is then derived a principle of action. In part one, the historical, genetic account of the rise of national languages led to the conclusion that "nature" engenders in us an "obligation" exclusively to our "native language." In part two, a characterization of contemporary culture (*die heutige Beschaffenheit der Kunst*), as well as a consideration of the central role of the "veil of language" in constituting linguistic meaning at all, together yielded an "argument in favor of learning several languages." Part three, however, has for its province the future, and thus there is nothing (yet) that could be the object of a statement of fact in the manner of the two preceding sections. The dominant concern of part three is rather to synthesize the two *principles* of parts one and two, and in that way to derive a program whereby what does not yet exist in fact—the ideal of humanity (*Humanität*)—may be, if not completely realized, at least approached.

At the same time, those two principles remain (and must, in a sense, always remain) contraries. The argument of part two, as seen, has assimilated and transformed major elements from part one. The earlier catalogue of disparate languages and cultures was recast in a single, extended organic image, as was the nature-governed process expressed by *ihre Familien und Dialekte verpflanzten sich* in the "natural artificiality" of *ich verpflanze mich*. Precisely that movement, however, contains the danger of accomplishing too much. The synthesis of native language and foreign languages may come to seem too simple and straightforward a matter, and to that extent we may lose sight of the tension that, in light of the argument of part one, must continue to inform it. Indeed, that there is a third section to the essay at all bears implicit witness to that consideration. The final paragraph of part two, and especially its last three sentences, expressed in broad terms a program for future action. At the same time, however (as perhaps only now begins to occur to us), the sense for the primacy of the "obligation" to the "native language" had faded considerably into the background. It is not mentioned explicitly at all in part two, and only at the very end of the section is there even an allusion to it, in the reference to "German diligence." The development of the argument in part two was indispensable, but it remains incomplete. Part three will complete matters (to the extent possible within historical limits). It will build on part two, elaborating and giving specific substance to the program announced in outline at the end of that section. In order to do so, however, it will first reinstate in full force the principle of part one. The direction of part three is accordingly at once counter to that of part two and yet, precisely in that capacity, the requisite continuation of it. The overall structure of the essay thus, again, embodies in itself the paradox of simultaneous continuity and disjunction that, for Herder, lies in the nature of developmental processes generally.

The relationship of statement to principle in parts one and two is, in effect, inverted in part three. From the synthesis of the principles of the two earlier sections will come a kind of statement. For reasons already indicated, this cannot, however, be a comprehensive and definitive description of what the future will be like. Rather it will take the form of an evocation of an idea and an exhortation to pursue that idea as an ideal. Herder never sees his task as limited to stating the facts of the matter on a given topic. He expects discovery and disclosure of the truth, properly carried out, to bring about real change in the world of human affairs. His works are always, at the most fundamental level, programmatic in nature. That quality, in turn, is no mere reflection of personal temperament but rather goes to the heart of his most basic philosophical convictions. In the first version of *On Knowing and Feeling in the Human Soul* (1774), he will state, "We live always in a world that we form for ourselves" (VIII, 252). As the analysis of *On Diligence* makes increasingly clear, however, the essence of that position was present in his thought from the beginning of his career. Reality, for him, is never simply there; it must always be brought into being. And thus, with respect to the movement of history in particular, the description of that movement must itself be involved at the same time in advancing it further in the direction of its goal.

That consideration has implications for the relationship of the text both to its audience and to itself. With regard to the latter, what we have seen thus far at every turn throughout the shifting course of the exposition, in its double-tiered, discursive-gestural structure, its exploitation of multiple connotations of key terms and images, its various foreshadowings and recapitulations—in the entire complement of rhetorical and conceptual techniques that have been brought to bear on the topic—is the implicit conviction that, if that exposition is not simply to make a point but to accomplish a task, its structure must reflect as closely as possible the nature of the process it is describing. Hence the tripartite form of the argument, the first two sections of which make contrary points. Herder, of course, knows the end toward which he is moving, in which the apparently irreconcilable contradiction will find a resolution; he is not composing the piece extemporaneously. Nonetheless, it must, in a sense, appear to unfold in that way. The argument must emerge as if guided by its own internal principle of development, and a chief object of his highly self-conscious artistry is to achieve precisely that effect. Nothing would be gained, in his view, if he were simply to lay out directly the conclusion of the argument, that is, the terms in which the synthesis in question is to be pursued (thereby letting the whole of the exposition consist in part three). That would, to be sure, appear to be the readiest way in which to answer the immediate question of *On Diligence* regarding the proper sort of language study to be undertaken in the schools. The audience, however, would be wholly unable to comprehend that answer in the requisite fashion. In accordance with the principle of the historicity of truth discussed earlier, in order to grasp all that is entailed in the conclusion of the exposition, it is necessary to have gone through the entire process by which that conclusion comes into being.

Thus the requirements imposed on the text's structure are, at the same time, requirements with respect to its relationship to the audience. The sections of the essay advancing the competing arguments for exclusive attention to one's native language and for competence in foreign languages must each embody the perspective appropriate to the argument at that stage, in order both that the course of the presentation keep strict pace with its material and that the perspective of the audience pass through those same stages. By the end of part one, the audience must find the argument for the native language compelling. In part two, it must feel the force of the argument for many languages. Only on this foundation can the synthesis in part three work in the way that it must in order to do justice to the problem. Only when the two poles of one language and many languages—and hence also the strict logical incompatibility between them—have actually been grounded in the audience's receptive *experience* can that audience be in a position genuinely to grasp the sort of synthesis toward which the exposition moves in part three, one that, again, both unites and yet preserves essential difference.

In order both to sum up the discussion to this point and to prepare for what is still to come, we can represent the overall structure of *On Diligence* in the form of a table (see page 94).

Part III, § 1

Part three begins, "But what a limitless sea I behold here before me, where, without a Palinurus of my own, I do not dare to venture—a labyrinth of languages, where, without a guide, I must surely go astray." We recall that part two has just concluded on a note of almost exuberant anticipation, having indicated a course of action that might well be taken, at least at first glance, as itself containing the solution to all the problems of the essay. That there is, however, more to be said—that it is, indeed, still necessary to confront squarely the issue that prompted its writing in the first place—is signaled with the first word of its third section. We have several times now noted the appearance of "but" or "however" (*aber*) to announce important junctures in the argument. It was the key element in constituting the

Structure of Herder's *On Diligence*

	part one	part two	part three
temporal dimension	past	present	future
linguistic dimension	"native language"	"several languages"	"manifold of languages . . . unity"; "uniqueness of every language"
cultural dimension	national	international	"goal of our fatherland"; "point of view of humanity"
philosophical dimension	*Natur*	*Kunst*	*Fleiß*
content	history: genesis of languages	cultural analysis: theory of language	project: idea of synthesis as ideal
logic	statement→ principle	statement→ principle	program (synthesis of principles)→vision

back-and-forth structure of part two; it marked the contrast between *Natur* and *die heutige Beschaffenheit der Kunst* in the transition from the first to the second section of the essay; and we now encounter it again, bridging sections two and three. Its function in each case has been to introduce a pronounced shift in the direction of the exposition.

The most direct route to the sort of synthesis envisaged in *On Diligence,* it turns out, is not a straight line in the sense of a straightforwardly linear and cumulative argument, but rather, as it were, a series of tacking movements in which forward progress is achieved by moving back and forth.[2] Thus the oblique structure of part two also provides in its way a guide to the reading of the essay at large, just as we saw was the case in somewhat different fashion with part one. And the same will prove true as well of part three. The structure of the concluding section combines linear and oscillating movements and so incorporates characteristics of both the historical-genetic account in part one, with its uniform chronology, and the zigzag pattern of part two. That circumstance, in turn, provides a degree of concrete corroboration to a point introduced in general terms at the outset regarding the relationship of reciprocal illumination between beginning and end of the essay. Just as it was necessary for parts one and two to unfold separately in order to reach part three, so it is only in part three that they appear in their proper relationship to each other and in that sense become for the first time fully intelligible.

We saw in part two that the movement of expansion and differentiation announced in the declaration *ich verpflanze mich* contained an implicit danger of dissolution of identity, and that some countervailing force would accordingly be required to guarantee the integrity and coherence of the self. That danger is rendered explicit in the images of the "limitless sea" (*grenzenloses Meer*) and the "labyrinth of languages" in the opening lines of part three. The term *Grenzen* has figured prominently in the essay, and, characteristically, Herder has exploited its ability to express more than one meaning, indeed, more than one sort of meaning. In the concrete sense of national borders it appeared at the beginning of part two; in the transition paragraph between parts one and two it expressed the abstract notion of limits of mental activity with the phrase "to determine the respective limits of that effort on which foreign languages and our native language have a claim." That phrase, in turn, recalled the title of the first draft of the essay, "To determine the limits of the effort that we should devote to our native language and to learned languages." The occurrence of the term at the beginning of part three, as part of an image expressing an *absence* of borders or limits, thus recalls the statement of the problem that occasioned the writing of *On Diligence* initially, and in so doing contributes further to the illumination of that problem and the full range of its implications.

The images of a "limitless sea" and a "labyrinth of languages" make clear that the determination of the "limits of our effort" called for here cannot be a matter simply of drawing a boundary, in the sense of setting aside one area for our native language and another for foreign languages—something that, in view of the association of language and thought established earlier, would entail a kind of bifurcation of the mind itself. (That implicit supposition was, for example, the fundamental problem with Clark's reading of the essay, discussed briefly earlier.) The need is rather to achieve a relationship between the two sorts of study, one that will unite the one with the other and yet at the same time preserve the difference between them. Confronted with a "limitless sea" or a "labyrinth," one will gain little by, as it were, remaining on the shore or at the threshold and drawing a line between the secure territory one already occupies and the sea or the maze beyond. The problem of how to find one's way on the sea or through the maze remains in this way untouched. But that is precisely what would result from supposing that determining "the limits of the effort that we should devote to our native language and to learned languages" meant simply establishing two separate spheres of activity, one the realm of our native language, into which we are born, the other the sea, or labyrinth, of foreign languages.

We must rather (to follow out the implications of the metaphors here) embark upon the sea, must enter the labyrinth. That is what the movement announced in part two with the declaration *ich verpflanze mich* amounts to. But if we are to do so—as both our own individual development and that of our nation and, indeed, humanity at large demand—we require a "guide" (*Leitfaden*) to impart organization and direction to our efforts. And that guide turns out to be our native language itself. "Well and good!" the text continues. "That guide will then be my native language, to which I must therefore sacrifice the first efforts of my diligence." The relationship between the native language and foreign languages is not, as it were, a geographical one, as between distinct territories bordering on one another, but rather a *functional* one. Our native language is not an area or domain, something of essentially the same order as other languages but merely the one we happen to occupy. Precisely by virtue of being our *native* language, that is, the embodiment of our distinctive *Denkungsart,* it is for us above all *mental activity.* The relationship between native language and foreign languages thus involves things qualitatively different from each other—a specific form of mental activity and the material that will constitute its object—and it is on the basis of that distinction that the connection between them will then be established.[3]

The images of a sea passage and of progress through a labyrinth, by evoking a sense of movement over time toward a goal, express implicitly the historical dimension of the project. Similarly, the use of the name "Palinurus" to refer to the need for a guide recalls, in correspondingly understated (though, for Herder's audience, entirely clear) fashion, the element of national purpose in that undertaking. Palinurus is the pilot of the Trojan fleet in the *Aeneid* and thus the man charged with guiding his countrymen to Italy, where Aeneas will fulfill his historical mission of founding Rome. Palinurus himself, of course, does not live to see the journey and the mission that it entails accomplished. In this, a part of the story of which the audience would also be aware, we have an additional, if even more understated, reminder of what we have seen to be a centrally important Herderian theme—that of the inevitable costs of progress. In this light, the fact that it is specifically the *Aeneid* that is referred to here appears all the more appropriate. For the whole of Virgil's epic is informed by nothing so much as precisely that sensibility, with its accompanying combination of melancholy and resolve.[4]

This image has, moreover, yet another function in the text, one that has less to do with Palinurus' role in the *Aeneid* in particular than with the general type of image that the invocation of his name represents. This marks the second time in the essay that recourse has been had to the name of a figure from a classical epic. In part one, the reference was to Proteus, from the *Odyssey*. Both cases represent appropriations of material from earlier authors and the transformation of it into imagery for the purposes of the present exposition. At the same time, however, there is a significant difference in the scope of these two images. "Proteus" referred to human language as a whole, specifically to the myriad forms assumed by language in the course of its development at different times and in different places. "Palinurus," on the other hand, as just seen, refers to the "native language" alone, and specifically to its ability to organize and direct the study of other languages.

Fundamentally the same focusing movement occurs repeatedly throughout part three of the essay. Elements of the exposition, and especially images, that earlier referred to other languages and cultures, either to one or another of them in particular or to language and culture generally, now recur with specifically national application. Concomitantly, first-person pronouns and possessive adjectives, present at important junctures earlier in the essay and becoming gradually more prominent as the exposition has proceeded, now tend to predominate. At the same time, the transition in the closing sentences of part two from first-person singular to plural forms becomes (with one exception) permanent. As he comes to evoke the terms of the synthesis toward which *On Diligence* has been moving, Herder continues the combination of discursive and gestural argumentation that has characterized the text throughout. In attempting to lay out for his audience—which, it is surely clear, he understands as ultimately the German people at large—a program for the future, he assumes implicitly, as suggested earlier, the status of a kind of voice of the nation. In relationship to the national entity, he is simultaneously object—brought into being as the specific individual he is within the framework that it defines—and subject—intent on moving it to bring itself fully into being by accomplishing the task latent in it. He is thus at once identical with his *Volk* and distinct from it. In this way, moreover, the question of whether it is the single, exemplary individual or the organically conceived national whole that provides the force driving the engine of history receives a characteristically Herderian resolution. In the way we are seeing, he finds a way to express, by exemplifying, the position that it is both—both, more-over, in a relationship that, again, at once unites and preserves differ-ence.

The conclusion that it is "my native language to which I must therefore sacrifice (*opfern*) the first efforts of my diligence" recalls another motif introduced in part one: "And it is to these foreign lan-guages that we must sacrifice (*aufopfern*) the days of our most vigor-ous flourishing . . ." We saw earlier how the structure of part one im-parted a double tone of voice, overtly condemning but implicitly approving, to the concept of *Aufopfern*. At that early point in the discussion, however, it was not possible to do much more than simply note that twofold quality and suggest in broad terms the reasons for it. Only now, with the reintroduction of the concept on the twin foun-dation of parts one and two, are we able to see the full import of what Herder was getting at obliquely in part one. The sacrifice contem-plated earlier was of "the days of our most vigorous flourishing, our liveliest memory, the freshest fire of our youth," these simply to be given up, in a kind of pedagogical fetishism, to "foreign languages" as if to an "idol." And it is in this sense, in which the sacrifice carried no prospect of achieving anything that would justify the loss incurred, that it was rejected. In the passage at hand from part three, however, the notion of sacrifice itself has undergone a decisive change. In the first place, it no longer appears simply as a matter of giving some-thing up, but rather as expenditure of energy—exercise of *Fleiß*—in a process of cultivation and development. Second, moreover, the im-mediate object of our efforts is no longer "foreign languages" but rather our native language itself, which in turn, as we become better able to make use of all the resources that it places at our disposal, will function as the mediator to other languages. Thus understood, "sacrifice" is not only necessary but positively to be encouraged.

Herder is beginning to give substance to the program announced in the conclusion of part two with the declaration, "With German diligence I seek to combine" the distinctive national characters of, for example, England, France, and Italy; "I gather the spirit of every people into my soul!" German *Fleiß* appeared there as the means by which the synthesis would be accomplished, and, as indicated in the schematic representation of the essay above, the concept of *Fleiß* does indeed provide the keynote of its third section, as did *Natur* for part one and *Kunst* for part two. The task of part three, delineated implicitly in the juxtaposition of parts one and two, involves achieving a particular sort of union of *Natur* and *Kunst,* and the concept of *Fleiß* appears well-suited to that end. It is represented, on the one hand, as a kind of natural endowment—for purposes of the essay a shorthand way of designating the distinctive mark of the German national character. At the same time, it is also related to *Kunst* in the broad but also most fundamental sense of that term. In binding together what was originally separate and thereby constructing new wholes, which the passage cited above suggests is to be understood as its characteristic mode of operation, it creates what does not exist already in nature. The Germans thus appear as that *Volk* whose "nature" it is to act in a fashion properly characterizable as at once artistic and artificial (*künstlerisch* and *künstlich*).

If this were all there were to the matter, however, we might wonder why it was then necessary to take the trouble of writing *On Diligence* at all—as Lessing says in a different (though related) connection in the *Hamburg Dramaturgy* (no. 80), "Why the onerous work . . ."—when, we might suppose, it ought to be sufficient to leave the Germans to the promptings of their own nature in order eventually to see everything needful accomplished. But this is, of course, not all there is to the matter. There are two other important aspects of Herder's outlook to be recalled in this connection—one general, the other specific to the Germans. First, as we have already more than once had occasion to note, no aspect of reality simply exists once and for all for him. A given nature must, like anything else, *develop* from potentiality to actuality. Secondly, the synthesis of *Natur* and *Kunst* represented by *Fleiß* must be a genuinely *dialectical* one, that is, one in which each pole functions actively in relation to the other. That condition, however, is not met, or is at best met halfway, by supposing that the German *Natur* will give rise of its own accord to an activity that is a form of *Kunst.* The distinctive *Nationalcharakter* of the Germans has yet to be realized in fact, and given the unique constitution of that character, it is not enough simply to wait for development to take its "natural" unaided course. For the German nation, as understood here, there can be no such thing as a development that is both natural and unaided. Precisely the *natural* realization of its character, in virtue of the inextricable linkage of *Natur* and *Kunst* involved therein, must take the form of active *cultivation* and thus be a function of *Kunst*. Hence the need for *On Diligence,* in order at once to represent to the Germans their nature (which is to say, for Herder, their vocation) and, precisely in so doing, to move them to undertake as a matter of conscious effort the task of fulfilling it.

The reference to the need to "sacrifice" to the native language "the first efforts of my diligence" (*meine Erstlinge des Fleißes*) gives implicit reinforcement to the point we have been considering here. Of particular significance in this formulation is the fact that *Fleiß* now appears as part of the grammatical *object,* while in the passage from the conclusion of part two cited earlier ("With German diligence I seek . . .") it designated the activity of the *subject.*[5] And we have now seen why that should be so. Even the notion of *Fleiß* encompasses more than one sense. It refers to the activity of synthesizing native and foreign languages, but also to the essential element of the German national character (the progressive synthesis of *Natur* and *Kunst*) that both makes that activity possible and realizes itself in the execution of it. As suggested earlier, that progression involves two different movements at once, one oscillating, the other linear, and we are now able to characterize those movements in more specific terms. The dialectical movement back and forth between the poles of *Natürlichkeit* and *Künstlichkeit* (reflected in the analogous, though not strictly parallel, movement between the poles of native and foreign languages) brings about a movement forward toward the full realization of national (and ultimately human) potential. (This same double movement will figure as well in the conclusion of the essay, in the relationship evoked there between the development of different peoples and the ideal of *Humanität,* which will in turn provide a key element in the effort to conceive a reconciliation of the competing notions of cultural autonomy and historical progress.)

With the "native language" established as the "guide" through the "labyrinth" of foreign languages, it must now be explained both what exactly that operation consists in and how our language is able to fulfill the role assigned to it. The question is approached by way of references, first to national heritage and the place of language in that tradition, and second to the integral relationship between our native language and the constitution of our minds. With regard to the first of these associations, "Just as the love for our fatherland generally enchains us with deeply felt bonds, so the language of our fathers also has for us charms that in our eyes surpass all others." This continues the pattern, noted above, of bringing back elements from earlier in the exposition and recasting them in specifically national terms. The image of "bonds" (*Banden*) linking us to "our fatherland" recalls the "bond of learning" from the first subsection of part two (as well as, of course, the key verb *verbinden,* "to combine," from the final subsection of that part, which, as noted a moment ago, is the word used to express the synthesizing activity that constitutes the essence of German *Fleiß*). *Band* will occur twice more in part three, and when it does there will be more to say about both the image itself and its wider implications for the essay as a whole.

The reference to "our fathers" similarly recalls a corresponding one to "our earliest forefathers" in the opening lines of the piece. As the exposition began with an evocation of the way of life of the ancestors of the human race generally, so the opening of its final section brings to the fore in the mind of the audience a sense for the tradition of the German nation in particular. The movement here, as with other such transformations of elements from earlier in the text, is one of contraction from the general to the specific, from the history of humankind at large to that of a single nation and its language. Out of that contraction, however, will come a new expansion, analogous to, though not of precisely the same order as, the first one, the movement in which national languages and cultures originated. Instead of fragmentation and dispersion, what is now in prospect is an expansion in the sense of an all-encompassing embrace in which will be realized the goal of united, but also differentiated, humanity.

Throughout its first two sections, the predominant pattern of movement in *On Diligence* has been one of expansion followed by contraction: in part one, from the one language of the Golden Age, to a multitude of languages born at the Tower of Babel, to the "obligation" to the native language; and in the first two parts taken together, from the national focus of part one, to the international perspective through most of part two, to the activity of the individual speaker at the end of that section. In part three, the pattern reverses: now, as we are seeing, contraction is to be followed by expansion. The German nation thus finds itself located implicitly at the point at which history comes to a head and out of which the future will emerge. At the same time, however, we recall that the movement at the end of part two from *ich verpflanze mich* to the implied *ich schaffe mich* was also one, first, of expansion and, then, of contraction, parallel to the pattern of part one (that parallel being, as we noted at the time, the key to the passage). And we also recall that it is the task of part three to elaborate and develop that movement. This is in fact precisely what it does. It does so, however, not by simply continuing in the same direction but rather by incorporating a countermovement as well. The pattern of movement and countermovement alluded to in general terms at the beginning of this chapter thus assumes concrete shape. In the end, the two movements of expansion-contraction and contraction-expansion occur together. We see again, from another vantage point, how the tenor of Herder's thought favors models that combine oscillation between opposite poles with linear progression and how he seeks to express that combination above all gesturally, by incorporating it in the structure of the text itself.

He now proceeds to say something about the relationship between a language and the constitution of each individual to whom it is native:

> They [the "charms" (*Reize*) that the "language of our fathers" holds for us] impressed themselves upon us first and were, so to speak, formed together with the subtlest ties and linkages in our sensibility. Or our native language has in fact the most profound harmony with our most sensitive organs of perception and their slightest modulations.

In person, number, and tense, the reflexive constructions here—"impressed themselves" (*druckten sich . . . ein*) and "were formed" (*bildeten sich*)—echo those of part one and thereby balance those of part two. In part two, the subject of such verbs had been the speaker, *ich*. At that point in the exposition the emphasis was on the role of the individual subject as active creator, even of his own language. Now, on the other hand, it is language that appears as the subject. In creating itself—we recall the (gestural) suggestion in part one that languages are animated by an internal principle of development—it also creates us. Thus the exposition preserves the dialectical reciprocity between the constitutive activity of the individual and the context in which alone that activity can arise and take concrete shape.

In his overview of Herder's thought and works, Irmscher emphasizes this point in particular in what he says about *On Diligence:*

> Herder sees very well that language is always already present, and he concludes from this that every new linguistic formulation will be decisively determined, in part, by this acquired context. This holds both for the individual's system of language and for that of a community. . . . Herder calls attention

emphatically to the value of this "already present language" (*Vorsprache*) . . . (*Über den Fleiß in mehreren gelehrten Sprachen*, 1764). In it the knowledge and wisdom of earlier generations is . . . fixed and lies ready to be called on by those who come after, who thus already have at their disposal a treasury of instruments for mastering existence (*Daseinsbewälti-gung*). At the same time, the *Vorsprache*, by making present to subsequent generations the reality of realized human potential, also calls to their attention the task that is set for them as well: namely, to explore for their own time the still unexhausted range of human possibility and to represent it in their own lives.[6]

Particularly apposite here is the emphasis on the unity of *tradition* and *mission* in Herder's thought and the recognition that that key idea already finds expression in so early a work as *On Diligence*. As we shall see presently, it in fact has a pivotal role to play in the move by which the central problem of the essay is to be resolved.

The third collection of *Fragments* returns to and develops further the ideas first enunciated in the passage last cited from *On Diligence:*

[Our native language] impressed itself upon us first, in our tenderest years, as by means of words we gathered the world of concepts and images into our soul. . . . Our distinctive mode of thought (*Denkart*) is, so to speak, rooted in it, and our soul and ear and organs of speech are formed with it . . . Like the fatherland, it surpasses in charm (*Reiz*) all other languages in the eyes of the person who was the son of its heart, the infant at its breast, the pupil under its direction, who is now the joy of its best years, and who is to be the hope and honor of its old age. (I, 400)

The parent-child relationship between language and the individual to whom it is native evoked in the images "son of its heart," "infant at its breast," etc. is striking for its suggestion that the language itself passes through a cycle of ages analogous to the ages of man in connection with each individual speaker of it. Not only, it seems, is any given person born into a particular age of language, in accordance, for example, with the schema in the section "On the Ages in the Life of a Language" in the first collection of *Fragments*. There is also a sense in which the entire cycle is played out in conjunction with the ages of each individual. The general influence of the eighteenth-century Neoplatonist revival as well as, in particular, that of Leibniz is apparent in this sort of microcosm-macrocosm model. In seeing that, moreover, and taking into account other aspects of Herder's thought that we have encountered in *On Diligence,* including especially the historical dialectic developed there, we begin to see something of the link that his thought establishes between Leibniz and Hegel. I have in mind here, in particular, the eighteenth- and early nineteenth-century development from the Leibnizian concept of the monad, according to which each of the basic elements of reality "represents" with greater or lesser "clarity" the whole, to the Hegelian notion of the concrete universal, in accordance with which the whole is embodied in each of its parts precisely as those parts in turn realize themselves in the constitution of the whole.[7]

The passage cited here from the *Fragments* not only reiterates but also expands on and makes explicit the thesis from *On Diligence* regarding the "bonds" between us and our native language. It says not merely that "our distinctive *mode of thought* is . . . rooted in it"; it adds that "our soul and *ear* and *organs of speech* are formed with it" as well. Not only is the structure of our minds determined by the character of our native language; a corresponding relationship obtains even between that language and parts of our physical constitution. Just as Herder is among the first to argue both that language and thought are ultimately identical and that the structures of language and mind vary widely among the peoples of the earth, past and present, he is also, so far as I know, the first to make a point of extending that relationship to include our vocal and auditory apparatus as well. As a matter of individual experience, no one who, as a native speaker of English, has attempted to master the phonology even of German (virtually as close a relative of English as there is in the family of languages), not to speak of the various sound systems of languages such as Russian or Arabic or Chinese, will, I think, be likely to find the position implausible. As a matter of empirical fact, moreover, it is, I believe, generally held by linguists to be correct. In Herder's own case, whatever basis he may or may not have had in actual observation for drawing this conclusion, he would surely have been led to it in any case on purely philosophical grounds. His rejection of the Cartesian separation of mind and body, or, to put the matter in positive terms, his conviction that the human organism is ultimately unitary in its constitution, seems clearly to entail the existence of such a fundamental continuity between the physical and mental aspects of our being.

The opening paragraph of the final section of *On Diligence* began with the assertion that the "native language" would provide the organizing principle for the study of foreign languages. References, first, to national linguistic tradition and, second, to the central role of our native language in both our mental and our physical development, have laid the foundation for stating how, specifically, that operation is to take place. On this basis, the paragraph now concludes with a description of the operation itself:

> Just as a child compares all images with its first impression, so our mind automatically matches all languages and dialects to our native language—and to what tremendous advantage! The great manifold of languages thereby has imparted to it unity; our steps in foreign realms become shorter and more certain when the goal of our fatherland shines steadily before our eyes. In this way the application of our diligence is facilitated; I swim with a support that bears me up.[8]

We noted earlier, in connection with the key image of the "veil of language," that linguistic structures function for Herder as do the categories of the understanding in Kantian epistemology. The claim perhaps seemed difficult to credit (despite what we saw to be the evidence for it in the text), in view of the still widely held belief that his thought is staunchly opposed to the "critical philosophy" of his one-time teacher.[9] In the passage just cited, he reasserts his position, now no longer in the figurative language of part two but rather in direct fashion. In so doing, he not only makes clear that his theory of language includes as one of its central elements an idea that will later be the foundation of Kant's philosophy, but he also anticipates even the Kantian vocabulary. In the *Critique of Pure Reason* Kant characterizes the synthesizing activity of the mind by saying that it produces "synthetic *unity* in the *manifold* of intuition" (emphasis added).[10] And as we see, that is precisely what, for Herder, "our mind" (*unser Geist*) does. In the case at hand, it applies the forms of "our native language" to the great "manifold of languages" and creates thereby "unity." In the *Treatise on the Origin of Language,* he continues to find the distinguishing, indeed, the defining, quality of human mental activity in its capacity to take "a manifold" and to constitute on that basis, in accordance with a "governing principle" (cf. the central importance for Kant of the notion of "rule," *Critique of Pure Reason,* A 105–06), "clear unity" (V, 97). And in the first version of *On Knowing and Feeling in the Human Soul* of 1774, he again asserts: "Sensations deliver raw materials to the soul, booty; the soul stamps its image on them . . ." (VIII, 252).

The entire tendency of *On Diligence* has made this conclusion virtually inevitable. Various points in the exposition have in one way or another argued, and the passage immediately preceding the one just cited has emphasized again in the strongest terms, that the mental activity that *is* "our mind" does not exist apart from the distinctive structures of our native language. Both the overall perspective and the specific forms of organization determined by our particular "veil of language" (equivalent to our characteristic *Denkungsart*) define the *Weltbild* that establishes the terms in which phenomena exist at all for us. Any "manifold," that is, any body of raw material that we may encounter, insofar as it becomes something that we actually apprehend, must have imparted to it the "unity" of that *Weltbild*. Thus, for Herder, there can be no question of grasping foreign languages in any way other than the one he describes here.

The analogy between the workings of "our mind" and the mental processes of "a child" again recalls, and at the same time transforms, an element from earlier in the exposition. The opening lines of the essay contained two references to "children." The first sentence, as part of the characterization of the Golden Age, spoke of "the small circle of our earliest forefathers . . . with the patriarchs, like children around their parents." We noted at the time that that age, when "all the world was of one language and one speech," was the early childhood of the human race and thus, notwithstanding the positive features of that primitive state (summed up in the image of "rough, simple contentment"), a stage that had to be left behind in order that the growth of the race at large not be stunted. That growth, however, though it moves away from childhood, nonetheless at the same time seeks always to recapture the condition of unity that characterized it, though at a higher, differentiated level. The link between the starting point and the (envisioned) culmination of human development lies in the fact that, although the childhood of the race lies in the distant past, we are all at some time children. Indeed, in our capacity as synthesizers of the "manifold" of other languages, we remain—so the suggestion of the analogy in *On Diligence*—in a sense always children. The *Treatise on the Origin of Language* recalls this image in order to express the phenomenon of continuous and expansive development that constitutes the essential mark of human nature, that which distinguishes us from all other forms of life precisely by virtue of our being creatures of language:

> It is of the essence of the human soul that we learn nothing in isolation, for itself alone, but rather either join it to what we already know or consider what in the future we will join to it. . . . That chain continues in this way until our death; one is, so to speak, never a *whole* person—always developing, in process, moving toward completion. . . . We are always emerging from childhood, however old we may be, are always underway, restless, unsatisfied; the essence of our lives is never enjoyment, but rather always progression, and we have never become fully human beings until—our lives are over . . . (V, 98)

The first sentence of the essay's second paragraph again employed the image of childhood, referring this time to "the children of dust" as they undertook to build "that edifice that threatened the clouds," the Tower of Babel. This was the situation that led to the rise of national languages, one of which, in turn, is to be the vehicle for imparting "unity" to that "manifold" in the way we are now seeing. The multiple use of the term "child" links the moments of disruption and synthesis and thereby reflects implicitly, again, the view that, precisely by being fragmented and dispersed, humanity also gained the capacity for achieving its own eventual reunification. In addition, the expression "children of dust" (*Kinder des Staubes*) looks even further ahead in the essay than the point we have now reached. It will be recalled again in the passage from Kleist's poem *Spring (Der Frühling)*, with its evocation of the activity of bees, at the conclusion of the exposition. "Children of dust" is, of course, a traditional epithet for mankind, alluding to the story of creation in Genesis. At the same time, however, *Staub* also means "pollen." Inherent in the nature of the "children of dust," as we shall see, is the vocation to be also, so to speak, "children of pollen," and this, moreover, in the double sense represented by the work of the bees—at once collectors of pollen, enriching their own homes, and pollinators of other organisms, stimulating further growth.

The analysis thus far of the concluding passage in the first paragraph of part three is, however, only half the story, as a moment's reflection makes clear that it must be. If there were no more to Herder's program than what we have seen to this point, it would amount, in effect, simply to a kind of translating of foreign languages into our own, and that is, of course, something against which he inveighed strongly in part two. What has still to be included here is the moment of *sich verpflanzen,* and it is to that that he turns next. The statement of synthesis, "The great manifold of languages thereby has imparted to it unity," continues, ". . . *our steps in foreign realms* become shorter and more certain when the goal of our fatherland shines steadily before our eyes." These two ideas, expressed in the same sentence, clearly represent for him two aspects of a single process.

In part one, arguing the case for study of the native language, he had said:

> I may perhaps be able to imitate stammeringly the languages of foreign nations, without, however, ever penetrating to the *core of their uniqueness.* I may perhaps, with much exertion, learn the words of dead languages from the monuments they have left, but *their spirit* has vanished for me. Fortunate it is that the peoples whose languages they were have passed away; otherwise who knows how much ignorance, coarseness, and violence to the original they would perhaps accuse me of.

Just as our native language reflects a distinctive *Geist,* a particular, characteristic form of mental activity, the same is true of every other language. Any language we may wish to learn will, like our own, embody an entire *Weltbild* in its own right. If we remain outside that world and concentrate merely on learning to mimic the external features of the language, we will, even "with much exertion" (*mit vielem Schweiße*), accomplish little, and nothing of what is essential. We must step outside ourselves and actually enter the "foreign realms" determined by other languages.

Genuine apprehension of foreign languages thus involves two movements, which occur simultaneously but in opposite directions. We must bring them to us, in the sense of grasping them from, and in the terms of, the perspective of our own language. At the same time, we must go to them, in the sense of achieving a perspective corresponding to theirs.[11] The final paragraph of part two began, "At once I raise myself to [every great mind] and extend my soul to the limit of every environment." That operation was, in turn, the necessary condition of being able to say at the end of the paragraph, "I gather the spirit of every people into my soul!" In dealing with other languages, we can synthesize only insofar as we extend our scope, can assimilate to ourselves only by going outside ourselves. And the same is true in the other direction. The activity of "transplanting" ourselves into other realms of language can function only when "directed," in the way we have seen, by the "guide" of our own. This is, again, the movement of simultaneous expansion and contraction that we have seen the exposition working throughout both to express and to exemplify in its own structure.

The result of that double movement is a step forward—again, oscillation issues in linearity—for it yields a perspective that is no longer exactly the one or the other, neither the original native perspective nor the foreign one, but rather, in a sense, both at once. Thus conjoined, however, both are also transformed from what they were initially. It is one of the most characteristic and, from the standpoint of the history of ideas, most important tendencies in Herder's thought that he consistently resists formulations of absolute alternatives. The challenge of existence is for him precisely the opposite of what it is, for example, for Kierkegaard. Not evasion, but rather acceptance of the "either/or" is, in his view, the temptation that must constantly be overcome. To accede in a given circumstance to the demand that one choose one position or the other is for him not, as it is for Kierkegaard, to ground one's existence authentically, but rather to admit defeat. As he sees it, reality repeatedly confronts us with polarities in which the opposed elements are at once mutually exclusive and equally necessary. In *On Diligence* that pattern appears, for the first time in his career, in the form of the opposition between fidelity to one's native language and the need to learn foreign languages, with all the wider implications that that issue has for the nature and development of the human race at large. Versions of the same pattern, formally for all intents and purposes identical, though varying widely in particulars of content, are also at the heart of those later works, from the *Fragments* to the *Ideas,* on which his reputation has always principally rested. And so too is the method that he develops in *On Diligence* for dealing with the problems that it raises.

Confronted with an apparent "either/or" situation, Herder sees the task as one of finding a way to say "both." Since the key to doing so, however, lies in conceiving things *historically,* under the aspect of change, the price of being able to say "both" is at the same time the obligation to say, in a sense, "neither." The process by which the contrary poles of native language and foreign languages are unified is not one of simple fusion (in which the differences between them

would be annulled), but rather of development, and hence of transformation. Our *Denkungsart* after learning another language is
clearly not the same as it was before doing so, and analogous considerations hold for the perspective of the language we learn. For it as
well is no longer precisely what it was in its original form, that is, the
sole embodiment of the *Geist* of the native speaker of that language.
In another, and equally fundamental sense, however, our *Geist* remains throughout this process the same one it always was. As Herder,
several years after *On Diligence*, makes explicit in a passage from the
Origin of Language cited earlier, our being is for him not something
fixed once and for all but rather (again, following Leibniz, and anticipating a host of later thinkers) activity, *Kraft*. In every linguistic act,
we both determine some part of our world and at the same time realize a further possibility latent in ourselves. When we learn another
language, we do essentially the same thing, but at the metalevel. For
the possibility we realize thereby is a part of our capacity for extending the scope of those very *possibilities* of world- and self-
determination. And in so doing, we come ever nearer to realizing, by
embodying in ourselves, the ideal of universal humanity as a unity-
in-difference.[12]

The overall structure of the opening paragraph of part three of *On
Diligence* has reinforced the point in gestural fashion. There was introduced first here the idea of the native language as the "guide" for
the study of foreign languages. That was followed by a reference to
the importance in this connection of national linguistic tradition, "the
language of our fathers . . . that in our eyes surpasses all others." This
Vorsprache both establishes the context and provides the means for
the synthesis to be carried out. Then came the description of the
process of synthesis itself in the passage beginning, "Just as a child
. . ." And the paragraph concluded on a projective note with the reference to "the goal of our fatherland that shines steadily before our
eyes." The single term "eyes" links the beginning and the end of the
paragraph, and thus the two moments of tradition and mission. To
look in the proper way to the past, to the heritage from which one
comes, *is* at the same time to look to the future, to the tasks yet to be
accomplished, for both the nature of those tasks and the ability to
undertake and complete them are latent in that tradition. And similarly, to proceed in the proper way into the future, which involves
stepping beyond the confines of one's initial situation and taking
"steps in foreign realms," *is* at the same time to return home, for
precisely by pursuing the "goal" of the "fatherland" that does not yet

fully exist, that is, by seeking to realize in fact what is still only potential in it, we reaffirm in genuine fashion the "love for our fatherland" that tied us to it "with deeply felt bonds" to begin with. And
between these reciprocal evocations of past and future, occupying the
middle of the paragraph, stands the statement of synthesis, now discussed at some length, by which specific content is given to that convergence of tradition and mission.

Part III, § 2

The second paragraph of part three develops further the theme of
twofold movement. It begins, "The more we cultivate our native language in active use, the more deeply will we be able to penetrate into
the uniqueness of every other language." The more we immerse ourselves in our own language, the sharper becomes our sense for the
differences among languages generally. Within the limits of *On Diligence*, it is not possible to follow out the implications of this idea in
detail. That would call for extensive consideration, backed by examples, of the expressive possibilities peculiar to various languages
(precisely the sort of discussion that, of course, does appear in Herder's later works). He accordingly limits himself on this occasion to
making the point in very brief and general terms: "Here we will see
gaps, there abundance, here riches, there a desert . . ." But, again, it
is not in the nature of the mind to perceive passively. Rather when-
ever we apprehend anything, we do so in an active process of constitutive synthesis, by imposing on what we can think of as a kind of
precognitive "raw material" specific, linguistically determined structures of mind. Thus the sentence just cited continues, " . . . and we
will be able to enrich the poverty of the one with the treasures of the
other."

The mention of "treasures" recalls an earlier reference, in part two,
to the "treasury of discoveries" represented by "every language of
learning," as well as the characterization in that same section of each
language as a "key to many treasure-vaults." The idea implicit in
those earlier passages, that the "treasures" specific to each language
have that status, not as discrete, self-contained entities, but rather by
virtue of their participation in an actively undertaken process of general enrichment, now becomes explicit. And that enrichment extends
to the instrument itself by which we gain access to these "treasures,"
our native language. In appropriating other languages, as seen, we

expand our own resources as well. Thus the text continues, following the sentence just cited:

> For how exact is the bond between a language and a particular way of thinking (*Denkungsart*)! Whoever surveys the full extent of a language takes in at the same time an entire field of thought; and whoever learns to speak that language with precision gathers into himself thereby a treasury of well-defined concepts. The first words that we stammer as infants are the foundation stones of our knowledge, and our nurses our first instructors in logic.

And if our "*first* words" (our national language) constitute the foundations of our knowledge, and if those who look after us as small children (and who thus, among other things, impart that language to us) are in that capacity our "*first* instructors" in the forms of thought, so these operations will be repeated with each new language that we learn. Each represents a "treasury of well-defined concepts," and the effect of assimilating such "treasures" to ourselves is, in a virtually literal sense, to expand our minds with regard to both what we know and, even more fundamentally, how we think.

In postulating an "exact bond" between language and particular way of thinking, Herder here asserts for the first time in entirely unambiguous fashion a thesis that, as noted earlier, is among the most fundamental (as well as best known) in his work. (In so doing, moreover, he all but explicitly expresses his conviction that theory of knowledge must be conceived and undertaken as theory of language.[13]) To appreciate the full import of this statement for the exposition of *On Diligence* in particular, however, it is necessary to see it as well in relation to a passage from earlier in the essay. In the fourth paragraph of part one, we recall, the bond between language and mode of thought was made the cornerstone of the argument for confining ourselves to study of our native language, an argument that culminated in the rhetorical question at the conclusion of the paragraph, "Would not things instead of words, and concepts instead of signs, nourish us far more?" The contrast intended here was evidently between the substantive content of our native language (actual "things" and "concepts"), which it has by virtue of embodying the distinctive form of mental activity peculiar to us, and the mere "words" and "signs" that are all foreign languages can be for us, failing contact with the *Geist* that animates them.

The key term "concepts" from that earlier point in the text recurs in the passage last cited from part three, now, however, as with other such elements from earlier stages of the exposition, with its function shifted in accordance with the overall direction of the concluding section. In seeing that transformation, we are better able to see how the essay, as it reasserts the bond between language and thought, also significantly modifies the conclusion drawn on the basis of it—no longer exactly the same one drawn in part one, but not exactly a different one either. The earlier argument is reinstated, but in a new form, incorporating the considerations of part two. Our relationship to our native language remains primary and unique, as it must, but that relationship can now no longer be understood as an exclusive one. In the course of the exposition, which has described in discursive terms the development of the human race under the aspect of language from its beginnings to the present, and which is now intent on laying the foundation for the next major phase of that development, the text has also—gesturally—brought about a *development in the concept of the native language itself*. Having not merely witnessed that development, but, as members of the audience, having actually contributed to bringing it about, we are now able to see that cultivating our own language in fact *means* exercising the ability it gives us to expand into other languages and assimilate them to ourselves. In this way we fulfill in genuine fashion *both* the "obligation" to our native language, established, as seen in part one, by nature, *and,* at the same time, the potential we have, by virtue of the present world-historical position of our language and culture, for contributing decisively to realization of the ideal of humanity at large.

Part III, § 3

The argument of *On Diligence* is now essentially complete. Before concluding, however, Herder takes a moment to touch on a theme that will go on to occupy an increasingly important place in his work, that of the possibility of a distinctive German national literature. The third paragraph of part three begins, "And to what end is our native language more indispensable than to poetry and eloquence, since with languages now dead the greatest strength of their thunder and the beauties of their most brilliant turns of phrase have died out as well." The latter half of this statement is puzzling, at least on first reading, for it appears to run directly counter to a centrally important position that we saw taken earlier in the exposition. In part two, it was precisely the "holy reliques of poetry and eloquence" preserved in languages themselves now dead that served as the chief examples in the argument against the use of translations. When translated, it was maintained, such works lose all the qualities of greatness peculiar to them; but those qualities themselves remain intact, and access to them is to be had by learning the languages in which they exist. What, then, can be meant by asserting here that the strength and beauty once expressed in those languages have died with them? The key to an understanding of the passage lies in seeing that it represents another instance of the overall pattern of part three. It does, in a sense, return to the position of part one (and, insofar, moves counter to part two), but at the same time it presents that earlier position in transformed fashion, as one growing out of the development of the exposition in parts two and three. The "native language" referred to here is now conceived as the simultaneous agent and object of a process of cultivation, in accordance with which it goes out into the worlds of other languages (*sich verpflanzen*), draws on their resources, and thereby realizes itself (*sich schaffen*).

It is, however, one thing to draw inspiration from a foreign model and another merely to imitate it, and that is the distinction underlying the passage at hand. To the extent that we succeed in "transplanting" ourselves into those other worlds, we shall certainly find that the strength and beauty of their literature still lives. If, however, we attempt simply to duplicate in our own language what was achieved, say, in Greek or in Latin, or, worse still, if we forswear our own language altogether in favor of another, we shall fail doubly, for we shall be neither our model nor ourselves. The paragraph continues, "The Homers, the Ciceros, the Voltaires, the Popes—did they become what they were in languages other than their own? With the exception, among the ancients, of a Terence, and, among us, of a few other writers, none of these repudiated his own native tongue." Our goal must be to achieve, again, not identity with the great models of the past, but rather a position analogous to theirs, to be to our own time what they were to their eras.

We saw in part two how this same idea functioned as perhaps the single most important element in the argument of the final stage of that section, and we noted at the time, with a passage from the *Fragments,* one example of how Herder returns to it at greater length in later works. Again in the *Fragments* he writes, with the same end in view, "Let us see the true ideal of the Greeks in each of their poetic forms for emulation, and their individual, national, and local excellences so that we may turn away from such imitations and be roused to imitation of ourselves (*Nachahmung unsrer selbst*)" (I, 294). He in effect inverts Winckelmann's famous maxim that the only way for us to become inimitable is to imitate the Greeks. For him, we imitate the Greeks (and every other great *Kulturvolk*) precisely by realizing ourselves as inimitable: "The more decisively our works are German and modern, the more related we will be to the Greeks. That which alone can enable us to equal them is the same open and genial power of creation."[14] "Only those middle periods" he writes in *On Diligence*,

> when we extricated ourselves from barbarism merely to become imitators of the ancients, when the Scaligers, the Buchners, and the Rapins were composing their works, only these times worshipped the Roman language as the sole monarch and left the native language on the slag heap. How good it is, though, that these times are no longer!

Both the tenor of the essay generally and, in particular, the fact that in the Germany of the 1760s a slavish imitation "of the ancients" was by no means yet a thing of the past make clear that the purpose of this statement, and especially the exclamation that concludes it, is as much hortatory as descriptive. It remains in large measure the task of the audience to bring into being through its own actions the "truth" expressed here.

Part III, § 4

That this is in fact the intention becomes still more apparent in the following paragraph, where features associated initially with "those middle periods" are spoken of as still to be seen in the present day:

> The scholar in foreign languages who remains a barbarian in his own, the Masorete of Priscian[15] who cannot write a line of a German letter without making himself ridiculous, who enumerates the verse forms of Horace, corrects the prosody of Anacreon and Lucretius, and who nonetheless (such a scholar is he) hardly understands the poets of his own language—a thousand years ago he would have been an apostle of wisdom among barbarians; today he is merely a ridiculous pedant.

The reference in the last clause but one to "barbarians" ties the end of this passage to its beginning and also links the whole passage to the description of "those middle periods, when we extricated ourselves from barbarism" preceding it. To note that connection is, at the same time, to see Herder expressing, in gestural fashion, an especially important aspect of his view of history. The status and value of human phenomena is for him (as it is, interestingly, again, for Marx) not determined exclusively, or perhaps even primarily, by their intrinsic nature. Rather it depends decisively on their historical position and, in particular, on the function that that position both enables and requires them to carry out.

There was a time when, in order to free oneself from "barbarism," it was necessary to become largely an "imitator of the ancients." Precisely for the sake of the *Bildung* of one's own *Volk,* it was necessary, paradoxically, to turn away from native resources and school oneself on the achievements of other peoples. At the same time, however, the necessity in question, despite its benefits in the long run, was nonetheless a disagreeable one—hence the expression of relief that the time when that necessity obtained now lies well in the past. Most important, of course, in the present connection is that this sort of development of one's own *Volk* through imitation of foreign models, with its concomitant virtual abandonment of the native language, must on no account be confused with the *functional* relationship of native and foreign languages that it has been the concern of *On Diligence* at once to describe as theory and to expound as program. The former was one stage that had to be passed through in order to reach the point at which the latter becomes possible, but they remain fundamentally different activities. Thus to persist in the one after history has moved on to a level that calls for the other is no longer to further development but to hinder it, and in that sense to become oneself a new "barbarian."

Making that point chiefly in connection with the relationship of German to "the Roman language," moreover, also recalls and completes a point the seed of which had been planted back in part one as part of the catalogue of national languages that sprang up in the wake of the Tower of Babel. Reference was made there to the way in which the Romans cultivated and refined their language by borrowing from Greek, and it was suggested, gesturally, that something analogous would prove necessary in the case of German. Had the Romans, however, modeled themselves entirely on the Greeks and so left their own native language "on the slag heap," there would never have arisen a Latin language in its own right, and hence the relationship of the Germans to Latin authors that was appropriate to "those middle periods" could not have occurred at all. Thus precisely the fact that that relationship was at one time possible (because Latin had gone on to realize its own distinctive potential as a language) contains, at the same time, the implicit message that such a relationship must never be regarded as more than a temporary expedient in preparation for the real task of realizing the unique vocation latent in one's own national character.

Herder begins the paragraph that we have been discussing, "Yet I am still speaking about the scholarly value of the native language and forgetting it from the point of view of humanity at large." He thus reintroduces explicitly the concept of learning and, in so doing, gives himself the opportunity to make the negative point just noted regarding a type of contemporary scholar in classical languages. At the same time, the rhetorical pose notwithstanding, it is quite clear that he has not "forgotten" anything here and that the audience is fully intended to see this. The phrase "scholarly value of the native language" (*gelehrten Nutzen der Muttersprache*) recalls the reference to "the burdens of our learning" (*unserer gelehrten Lasten*) in the opening paragraph, and a principal object of the exposition that has taken us from the one to the other has been precisely to demonstrate that we can form a true notion of the value of studying our native language only, so to speak, *sub specie humanitatis,* that is, in light of the advancement of the entire race and the special role we are called on to play in it. With the audience thus gesturally reminded of that central strain in the argument, the essay can conclude:

Part III, § 5

Our learning must cultivate both sorts of language, must link both together in a bond of knowledge. Thus, when we depart from our homes, we must often imitate the bees,

. . . . who in scattered hosts
hum through the air and fall upon clover and blooming
    plants, [t/o]
and then return home to the hive, laden with sweet booty,
and bring forth for us the honey of wisdom. . . . [16]

This final paragraph draws together the principal themes sounded in the work. It at once sums up the conclusion the argument has developed and incorporates into that summation, by recalling and restating key images and motifs from throughout the text, the course by which it was reached. The result is a web of ideas and images in which the individual threads are all discernible but which at the same time resists articulation of its structure solely in discursive terms by considering each thread independently of the others. As it has been necessary to construct the exposition throughout on two levels at once, one discursive, the other gestural, so that double-tiered structure is preserved in exemplary fashion here in its closing lines. The paragraph has built into it a field of multiple associations and resonances that carry the mind of the listener or reader back and forth in the text in several directions at once and that depend for their full meaning on being apprehended in that nondiscursive fashion. Even the discursive sense of the first sentence, the comparatively straightforward and more or less readily paraphrasable proposition it expresses, is put together of elements that, by virtue of the various structural roles they have already played in the exposition, cannot be understood simply as we would ordinary language. The sentence is thus simultaneously discursive and nondiscursive in character, and analogous considerations apply as well to the remainder of the paragraph (beyond the obvious sense in which it expresses an image in its own right) in that it, too, draws on and restates elements from earlier in the text.

In noting this structure and how it functions, we also see the culmination of Herder's effort to realize in *On Diligence* a true union of theoretical explication and programmatic efficacy. As noted earlier, it is for him never sufficient merely to state what is to be done and why. Rather he seeks to exemplify in the structure of the text itself both the nature of the task to be undertaken and the means required to do so. To the extent that the audience genuinely *understands* his description of the problem to be resolved, it has accordingly, by that very fact, undergone a kind of *preparation* for dealing with it. For in order even to comprehend what he is saying here, it is necessary, as we have seen, to hold in one's mind a range of different, even contrary, interpretations of key terms and to sustain in a kind of constant oscillation the tension between them. And coming to grips with the problem of the One and the Many, as conceived and presented in *On Diligence*, requires precisely that sort of mental agility. Thus, as we come to assimilate all that is entailed in the goal that the text sets for us, we at the same time find ourselves already embarked on the path toward achieving it.

The first major term in the concluding paragraph, "learning" (*Gelehrsamkeit*), occurred several times in the essay's second section. Reference was made there, first, to a "bond of learning" (*Band der Gelehrsamkeit*) that came into being as a kind of by-product of international commerce—in order to acquire from other peoples "booty" of all sorts, it proved useful to know their languages. The situation thus brought about, however, though in the first instance simply an outgrowth of economic interests, contained the potential for activities of a sort and scope not contemplated by those initially responsible for it. Thus that section of the text went on to speak of the "treasury of discoveries" that has been achieved by "every language of learning" and that can now be shared among other peoples "as booty." The ability to pass back and forth across linguistic frontiers, and the resulting dissemination of the discoveries and advances of any one nation among all the others, has to an extent brought the peoples of the earth closer together and has insofar advanced the overall development of the race. The degree of unity that can be achieved in this way is, however, fundamentally limited. As long as languages remain only repositories of learning and the media in which it is conveyed, they themselves undergo no development. Thus, while the possibilities for contact among different peoples have become more extensive, this remains essentially contact among discrete national-cultural centers.

Realizing the ideal of humanity as a unity-in-difference requires that languages themselves become objects of cultivation, in the way the essay has described. "Learning," as specifically "*our* learning," is thus no longer a by-product of some other activity or a particular sort of content to be transmitted. Rather it assumes the function of principal agent of development. Development, in turn, becomes something that no longer merely occurs, but is rather now undertaken as a matter of conscious intention. Thus "our learning" is in fact equivalent to "our diligence" (*Fleiß*) and hence to the capacity for expansion and assimilation that is the hallmark of our native language. Animated by the "bond" of tradition and exemplified in the "bond" uniting language and mode of thought, it realizes its vocation—the mission inherent in both those "bonds"—by cultivating both itself and foreign languages and thereby linking them together in a new "bond of knowledge" (*Band der Wissenschaften*).

The first principal verb in the final paragraph's opening sentence, *bauen,* which I render here as "cultivate," draws together a still wider range of themes and motifs. It recalls "that edifice (*Bau*) that threatened the clouds" from part one, the project whose failure resulted in the fragmentation of the human race, but which thereby also set in motion the chain of events leading to the point at which, through the agency of one people in particular, it begins to undertake consciously the task of its own reunification. One might almost suppose that Herder were thinking of Dante here. Just as the Pilgrim's attempt at the beginning of the *Comedy* to ascend directly to heaven is blocked and he is obliged to pass by stages, first of descent and only then of ascent, through all the realms of the afterlife before finally attaining his goal, so the Tower of Babel was also a kind of impermissible shortcut. It represented an attempt, this time by the race at large rather than a single individual, to pass directly from the earthly to the divine realm without first proceeding through the stages of development and differentiation in which all the myriad possibilities of human nature are realized, as they must be.[17] However this may be with respect to Dante, though, it is clear that Herder does anticipate Hegel here. We think, for example, of Hegel's criticism of Schelling, that the latter's method of philosophy amounts to an attempt to proceed directly to the goal of the Absolute without establishing concretely and specifically all the intermediate stages that are necessary if that goal is to have a substantive (as opposed to merely nominal) existence. What such an approach gives us in the end, says Hegel in a famous phrase, is merely "the night in which, as one says, all cows are black."[18] For him, on the other hand, as for Herder before him, the end of the process of development exists only as the totality of the process itself, and thus none of its stages may be omitted, either in fact or (as we have seen, for ultimately the same reason) in the exposition that describes it.

In addition, the verb *bauen* itself, used in the sense of "to build," occurred in conjunction with the "work (*Gebäude*) of so many hands" in part two. The particular significance of *bauen* in that connection was that it marked the point at which the exposition shifted from characterizing the development of the race simply as a process of natural, organic growth (as in the extended image beginning "Thus the seeds that were germinated in Asia . . .") and introduced the image of construction. That was also the point at which modern peoples appeared on the historical scene ("In the same way, the people of today can build on the foundation of the ancients . . ."). What had been a substantially unconscious progression, analogous to the growth of plants, becomes, over time, conscious. We reach the stage at which we are able to survey the path by which we have come, to comprehend the development that it represents, and, on that basis, to understand our own nature not as something given but rather as something still to be realized. Accomplishment of the tasks latent in that nature is henceforth a matter of conscious execution of them. Each of us becomes, in a formulation noted earlier from the *Origin of Language*, "the purpose and goal of his own cultivation" (V, 28). Of the longer passage in the *Origin of Language* that culminates in this phrase, Irmscher says, "Without actually employing the term itself at this point, Herder expresses here the core of his conception of *Humanität*, which the *Ideen zur Philosophie der Geschichte der Menschheit* (1785ff.) and the *Briefe zu Beförderung der Humanität* (above all Letter 25; 1793ff.) take up again and develop further."[19] In light of the ways that, as we continue to see, *On Diligence* in turn lays the foundation for the *Origin of Language*, Irmscher's observation lends further support to the thesis of the present study that the essay represents to a large extent the source from which the bulk of Herder's subsequent work proceeds.

Employed in its meaning of "to cultivate" in the concluding paragraph, *bauen* reemphasizes the point in question here. At the same time, however, this usage has associations with the organic realm— that of naturally growing things—that were not part of the earlier use in the sense of "to build." By thus exploiting what I earlier termed the conceptual range of a single key term, the exposition is able to bind together its several sections without undoing the distinctions and contrasts it has established. It emphasizes that the status of the contemporary age in the overall development of the race represents a qualitative change from what has gone before and yet at the same time, again, preserves the sense that that development remains nonetheless a single, continuous process. *Bauen,* moreover, again in the sense of "to cultivate," expresses the combination of natural and artificial, *Natur* and *Kunst,* that as we have seen is henceforth to be the key to continuing the development of the race in the direction of its goal.

The object of cultivation referred to in the sentence at hand, "both sorts of language" (*beiderlei Sprachen*), also harks back to an earlier formulation and again, as with other such instances of the same structure in part three, illuminates it retroactively by developing aspects of it that could not have been elaborated in the requisite way at that earlier stage. In part two, the question was posed rhetorically and, as we noted at the time, with more than a hint of disdain, "But how much do our glittering needs of today not require that we move in both sorts of world (*in beiden Welten*)?" The immediate reference in the context of part two was to the desire of contemporary society for luxury items of all sorts and to the corresponding need to travel to "distant worlds" in order to meet that demand. It has turned out, however, as we have gone on to see in the remainder of part two and in part three, that the present age, by virtue of its historical position and the mission thereby latent in its nature, does have a real need to meet. And accomplishing that mission, by cultivating "both sorts of language," does require, moreover, that we in another sense "move in both sorts of world," the *Weltbild* of our own language and those of other languages.

The activity of bees provides an apt concluding image to the exposition (one, interestingly, that finds a place in the writings of many eighteenth-century authors, most notably, perhaps, Mandeville, with his use of it to illustrate the principle of "private vices, public benefits," but more than a few others as well). Oscillating continually between hive and field, bees nonetheless, in a sense, never leave home, for the community of the hive, as embodied in its productive activity, is wherever the bees are at work. To put it another way, for a bee, to be "at home" means to be engaged in a constant movement back and forth by which both home in the narrower sense, the hive, and the world outside are changed. At the same time that the bees collect the material necessary to sustain and expand their community, they also play a central role in the growth and renewal of organisms in the outside world on which they in turn depend. Each aspect of their activity supports the other, and thus the whole, comprising hive and outside world together, advances.

So with us and the work envisaged for us in *On Diligence*. To *be* ourselves means to *fulfill* the vocation inherent in our character, and that means, in turn, always going beyond what we are in the narrower sense of the language and *Weltbild* from which we begin. At the same time, "when we depart from our homes"—for which, of course, there could also have been written "when we transplant ourselves," *wenn wir uns verpflanzen*—we are always also, in the perspective of the whole, returning home. *Sichverpflanzen* leads to *Sichschaffen*. In journeying in foreign realms, the "goal of our fatherland," which is at the same time ultimately the goal of humanity at large, remains always before us. As with the bees, action in accordance with our nature involves an oscillating movement that is at the same time a progressive one. For the poles between which we move do not remain unchanged but are rather themselves altered in the very process of that movement. In drawing on the "blooming plants" of other languages and cultures, we cultivate "both sorts of language" and in that way derive a new kind of "booty." This "honey of wisdom," the text's concluding image for the fruit of our efforts, represents, like Faust's declaration in his final speech of "wisdom's last verdict" (v. 11574), the essential contribution that we are called on to make to the next great *Aufblühen* of the race in the form of the ideal of fully realized humanity.

As noted a moment ago, in *On Diligence* Herder already expresses, in Irmscher's phrase, the "core of his conception of *Humanität,*" which he will later elaborate in, among other works, the *Ideas* and the *Letters for the Advancement of Humanity.* In view of that fact, it is all the more interesting to note the way in which Irmscher's discussion of the *Ideas* provides implicit additional support for the thesis regarding the link between Herder's first work and the one generally viewed as his magnum opus. It turns out, that is, that the *Ideas* incorporate not only the substance of the thought introduced in *On Diligence* regarding the development of the human race but also the structural terms in which it is formulated there, as a movement combining oscillation and linearity. Irmscher notes that, for Herder, the nature of the individual human being and the overall movement of history manifest essentially the same structure. Just as the former is constituted as a "tension-filled product in which opposing forces achieve balance,"[20] so also is the latter:

> Herder defines . . . the law of history . . . as a development toward an "equilibrium of opposing forces" (XIV, 250) . . . , in which the unique character of each people emerges and becomes historically effective (XIV, 227). . . . He attempts to comprehend the process of development of peoples . . . as one of dialectical growth and formation. This cultivation (*Bildung*) of peoples, however, is overlaid by a higher, linear development toward a definable goal (XIV, 235ff.). . . . The principle of balance, which Herder also terms reason, equity, and humanity, gains ever more influence among people. . . . The "collective reason" (XIV, 249) of mankind will finally bring about the age of happiness for all.[21]

Some of this, to be sure, has application almost exclusively to the later Herder and is thus not reflected in *On Diligence*. For example, the notion of an explicitly "definable goal" (*definierbares Ziel*) to human development is, as noted earlier, incompatible with the theory that he enunciates in the earlier essay. The possibility of such a definition can arise only as he comes, in later years, to construe the ideal of *Humanität*, in Irmscher's words, less in terms of "the inexhaustible potential of human nature" and more as "a system of ethical norms"[22] admitting of more or less exact specification. In keeping with this movement in his thought, he then tends to place the emphasis in his work less on the comprehensive project of realizing humanity as a great unity-in-difference, and more on the comparatively modest (though, obviously, scarcely inconsiderable) goal of bringing about an "age of happiness for all." Nonetheless, the basic structure that Irmscher describes for the *Ideas* remains fundamentally the one that we have seen developed initially in *On Diligence*. The one major element necessary to complete the picture with respect to the *Ideas* would be an indication—something not provided (nor, of course, intended to be) by the lone verb "overlaid" (*überlagert*)—of how, specifically, the two sorts of movement, oscillating and linear, and thus the two sorts of development, those of individual *Völker* and that of *Humanität* at large, function in relationship to each other. I hope the analysis here of *On Diligence* has, among other things, contributed to an understanding of how Herder conceives that relationship.

The resultant of endless oscillation and ultimately linear progression can be regarded as a single great circle. Such a circle, as we have several times noted in the course of the discussion, represents for Herder the overall structure of human history and is, accordingly, the form he seeks to exemplify in the text of his essay. The movement thus depicted, however, although it may be entering its final stage, is, as we have also noted, not yet complete. Our journey, represented in the closing image by the work of the bees, is announced, and the goal is characterized in general terms, but the circle is still open. And insofar as the end of that journey coincides with the realization of an *ideal,* that is, something inherently *infinite* in nature, or in other words, insofar as the potential of human nature is indeed inexhaustible, it must always remain open. The notion of an asymptotic approach to a given value also suggests itself in this connection, and Herder was in fact to employ that model as well much later in his career, in the section "Love and Selfhood" ("Liebe und Selbstheit") in the first collection of *Scattered Leaves (Zerstreute Blätter)* (1785), to restate the theme introduced here in *On Diligence:*

> As far as enjoyment of the highest being is concerned, there it remains always "hyperbola with its asymptote" . . . and must remain so. The hyperbola approaches the asymptote, but never reaches it. To our supreme happiness, we could never lose the sense of our own existence and attain the sense that we are God. We remain always creatures, even when we become the creators of great worlds. We approach perfection; infinitely perfect, however, we never become. The highest good that God could give all creatures was and remains their own existence, in which he is to them, and by stages becomes ever more, all in all. (XV, 326)

The conclusion of *On Diligence* thus adumbrates yet another of the fundamental elements of the sensibility of German Romanticism, namely the notion that, in the case of an infinite project, the way to the goal converges ultimately with the goal itself. The ideal of the synthesis in which all humanity is comprehended as a single community, a unified totality in which differentiation and particularity are nonetheless preserved, is realized precisely as a continual effort to achieve that end. Essentially the same relationship between goal and progress toward it is at the heart of the vision evoked by Faust in his last speech, as well as in the continuing ascent toward heaven (a progression clearly to be understood as infinite) on which the play ends. Substantially the same sensibility runs as well through the work of the first great theoretician of German Romanticism, Friedrich Schlegel (for example, in the famous description of "Romantic poetry" in the 116th *Athenäums-Fragment*). The expression of this idea by means of the imagery of departure and return, moreover, anticipates what is probably the most characteristic Romantic way of formulating the notion. It requires, for example, no great leap of imagination to hear in the perpetual return home of the concluding image of *On Diligence* the forerunner of the answer to Heinrich von Ofterdingen's question, "Where, then, are we going?—Ever homeward."[23]

For Herder, however, as for his successors, the "home" to which we return is itself irreducibly twofold in nature: on the one hand, the condition of unity from which we began; on the other, by virtue of incorporating multiplicity and diversity—indeed, contrariety—differing qualitatively from that original state. It is thus, in structure, an exact counterpart of the form that we have seen him impart to his essay. Accordingly, as noted earlier, as we gain proficiency in the sort of balancing act necessary even to understand him here, as our minds assimilate all that is involved in the problem of the One and the Many and what is necessary to resolve it, we at the same time come to embody in ourselves a condition analogous to the one inherent in the object of our efforts. Thus not only can we say that the way and the goal are, ultimately, one. Precisely in virtue of being able to formulate that conclusion on the basis of Herder's exposition, that is, precisely to the extent that we *comprehend* his conception and representation of the goal of *Humanität,* we have already begun to *exemplify* in ourselves an image of it.

4

After *On Diligence*

Four years after *On Diligence,* in 1768, Herder writes in the second edition of his *Fragments,* "In our education we learn thoughts through words, and the nurses who teach us to speak are thus our first instructors in logic" (II, 16). That idea, expressed in part in virtually identical terms, had already figured, as we have seen, in *On Diligence.* The *Fragments,* as their title indicates, represent a very different sort of work from *On Diligence.* In particular, their much looser structure affords the necessary latitude for developing topics at whatever length seems appropriate. And thus we find here the explicit elaboration of a theme the core of which had been formulated initially in the earlier work:

> If it is true that without thoughts we cannot think and that we learn to think through words, it follows that *language determines the entire scope and limits of human knowledge.* . . . This general way of regarding human knowledge from the standpoint of and in terms of language must yield a *negative philosophy:* how far human nature should rise in its ideas, because it cannot rise higher? how far one should express and explain oneself, because one cannot express and explain oneself further? How much would one be able to sweep away here of all that we say, without thereby thinking anything; that we conceive incorrectly, because we say it incorrectly; that we want to say, without being able to think it. The man who would develop this negative philosophy would stand at the furthest extent of human knowledge, as if at the edge of the world; and

though he would be unable to raise his head over these limits
and look around in the open air, he would nonetheless extend
his hand in that direction and proclaim: Here is emptiness, and
nothingness! And he would have attained, in another sense of
the term, the highest Socratic wisdom: that of knowing nothing. (II, 17; emphasis added)

Herder's program of "negative philosophy" corresponds closely to
Kant's conception of the task of the *Critique of Pure Reason*. In the
preface to the second edition, for example, Kant writes:

Metaphysics has to deal only with principles, and with the limits of their employment as determined by those principles
themselves. . . . But, it will be asked, what sort of treasure is
this that we propose to bequeath to posterity? What is the
value of the metaphysics that is alleged to be thus purified by
criticism and established once for all? On a cursory view of the
present work it may seem that its results are merely *negative,*
warning us that we must never venture with speculative reason beyond the limits of experience. Such is in fact its primary
use. (B xxiv)

A version of the theme of "the positivity of the negative" also appears
in Kant's thought in this connection. The passage cited here from the
preface to the second edition of the *Critique* continues:

But such teaching at once acquires a *positive* value when we
recognize that the principles with which speculative reason
ventures out beyond its proper limits do not in fact *extend* the
employment of reason, but, as we find on closer scrutiny, inevitably *narrow* it. These principles properly belong [not to
reason but] to sensibility, and when thus employed they
threaten to make the bounds of sensibility coextensive with
the real, and so to supplant reason in its pure (practical) employment. So far, therefore, as our Critique limits speculative
reason, it is indeed *negative;* but since it thereby removes an
obstacle which stands in the way of the employment of practical reason, nay threatens to destroy it, it has in reality a *positive* and very important use. (B xxiv–xxv)

Much of what has been written about the relationship of Herder's
thought to Kant's has been unduly colored by the well-known, not to

say notorious, facts of their personal relationship. Allusions in the
literature to the bad blood between the two in later years often seem
to outnumber efforts to compare what they actually say in their
works. Or when reference is made to these, in Herder's case it is frequently only to two very late pieces, the *Metacritique* (1799) and
Kalligone (1800), discussion of which, moreover, sometimes appears
more concerned to emphasize Herder's overt intention—to overthrow
Kantian epistemology and aesthetics (or what he took these to be)—
than to examine closely the texts themselves. This tendency in Herder studies has meant that both an important respect in which he
breaks new ground in the history of ideas and a significant point of
contact (in a manner of speaking, before the fact) between his work
and Kant's have tended to be overlooked.[1]

Historians of philosophy identify two major "turns" in philosophical thinking since the eighteenth century, one "epistemological," the
other "linguistic." Each of these involves a fundamental reordering of
the ways in which philosophers frame their questions and the meth-
ods by which they seek to resolve them.[2] The "epistemological turn"
occurs in the eighteenth century and is generally regarded as the
work of Kant. In his commentary on the first *Critique,* Robert Paul
Wolff explains what this entails:

> The epistemological turn is the progressive substitution of
> epistemological for ontological or metaphysical considerations.
> It is the recognition that the knowing subject can never be
> ignored, or bracketed out. Since all knowledge is the knowl-
> edge by a subject, even the most general investigation of the
> modes and categories of being will have to begin with an anal-
> ysis of the limits and preconditions of knowing. . . . If there are
> forms of perception and cognition which are inherent in the
> fact of consciousness itself, then these will constitute the limits
> of Being, so far as it can be discussed at all. To extend our
> investigation beyond those limits will involve us in an empty
> play of words for which no content can ever be provided.[3]

As Kant himself puts it succinctly, ". . . the proud name of Ontology
that presumptuously claims to supply, in systematic doctrinal form,
synthetic *a priori* knowledge of things in general . . . must, therefore,
give place to the modest title of a mere Analytic of pure understanding" (A 247, B 303).

Kant's substitution of, in Wolff's words, "certain logical character-

istics of judgments for the illegitimate notion of an independent universe of objects"[4] has implications for language insofar as it disquali-
fies from the domain of intelligible discourse propositions now shown
to be neither true nor false but simply meaningless. The Kantian
argument is not, however, itself primarily a linguistic one. The "logical characteristics of judgments" that it analyzes are ultimately categories of mind, not structures of language. The distinction between
these two notions is a fine one in Kant. He does, after all, derive the
Table of Categories (that is, the pure concepts of the understanding)
from the Table of Judgments, a schematic listing of the various forms
that propositions may assume. Nonetheless, the distinction exists, and
it is clear where for him the priority lies. The Table of Judgments is,
as he says, merely "the transcendental clue (*Leitfaden*) to the discovery of all pure concepts of the understanding" (A 67, B 92). It is, to
put it mildly, a less-than-exhaustive description of human language,
and in any case, as Wolff reminds us, "Kant quite evidently adjusted
the Table of Judgments so that it would yield the desired Table of
Categories."[5] Once the latter Table has been derived, the argument
of the *Critique* can proceed to its principal concern, the transcendental deduction of the categories—the demonstration, that is, that the
pure concepts of understanding, especially the concept of causality,
are objectively valid for our experience precisely because they constitute that experience in the first place—without concerning itself
further with questions of language.

The "linguistic turn" in philosophy stands in relation to the "epistemological turn" as that watershed stood to the way of doing philosophy that it succeeded. Just as Kant reanalyzed questions of Being
as questions of knowledge, modern linguistic philosophers reanalyze
questions of knowledge as questions of language. In his introduction
to the collection of essays entitled *The Linguistic Turn*, Richard
Rorty characterizes "linguistic philosophy" as "the view that philosophical problems are problems which may be solved (or dissolved)
either by reforming language, or by understanding more about the
language we presently use."[6] In our century, and especially in the
last two to three decades, versions of that view or derivatives of it
have become either the dominant paradigms or major competitors for
dominance not only in philosophy but in one field after another
throughout the humanities and social sciences. And the most vigorous
and stimulating forms taken by this broad tendency have been those
developed by thinkers who, like Wittgenstein, Cassirer, Heidegger,
Habermas, and Lévi-Strauss (to mention only a handful), have in one

way or another preserved intact the advance achieved with the "epis-temological turn" and built upon it.[7] Wittgenstein's entire philosoph-ical career, and perhaps most especially his notion of *Weltbild*, devel-oped explicitly in some of his last work[8]; Cassirer's "philosophy of symbolic forms"; Heidegger's early analysis, in *Being and Time,* of the phenomenon of posing the question of Being, as well as his rein-terpretations of key terms in the language of the pre-Socratics, and his later meditations on the special relationship of poetry to Being; Habermas's reflections on the various implications and presupposi-tions of correspondence, coherence, and consensus theories of truth[9]; and Lévi-Strauss's "science of the concrete"—each of these repre-sents both a continuation of the fundamental insight that reality is not simply given but is rather constituted by the experiencing sub-ject, and an attempt to analyze that constitutive activity as grounded ultimately in the workings of language.

It is customary, as noted a moment ago, to regard this general out-look as having developed in two principal stages over the last two hundred years. There is, on this view, first the "Copernican revolu-tion" of Kant's "critical philosophy" (to use his own terminology), which transforms our understanding of the world of objective fact from something existing independently of us to something that we ourselves bring into being, and second, in the twentieth century, a reinterpretation of that revolution in thought in linguistic terms. Both our reading of *On Diligence,* however, and what we have seen of a number of other works in which Herder builds on the foundation laid in that essay, including the *Fragments,* the *Travel Journal,* the *Trea-tise on the Origin of Language,* and *On Knowing and Feeling in the Human Soul,* make clear that, in the 1760s and 1770s, he had al-ready accomplished in his own thinking the essence of the "episte-mological turn"—the conception of the constitutive role of the ac-tively knowing subject in relation to reality—and that he had done so, moreover, in the terms of the "linguistic turn," ordinarily located by historians more than a century later.

Commenting on the passage from the *Fragments* cited above, in which Herder outlines his program of "negative philosophy," Irmscher notes:

> [Language] sets limits to our capacity for knowledge by estab-lishing the perspective under which reality can be experienced and known. Whoever therefore wishes to determine the limits of knowledge will find in a given language the conditions of its

possibility. Thus already in 1768, Herder conceives the idea
of a critique of knowledge as critique of language (*Erkenntnis-
kritik als Sprachkritik*.)[10]

Irmscher's formulation of the matter underscores further the affinity
noted earlier between Herder and Wittgenstein (in many respects the
Kant—or Herder—of the twentieth century). For the *Tractatus
Logico-Philosophicus* is, in essence, nothing other than (in Herder's
words from the *Fragments*) "a general way of regarding human
knowledge from the standpoint of and in terms of language." In it,
Wittgenstein develops an exemplary expression of what Herder
clearly envisages, a "critical" philosophy (in the later, Kantian sense
of that term), in which the structures constitutive of reality are shown
to be those of language. And, near the end of the *Tractatus,* he outlines a program with a distinct resemblance to the "negative philosophy" of which Herder had spoken earlier:

> The correct method in philosophy would really be the follow-
> ing: to say nothing except what can be said, i.e. propositions of
> natural science—i.e. something that has nothing to do with
> philosophy—and then, whenever someone else wanted to say
> something metaphysical, to demonstrate to him that he had
> failed to give a meaning to certain signs in his propositions.
> Although it would not be satisfying to the other person—he
> would not have the feeling that we were teaching him philos-
> ophy—*this* method would be the only strictly correct one.
> (6.53)

In the same vein, Herder follows the section of the *Fragments* cited
above with, "If I am not mistaken, from our entire metaphysics, from
ontology to natural theology, ideas would at once be forced to with-
draw to which mere words had afforded entry and a false right of
belonging" (II, 17).

If, however, Herder's conception of his philosophical program as
ultimately *Sprachkritik* thus places him even closer to Wittgenstein
than to Kant, the opposite is true with respect to diagnosis of the
circumstances that make such a critique necessary. The *Tractatus*
does not address the question of why anyone would want to say (or
try to say) "something metaphysical" in the first place. Kant, on the
other hand, opens the preface to the first edition of the *Critique of
Pure Reason* with just such a diagnosis:

Human reason has this peculiar fate that in one species of its knowledge it is burdened by questions which, as prescribed by the very nature of reason itself, it is not able to ignore, but which, as transcending all its powers, it is also not able to answer. (A vii)

Herder had already expressed essentially the same insight in the 1760s. His programmatic sketch of the nature and goals of his envisaged "negative philosophy" concludes:

> . . . and just these [the pseudo-ideas referred to in the passage last cited] are the ones over which there has been the most argument. Nothing is easier to quarrel about than what neither party understands, and unfortunately the human race is drawn to nothing so much as wanting to explain what it finds impossible to explain. (II, 17)

In the section of the *Fragments* immediately preceding the one in which he formulates the notion of a "negative philosophy," Herder writes:

> There is a symbolism common to all people—a great treasure-vault in which is preserved the knowledge belonging to the entire human race. The true philosopher of language, whom, however, I have not yet seen, has the key to this dark vault. When he comes, he will open it, throw light on it, and show us its treasures. That would be the true *semiotics,* something that we now find in name only in the indexes of our philosophical encyclopedias: *a deciphering of the human soul through its language.* (II, 13; emphasis added)

The history of the term 'semiotics' is a longer one than is sometimes supposed. The sense in which it is for the most part currently used, as the name of the general science or theory of signs, seems by and large to be regarded as stemming from the work of C. S. Peirce and F. de Saussure at the turn of the century.[11] Reference is also regularly made in this connection to the somewhat later work of Charles Morris, who, influenced in particular by Peirce, established the division of semiotics into syntactics, semantics, and pragmatics—the studies, respectively, of "the formal relations of signs to one another," "the relations of signs to the objects to which the signs are applicable," and "the relation of signs to interpreters."[12] Franz von Kutschera, however, in his survey of linguistic philosophy, reminds us that *Semiotik* was also an "old Stoic designation,"[13] and he notes as well that 'semiotics' occurs in the seventeenth century in the work of the British empiricist philosopher John Locke.[14] Before it became a linguistic or philosophical term, though, 'semiotics' was, in English at any rate, a medical one. In fact, the Oxford English Dictionary still gives for 'semeiotics' only "the branch of medical science relating to the interpretation of symptoms."[15] One of the examples given by the OED to illustrate this usage, moreover, taken as it is from Lavater, indicates that it was also at least one of the meanings of the German *Semiotik* in Herder's time.[16] In addition, however, the term also appears in Germany at this time in a linguistic connection, as the title of the third section of J. H. Lambert's four-part *Neues Organon* (published, interestingly, in 1764, the same year as *On Diligence*).[17]

Herder's use of the term to refer to the study of language *as the key to the understanding of human nature* seems, however, to be his own invention.[18] The idea for such a program follows naturally from the conception of language that we have seen introduced in *On Diligence,* a conception, as we have also noted, that is developed at length in, among other writings, the *Treatise on the Origin of Language.* The aim of the latter work is, in Irmscher's words, to demonstrate "that human nature does not merely, of necessity, produce language, but rather, moreover, that it constitutes itself *in* language and *as* language."[19] Language thus represents, as Herder says in the *Treatise,* "a dictionary of the soul" (V, 56), and the study of it in all its aspects accordingly represents the first and best key to a comprehensive science of man.

If Herder is the first to use the term *Semiotik* to designate the sort of program he envisages here, he does have at least one forebear with respect to the substance of that program. That is the Italian philosopher and jurist Giambattista Vico. Paraphrasing a central tenet of Vico's thought (which, like Herder's, is at once philosophy of history, anthropology, epistemology, and a good deal more), Berlin says:

> [T]he creations of man . . . are natural forms of self-expression . . . [and] natural ways of conveying a coherent view of the world. . . . [T]he way to understand . . . men and their worlds is by trying to enter their minds . . . by learning the rules and significance of their methods of expression—their myths, their songs, their dances, the forms and idioms of their lan-

guage. . . . [O]ne needs to understand what they lived by, which can be discovered only by those who have the key to what their language, art, ritual mean . . . [20]

Implicit in Berlin's repeated use of the grammatical plural here is a related respect in which Herder's and Vico's outlooks broadly coincide. For both of them, the human race presents the observer with a multitude of different forms of self-expression and organization of experience. These, says Berlin, continuing his presentation of Vico's position, "must be understood, interpreted, evaluated, not in terms of timeless principles and standards valid for all men everywhere, but by correct grasp of the purpose and therefore the peculiar use of symbols, especially of language, which belong uniquely to their own time and place . . . "[21] Herder, of course, could not agree more. The passage last cited from the *Fragments* continues:

> Every nation has its own storehouse of thought rendered into signs; this is its national language: a store to which the centuries have added, that has waxed and waned like the moon, that . . . has experienced revolutions and transformations, . . .—the treasury of the thought of an entire people. (II, 13)

We have seen that for Herder, as for Kant, reality is never simply given, but is rather constituted by the human beings whose reality it is. We have also seen that, where Kant analyzes that constitutive activity as the workings of categories of mind, Herder locates the structures that organize, and so create, experience in the various forms of linguistic expression and communication. Up to this point, then, the basic outlooks of the two thinkers have, as suggested, a substantial amount in common, with the difference between them being, if not merely one of emphasis or formulation, not a substantial matter of primary doctrine either. Going a step further, however, we come to a point on which the two genuinely do disagree. We saw that there is a sense, if an extremely limited one, in which linguistic structures are fundamental for Kant as well, inasmuch as he purports to derive the Table of Categories from the Table of Judgments. To offer the latter as an even remotely adequate representation of how language works, however, is, from Herder's perspective, simply not to take seriously the enormous diversity in the languages actually used by different peoples. It is, for him, a cardinal principle that one must take the manifold phenomena of human linguistic behavior as one finds it and attempt to understand each of its manifestations on its own terms, not reduce them all to a single, uniform set of possible forms of the proposition. In this respect, he differs not only with Kant but also, of course, with the Wittgenstein of the *Tractatus*. One part of the argument of the *Tractatus* takes as its task the formulation of "a description of the propositions of *any* sign-language *whatsoever* in such a way that every possible sense can be expressed by a symbol satisfying the description" (4.5). This part of the text culminates in Wittgenstein's statement of "the general form of the proposition" (6). The relationship between the two thinkers in this respect appears in a different light, however, if we consider Wittgenstein's later thinking on language, from the time of *The Blue and the Brown Books* and the *Philosophical Investigations* on. The starting point for this second period of his philosophical work—the thing that provided the impetus for his return to doing philosophy at all—was precisely his growing awareness of the limitations of the analysis of the *Tractatus*. Though adequate to certain kinds of language use, the model that it presents, as he came to recognize, is by no means able to account for all of them.[22]

For Kant, on the other hand, the human mind is essentially the same at all times and in all places, and therefore it should in principle be possible, in a work like the first *Critique*, to formulate a comprehensive and definitive description of the structure of its activity. Kant was (and is), of course, far from the only one to hold this view of the mind. Indeed, it is likely that until well into the eighteenth century most people, by a wide margin (and whether philosophers or not), simply assumed it to be true. Herder, along with Vico, is among the first to challenge that assumption. A generation later, carried by the twin waves of Romanticism and post-Kantian Idealism, the challenge will have grown into a full-scale assault. Where Kant, in other words, is a universalist (cognitive, no less than ethical), Herder's inclinations are, at least initially, relativist. In the terms of a well-known opposition in twentieth-century linguistics, Kant appears to side with Chomsky, Herder with Whorf. Versions of this dichotomy, with Herder located on only one side of it, constitute another aspect of a kind of received image of him. That image, however, though it may come somewhat closer to the truth than, for example, the view that his thought is fundamentally opposed to the critical philosophy of Kant, is nonetheless, as suggested in chapter 1, no more than half the picture and thus, taken by itself, misleading at best. In particular, it leaves out of account what we have seen to be the centrally important

/ *tension* in his thought between relativist and universalist tendencies and so also fails to consider the distinctive approach that he takes to dealing with that tension.

Herder recognizes that there is no plausible alternative to regard-ing humanity as, ultimately, a unity. It must accordingly be possible to characterize that unity in terms of the most distinctive, in fact the defining, feature of humankind—its language. At the same time, the human race presents, both historically and at any given moment, a panorama of qualitative differences, and this most vividly, again, in the form of language. Hence the path to a genuine *Semiotik*, in the sense of an adequate characterization of the "symbolism" (*Symbolik*) common to all people, must proceed through each particular "store-house," each "treasury of the thought of an entire people," which is to say, through the myriad national languages of the different peoples of the earth, past and present. The passage last cited continues:

> Everything that is peculiar to this national treasure—origin, history, the true character of its uniqueness in all respects [there follows a long list of examples]—all this and a hundred more unheard-of things would be disclosed to us about the store of the thought of a given people . . . (II, 13–14)

"The true philosopher of language," who is to accomplish all this, and, moreover, not for a single language only but ultimately for all of them, clearly has his work cut out for him. Apart from the sheer enormity of the task, however, there is a still more fundamental difficulty associated with it, one inherent in the very nature of the project itself. The individual undertaking it must develop a comprehensive, universal statement, but must pursue that objective by means of a method based on the principle of particularism. Such a person must, so to speak, become Chomsky by working as hard as possible at being Whorf. In addition, compounding the problem further, there is the consideration that this individual will himself of necessity be situated in one such "storehouse" in particular. The specific nature of the "treasury of thought" it contains will therefore be the primary determinant of that person's world, indeed, of the basic fabric of his existence, and accordingly cannot escape being reflected in his dealings with other languages. With all this in mind, Herder goes on to say:

> However, such a position of investigator of language is, of course, a difficult one to fill, because it calls for a man . . . who

> has traveled through foreign nations and among their peoples,
> has learned foreign languages and dialects, . . . who is, how-
> ever, at the same time . . . able to refer everything back to his
> native language, in order to be a man of his people. (II, 14)

The problem indicated here is the same one that, as we have seen,
stands at the center of *On Diligence:* how to reconcile the competing
demands of universalism and particularism, and how to do so, moreover, from within the problem itself. The latter requirement, however, as we have also seen, does not merely form part of the definition
of the task to be undertaken. Precisely in so doing, it also presents
us, implicitly, with the key to accomplishing that task. For Herder
there is (for human beings, at any rate) no such thing as an Archime-
dean point outside the whole system from which a definitive survey
of that whole would be possible. Given what we have seen of his
theory of mind and its foundation in the principle that perception and
cognition are based always in some *Denkungsart* (and thus some
Nationalcharakter) in particular, such a vantage point must clearly
be in his view an impossibility. Since linguistic-cultural perspectivism
is a fundamental fact of human life, the need is rather, as Irmscher
remarks in a slightly different connection, "to think the notion of per-
spectival knowing . . . through to the end. Since the philosopher also
. . . exists historically, his own situation goes as well into the image
that he constructs of history . . ."[23] To "historically" (*geschichtlich*) we
can add "linguistically" without altering the basic point. If it is true
that the thinker finds himself within the problem to be resolved, it
must also be the case that the specific nature and structure of the
problem is in turn determined in accordance with that "treasury of
thought" in particular that is peculiar to him by virtue of his native
language. The thinker thus at once encloses and is enclosed by the
problem. The One-Many problem itself, in the specifically linguistic-
historical form that it assumes for Herder, emerges, so to speak, from
within one of the Many. Corresponding to the One, in the sense of
the universal synthesis that is the ideal object of our efforts, there is
another "one"—for Herder, his native German language, culture,
and tradition—and between the two there exists a fundamental
analogy.

At this point, the influence of Leibniz on Herder becomes especially apparent. Just as, for Leibniz, each monad "represents," or
"reflects," the whole with the degree of clarity appropriate to it, so
Herder's particular "one" from among the Many has an analogous

capacity for expressing the One. The native language is itself an image of unity-in-diversity, as his characterizations of it, for example, in the passages from the *Fragments* cited above, are calculated to emphasize. At the same time that he is influenced by Leibniz, however, he also takes a number of important steps beyond his great predecessor. In particular, he takes the Leibnizian theme of development, the notion of actualization of potential, and incorporates in it two additional ideas of his own—first, the understanding of the mind as constitutive mental activity, and second, the concept of historicity. In so doing he imparts to the notion of development a degree of scope and power apparently not contemplated by Leibniz. That advance, in turn, marks an important stage in the emergence of German Idealism generally, from its beginnings in Leibniz to its culmination in Hegel.

In the Leibnizian scheme, each monad, in accordance with a law immanent to it and uniquely its own, develops as far as it can toward reflection of the whole. That development occurs in relation to something given as fixed and complete in advance, for the universe, conceived as everything that is, ever was, or will be, has of necessity existed from all eternity in the mind of God. Coordination of the various developments, each of which is in itself not only distinctive but also distinct from all the others, occurs through a divinely preestablished harmony among them. The properties of monads, which Leibniz deduces as the irreducibly fundamental units of reality, preclude the possibility of real contact between them. Thus no monad really influences, or is influenced by, any other. What we take to be, for example, causal relationships are in actuality independently occurring changes in the representations of different monads. God, however, has arranged these to take place in such a way that the one appears to us as the cause and the other as the effect.

In the Hegelian system, each moment of the dialectic also develops as far as it can in accordance with the nature and limits of the concept peculiar to it. Unlike the Leibnizian scheme, however, matters do not end there. The very incompleteness of any given moment (before the final one), that is, its inability to provide in itself an adequate representation of the whole, is at the same time what generates the next moment in the dialectic. That new moment then repeats the process at the next higher level, and so the overall system unfolds. Individual centers of development remain individual. Yet at the same time, precisely by virtue of the nature of that individuality (that is, incomplete), they together constitute a single, comprehensive chain. The culmination of that progression occurs in the self-realization of Absolute Spirit, the status of which within the framework of Hegelian thought corresponds broadly to that of God in Leibniz's system.

To put the matter in Leibnizian terms, God remains for Hegel the supreme monad, embracing all the others, but he is no longer the one monad exempted from the principle of development. Rather he becomes actual precisely in and through the actualization of all reality. The Leibnizian preestablished harmony thus becomes, in Hegel's system, a strict logic of development (which, however, interestingly, continues to yield a conclusion formally identical to one reached earlier by Leibniz, though now construed in substantively quite different terms, namely the ultimate identity of the rational and the real). The key to the whole development, for Hegel, occurs, paradoxically, very near its end, with the historical emergence of human consciousness. A point is reached at which an individual (Hegel) is able to render explicit the entire process by articulating each of its stages in a philosophical system and so bring about its completion in the form of self-conscious self-realization.

Between these two end points stands Herder, influenced by the one, but at the same time transforming his thought and thereby moving in the direction of the other. In Herder's theory, individual nations or peoples have a status roughly analogous to that of Leibniz's monads. Each is an autonomous and unique linguistic-cultural center, governed by principles of development immanent to it and reflected in its particular national history. At the same time, however, the idea of humanity requires that there be, in some sense, a unity to that multiplicity, just as, for Leibniz, each monad has its place within a single, harmoniously integrated whole. For both thinkers, the ultimate source of that unity is God, though in markedly different senses. For Leibniz, as noted, the whole exists timelessly as divine creation. The relationship of any monad to it consists in striving to reflect more perfectly what is itself eternal, to achieve, within the limits of its potential, the most adequate representation possible of intelligible reality. We have seen, however, that for Herder human beings in particular, as *homo loquens,* are defined (or rather, define themselves) by the intentional, constitutive activity that is the mind. Our development toward realization of ourselves and our (linguistic) construction of our world are two aspects of a single process. Hence, with respect to the ultimate unity of the human race, there can be no question of simply reflecting an idea already completely formed in the mind of God. Rather that unity must be brought about through a process of active synthesis, the field of which is history. We noted earlier the assertion in the *Origin of Language* that it is in our nature to realize ourselves progressively; one is "never a *whole* person—always developing, in process, moving toward completion" (V, 98). And what is true for the individual holds as well, by analogy, for the race at large.

We have seen that from the beginning of his career, in *On Diligence*, Herder conceives this overall historical progression as a movement in three principal stages, from a condition of original, undifferentiated unity, through a phase of fragmentation and dispersal, coming finally to restoration of unity, now as articulated unity-in-difference. For him, as later for Hegel and others, as we have also seen in that early essay, there comes a point in this development at which the self-realization of the individual—the acts of synthesis by which he determines at once himself and his world—coincides with that of the entire race. And thus he writes, for example, in *Another Philosophy of History for the Cultivation of the Human Race:*

> If I could succeed in connecting the most disparate scenes, without confusing them—showing how they all refer to each other, grow out of each other, lose themselves in one another; regarded as individuals, only isolated moments; in the context of continuity, however, means to ends—what a sight! What a noble application of human history! What encouragement to hope, to act, to believe, even where one sees nothing, or not everything! (V, 513)

The reference here to an "application of human history" does not mean merely the use of historical studies as a kind of spiritual tonic for one's contemporaries. While it may be legitimate to see something of that thought in this passage, it constitutes, at most, a relatively small part of a much larger notion. In reading Herder, it is important that we take as seriously as he evidently does the idea that history truly is the fundamental stuff of our existence, the medium in which whatever we do assumes concrete form, and thus a process that generates us even as we create it. There is, even in principle, no point that we could occupy outside of history, from which we could then, so to speak, "apply" it as in some sense a means to an end while at the same time remaining ourselves distinct from and so essentially unaffected by it. The "application of human history" in question here must accordingly be understood as, ultimately, the application by history of itself, in the person of the speaker (Herder), toward its own completion. And because that process is still underway—for reasons that we have seen, will always be underway—his role cannot consist simply in developing a body of theory that would then stand once and for all as the exemplary representation of the whole. Rather his work is charged, in a kind of implicit historical imperative, with assuming the programmatic function of arousing others to action toward the concrete realization of that end. In the nature of the case, however, not even he is able to produce a depiction of the goal complete in all respects (hence the qualification at the end of the passage, "even where one sees nothing, or not everything").

In characterizing the step that Herder takes beyond Leibniz, from representation to constitutive synthesis, we thus also come to the step that he does not take and that is thereby left for the post-Kantian Idealists, above all Hegel, namely the ultimate identification of God with the historical-logical process in which the whole of reality comes into (self-conscious) being. He retains, as Hegel does not, much of the traditional Judaeo-Christian conception according to which God acts upon history but is himself independent of it. As its creator, God knows already the course of history; he does not first come to be within it. Thus there is, in Herder's view, the possibility—indeed, the reality—of a complete grasp of the whole from a position outside it. That position, however, and hence the view it affords, is beyond the capacity of any human being to achieve. In *Another Philosophy of History,* he states, "It is the Creator alone who conceives the entire unity of one and all nations, in all their multiplicity, without thereby losing sight of their unity" (V, 505). And again, from the early piece *On Baumgarten's Mode of Thought in His Writings (Von Baumgartens Denkart in seinen Schriften):*

> A completely philosophical language would have to be the discourse of the gods, who watched as the things of the world were formed, who looked upon all beings in their state of origin and becoming, and who thus created every name of every entity genetically and materially. . . . Thus here as well one must distinguish, in accordance with that ancient Greek expression, the language of the immortal gods, who dwell in the blessed abodes, and the language of mortals, with their perspective bound to the earth. (XXXII, 180)

In this he remains closer to Leibniz and the latter's conception of the necessarily imperfect reflection of the universe by any monad other than the divine one. Herder's belief in the inevitable discrepancy between human perspective, bound always to some situation in particular, and divine omniscience means, in conjunction with his views on the nature of the mind and the character of historical development, that, on the one hand, the development of the human race assumes for him a structure similar to the one later described by Hegel, but that, on the other, that development remains, in contrast to Hegel's closed system, open-ended. This pattern for his work at large was established in what we have seen to be the structure and import of *On Diligence,* with its evocation of the ideal of humanity as the concrete embodiment of the resolution of the One-Many problem and its aim of instilling in the audience both the resolve and the ability to take upon itself the mission of realizing that ideal. Neither there nor in later works, however, does he in fact achieve the synthesis he is pursuing. Thus it is not only the larger works, from the *Fragments* to the *Ideas,* that remain incomplete. In a sense, and one that anticipates the Romantic conception of the fragment (as enunciated, for example, by Friedrich Schlegel[24]), all his works are fragmentary by their very nature, never the monuments to completion erected by Hegel. In the terms of a famous hypothetical alternative formulated by Lessing—either possession of the whole truth or an endless quest for the truth[25]—he chooses with Lessing the latter, and for much the same reason.[26]

Fundamentally the same difference between Herder and Hegel that we have been considering here appears as well from a slightly different point of view. The linguistic-cultural terms in which Herder primarily conceives his version of the problem of the One and the Many create for him, in his effort to realize the synthesis that would mark the completion of human development, requirements of a sort that Hegel's system does not oblige him to meet. When Hegel describes the essential character of a given culture and thereby locates it within the overall historical development of the *Weltgeist,* he does so in his own language, from his own perspective. Since that is, however, by hypothesis also the perspective of the whole, the fact that that description has captured everything necessary about its object is guaranteed. Hegel does not feel constrained to evoke a flesh-and-blood sense for what it felt like to be, for example, a Greek in the age of Pericles or a Roman in the era of the Republic, much less for the way of life of the Eskimo or the Tibetan or the American Indian. Herder, however, feels precisely that obligation.

In *On Diligence,* prompted initially by the question of how to relate the study of foreign languages to one's native language, he begins to grapple with the difficulty inherent in the attempt to meet that requirement. A decade later, in *Another Philosophy of History,* he provides an explicit formulation of the same difficulty:

> Has anyone truly appreciated how inexpressibly difficult it is, with the unique qualities of an individual, to express distinctly that which distinguishes him? how he feels and lives? how different and unique all things become for him through being seen by his eye, measured by his soul, felt by his heart . . . (V, 502)

In connection with this passage, Irmscher comments:

> Since the general conception thus dissolves into nothing but distinct individual entities, there arise difficulties in principle in the attempt to grasp and express the particular with language, which in the nature of the case unavoidably generalizes. Herder was intensely aware of this problem, but was not able to find a solution to it.[27]

As we have seen, there is indeed a problem here, one that Herder may have felt more acutely than anyone before him, even Vico. I want to suggest, however, a slightly different way of describing what that problem consists in.

We need to distinguish two senses in which language "generalizes." The one is not a necessary quality of language but rather a contingent one, manifested, for example, in an inordinately abstract style or a failure to make necessary distinctions. Herder certainly does not regard this as true of all language—his works include a wealth of examples that in his view, as he makes clear, manifest precisely the opposite qualities—but he is at the same time well aware of how difficult a fault it is to avoid, especially when one is attempting, as he is, to survey and organize large bodies of the most diverse material without distorting it in the process. The passage just cited from *Another Philosophy of History* is preceded immediately by:

> No one in the world feels the weakness of general characterizations more than I. One depicts an entire people, age, region—what has one depicted? One brings together successive peoples and periods, in an endless variation like waves of the sea—what has one depicted? what has the descriptive word

actually caught?—In the end, one brings them together in nothing but a generalization, where everyone perhaps thinks and feels whatever he pleases—defective means of description! How much can one be misunderstood! (V, 501–02)

The possibility of being *misunderstood*, however, necessarily entails a corresponding possibility (however difficult to realize in fact) of being understood correctly. And that, in turn, is, for Herder, equivalent to saying that there exists the possibility of finding the right words. Following the first of the passages just cited from *Another Philosophy of History*, he makes that point all but explicitly:

> . . . is that not as if one should survey the entire ocean of the world's peoples, ages, and countries and grasp them with one glance, one feeling, one word! Dull half silhouette of a word! *The entire living portrait of way of life, customs, needs, geography and climate would have to be added, or have come first; one would first have to achieve a sympathetic identification with the nation in order to feel its inclinations and actions, individually and all together; one would have to find a Word, in whose fullness one could conceive everything;* or one reads merely—a word. (V, 502; emphasis added)

We recognize in this a point already familiar from *On Diligence*, namely the need to grasp a culture in its entirety in order to gain access to any part of it. In addition, and as important, this passage and the one cited just before it here are together governed by one of Herder's most characteristic images, that of the sea and its waves. In the *Treatise on the Origin of Language*, he employs the same image to depict the process by which human language first comes into being. This occurs when the mind[28] abstracts a single "wave" from the "ocean" of sensations in which it is immersed and posits that element as the distinguishing feature of one thing (or rather, one class of things) in particular. That abstracted sensation yields the name, and, with it, the "clear concept," of the thing in question (V, 34–35). This is the second of the two senses in which language "generalizes," and unlike the first it is not a contingent aspect but rather one that is essential to there being language at all. In this sense, however, there cannot be any ultimately unbridgeable gulf between the "generalizing" quality of language and the particularity of phenomena. For any such elusive particular would naturally have to be a part of our world.

If it were not, there would be no way in which it could even be intelligibly referred to. But for Herder, as we have emphasized repeatedly, it is only as our own specifically *linguistic* construct that we have our world at all.

The problem at issue stems not so much from a gap between the general and the particular with respect to language as such, but rather from the existence of a plurality of languages. In the form of the myriad ways of constructing reality that they embody, these constitute a plurality of worlds of human beings. We occupy, by virtue of our own national heritage, one of those worlds. There is one conceptual framework native to us, and the task is to bridge the gap between it and every other such framework. The locus of the problem is the conflict between the means we are obliged to employ and the end set for us in the nature of the task. There is no alternative to proceeding by means of our native language, and yet with that instrument we must somehow achieve an understanding and a characterization of other peoples comparable to the self-representation that each of them gives by nature (which is to say, a representation analogous to the one that we constantly give of ourselves in the form of our own language, culture, and overall way of life, whereby every part embodies and reflects the whole). We cannot change the nature of language as an activity of abstraction and constitutive synthesis. At the same time, we cannot simply assimilate another culture, and thus another *Weltbild*, to our own without distorting it beyond recognition. It is in this light that we must understand the expressions of frustration just seen in *Another Philosophy of History* regarding the possibility of giving an adequate representation of the distinctive qualities of other peoples. The objection is not to the use of words as such—in the nature of the case, it cannot be—but rather to one particular sort of word. What Herder finds inadequate is a description that merely surveys and summarizes and that thus reflects only the conceptual framework of the individual doing the describing, not that of the object of description as well. We must find "a Word"—there is no other resource available to us—but it must be one that somehow evokes a sense, so to speak, for how the "endless variation" of the waves goes to make up the sea and at the same time how the whole sea is, in one way or another, present in each wave. To accomplish this sort of description, however, it is necessary that one first have achieved a kind of sympathetic identification with that other people (and eventually with all other peoples).

The sort of "Word" envisaged here is clearly one that is capable of more than can be accomplished with ordinary, discursive language. While remaining within the bounds of a single linguistic framework, and limited still further by the inherently finite character of all linguistic expression, it must nonetheless be able to grasp and reflect within those limits the manifold entirety of another people and its culture. Functioning in this way as the link between different cultures, it thereby also serves as the mediator between the finite individual, determined always by some national-cultural context in particular, and the infinite ideal of humanity as an all-embracing unity-in-difference. It is thus called on to contribute to the attainment of essentially the same goals that were set initially in *On Diligence*. And just as it was necessary that the structure of that early essay go beyond the merely discursive and incorporate in its exposition a second, poetic-gestural dimension, so something similar holds as well for the kind of "Word" that we see called for here in *Another Philosophy of History*. That possibility of language, moreover, looks ahead to the development of German thought and literature in the generation to follow. Both aspects of what we have seen to be the twofold function of this "Word"—comprehension of the general in the particular and, on that basis, mediation between the finite and the infinite—anticipate the conception of the poetic symbol as it will be developed, in particular, by the German Romantics.[29]

Referring to the "entire nature of [a people's] soul, that which in everything is the dominant force, which shapes all other inclinations and powers of the soul in accordance with itself, which colors even the actions furthest removed from one another," Herder goes on to say, ". . . in order fully to sympathize with that nature, look not to the word, but rather enter into the age, the region, the entire history; feel yourself into everything (*fühle dich in alles hinein*)—only then will you be on the right path to understanding the word . . ." (V, 503). And thereby also, "to find[ing] that Word" (V, 502) in the first place. The need to "feel oneself into" other ways of life and worldviews as the only way genuinely to understand them is here asserted a generation before that same idea would be given fresh currency in the philosophy of German Idealism, especially that of Schelling. That was in turn, of course, as is well known, the source from which Coleridge appropriated it (coining in process the English word 'empathy'). Herder's call for a movement of *Sichhineinfühlen* is also (along with Vico's earlier version of it) the ancestor of Dilthey's notion of *Verstehen*, conceived, in contrast to the *Erkennen* characteristic of the natural sciences, as the epistemological mode appropriate to the humanities.

The concept of *Sichhineinfühlen* appears as well in a more explicitly metaphysical-epistemological connection elsewhere in Herder's writings. In the "Studies and Sketches for the *Plastic Arts*" ("Studien und Entwürfe zur *Plastik*") of 1768 and 1769, he writes under the heading "Philosophy of the True, the Good, and the Beautiful, derived from the Sense of Feeling" ("Philosophie des Wahren, Guten und Schönen aus dem Sinne des Gefühls"): "Feeling is the first, the most profound, and almost the only sense of mankind; the source of most of our concepts and sensations; the true, and the first, organ of the soul for gathering representations from outside it. . . . The soul feels itself into the world" (VIII, 104). And also, from *On Knowing and Feeling, the Two Principal Powers of the Human Soul:* "A man who is strong in himself feels himself deeply into everything. . . . what an image of the strength of the Creator!" (VIII, 309).

The exhortation *fühle dich in alles hinein* restates a principle announced originally in *On Diligence* in the form of the notion of *Sichverpflanzen*. Though the later formulation is certainly far the better-known one, as a vehicle for expressing as many aspects as possible of what Herder wants to say in this regard, its earlier counterpart is, for two reasons, at least slightly preferable. First, its use to refer both to the emergence of national languages and to our learning of languages other than our own expresses implicitly, as we have seen, a parallel between those two movements. This in turn brings into sharp focus a point that we to some extent have to deduce from the overall context of the corresponding passages in *Another Philosophy of History*, namely that the unification of the human race for which we are meant to be striving is to be accomplished in the first instance through language. When Herder speaks of the need "to achieve a sympathetic identification with," or "to feel one's way into," another culture, he does not mean by this simply a kind of mystical intuition in the sense of something that in principle defies articulation and to which one therefore either catches on or does not. He has in mind rather the necessity of comprehending that culture as a whole and thus of approaching as closely as possible to the way in which those who are themselves native to it experience it. And that, in turn, entails above all knowing their language, for there is, in his view, no more complete or more fundamental embodiment of the character of a culture than that. Significantly in this connection, he follows both the phrases from *Another Philosophy of History* mentioned above with a reference to "a Word" or "the word," to which the actions expressed in those phrases are to provide access.

Secondly, when *sich verpflanzen* occurs in *On Diligence*, it is always in conjunction with *sich schaffen*. In this way the text emphasizes that the process by which we extend ourselves into other cultures is, and must be, at the same time an activity of self-realization. The medium of that activity is our own language and thus our own culture. These are also, however, at the same time its goal, though in a sense that extends both of them well beyond what they were initially. We have seen that, for Herder (as for Hegel), there comes a point at which the development of the individual converges with that of the race at large. In that individual the historical process comes to self-awareness and so becomes the conscious agent of its own fulfillment. The locus of that convergence is the individual's *Volk*, with its capacity to undertake an endless process of self-cultivation.

A parallel is thus established between individual, *Volk*, and human race, in that it is in the nature of each to be never complete but always underway to completion. The parallel, however, is not between three lines, each separate from the others, but rather between concentric circles, each nested within the next larger. The *Volk*, accordingly, faces in two directions at once (as does the individual in a different, though related, sense seen earlier in *On Diligence*). In relation to the individual, it is the context that has generated that person and that he (or she) in turn calls to further development precisely in the act of striving for self-realization. In relation to the race, it is itself the individual entity. It stands to that still greater context in the same relationship as does the individual to it, as simultaneously object and subject, and thereby links the person to the race at large. The effective relationship that the *Volk* assumes to humanity as a whole depends on the individual's assuming the same relationship to it, just as, in the opposite direction, the possibility of that individual in the first place, and hence the ability to take on the role in question, is grounded in the position occupied by that person's *Volk* in the overall historical pattern.

This state of affairs is at once the source of and the key to the peculiar double status of Herder's One-Many problem. That problem, as we saw earlier, is both the framework of history and a product of it, and precisely in virtue of that, so also is the path toward its resolution. The same national-cultural *Denkungsart* that experiences history in this way, that is, the specific linguistic form in which history becomes conscious of itself as a problem of the One and the Many, is by that fact also the one in terms of which the effort to resolve the problem must be undertaken. For Herder, as we have emphasized, there are no merely theoretical problems, and hence no solutions that can be accomplished solely in the mind of a single thinker. The issues he confronts grow out of and reflect the real historical development of the human race, and their resolution therefore depends decisively on furthering that development. The attempt to *represent* a unified but at the same time differentiated humanity can thus succeed, again, only if it is at the same time an effort to *realize* that unity-in-difference in fact.

Appendix

Über den Fleiß in
mehreren gelehrten Sprachen

Part I, §1

Jene blühende Zeit ist dahin, da der kleine Kreis unserer Ur-
väter, um die Patriarchen, wie Kinder um ihre Eltern wohnten:
jenes Alter, in dem, nach der einfältig erhabnen Nachricht unsrer
Offenbarung alle Welt nur eine Zunge und Sprache war. Da
herrschte statt unserer gelehrten Lasten, und statt der Masken   5
unsrer Tugend, rauhe, einfältige Zufriedenheit. Doch was
schildre ich ein verlornes Porträt von unersetzbaren Reizen? sie
ist nicht mehr, diese goldne Zeit.——

§2

Da die Kinder des Staubes jenen Bau, der den Wolken drohete,
unternahmen: da wurde der Taumelkelch der Verwirrung über   10
sie ausgegossen: ihre Familien und Dialekte verpflanzten sich in
verschiedne Himmelsgegenden; und es schufen sich tausend
Sprachen nach dem Clima und den Sitten von tausend Nationen.
Wenn hier der Morgenländer unter einem heißen Scheitelpunkt
glühet: so strömt auch sein brausender Mund eine hitzige und   15
affektvolle Sprache fort. Dort blüht der Grieche in dem wollüstig-
sten und mildesten Himmelsstrich auf: sein Leib ist, nach Pin-
dars Ausdruck, mit der Grazie übergossen: seine Adern fließen
von sanftem Feuer: seine Glieder sind ganz Nerven: seine

Sprachwerkzeuge fein, und unter ihnen entstand also jene feine   20
attische Sprache, die Grazie unter ihren Schwestern.

§3

Die Römer, die Söhne des Mars, sprachen stärker, und holten
erst aus Griechenland Blumen, ihre Mundart zu verschönern.
Noch männlicher redet der kriegerische Deutsche; der muntre
Gallier erfindet eine hüpfende und weichere Sprache; der Spa-   25
nier gibt seiner ein gravitätisches Ansehen, sollte es auch bloß
durch Schalle sein: der träge Afrikaner lallet gebrochen und hin-
sinkend, und der Hottentotte verirret sich endlich in ein Stamm-
len kalekutischer Töne. So verwandelte sich diese Pflanze nach
dem Boden, der sie nährte, und der Himmelsluft, die sie tränkte: 30
sie ward ein Proteus unter den Nationen. —

§4

Hat also eine jede Sprache ihren bestimmten Nationalcharakter,
so scheint uns die Natur bloß zu unsrer Muttersprache eine Ver-
bindlichkeit aufzulegen, da diese vielleicht unserem Charakter
angemessener ist, und unsre Denkungsart ausfüllet. Fremden   35
Nationen werde ich vielleicht ihre Sprache nachlallen können,
ohne bis auf den Kern ihrer Eigenheit zu dringen. Gestorbne
Sprachen werde ich vielleicht den Worten nach aus ihren Denk-
mälern mit vielem Schweiße erlernen, aber ihr Geist verschwand
mir. Glücklich, daß die Völker, denen sie eigen waren, verlebt   40
sind; sonst würden sie mir vielleicht, wer weiß, welche Unwissen-
heit, Rauhigkeit und Zwang Schuld geben. Und diesen fremden
Sprachen müssen wir unsre blühendsten Tage, unser lebhaftestes
Gedächtnis, unser frischestes Jugendfeuer aufopfern, wie man
jenem Abgott die Blüte der Jugend in seine glühenden Arme   45
gab. Würden nicht Sachen statt Worte, und Begriffe statt Zei-
chen uns weit mehr nähren.

§5

Alle diese Einwürfe wider die Sprachen unseres Fleißes scheinen
wirklich sehr die Natur auf ihrer Seite zu haben, weil aber die

heutie Beschaffenheit der Kunst sich sehr davon entfernt: so ists   50
beinahe der Mittelpunkt unserer Schulwissenschaften, die Grenzen des Fleißes zu bestimmen, auf den fremde und eigne Sprache ein Anrecht haben.

Part II, §1

Genösse jede Nation, in ihre Grenzen eingeschlossen, und an den
Boden ihres Landes geheftet, die Gaben der Natur aus dem   55
Schoß ihrer Erde, ohne von andern Völkern den Tribut des
Reichtums widerrechtlich zu fordern; so würde vielleicht niemand das Bürgerrecht seines Vaterlandes gegen ausländische
Vorzüge vertauschen dürfen. Ich brauchte es nicht, andern ga-
lante Sprachen und zweideutige Höflichkeiten nachzuäffen, und   60
keine Stadt würde ein Gemisch von zehn Handelssprachen. Aber
was brauchen unsere jetzige glänzende Bedürfnisse nicht für Be-
wegungen in beiden Welten? Das Gold auf den Königsdiademen,
die Delikatessen unserer Tafeln, alle die Geräte der Pracht und
des Luxus, den man mit der Maske der Bequemlichkeit ver-   65
hüllet: sind ein geplünderter Raub ferner Welten. Je teurer die
Beute wird, desto mehr steigt ihr Wert, und die Staatsklugheit
des Handels erlernet also Sprachen, um andre Nationen wenig-
stens mit Worten ihrer Zunge zu hintergehen. Hier knüpft die
Politik des Staats die Sprachen zur allgemeinen Kette der   70
Völker, und eben so werden sie ein großes Band der Gelehrsamkeit. So lange über die zerstreute Menge der Gelehrten kein Mo-
narch herrscht, der eine Sprache auf den Thron der Ruinen so
vieler andern erhübe: so lange die Pläne zu einer allgemeinen
Sprache unter die leeren Projekte und Reisen zum Monde ge-   75
hören: so lange bleiben viele Sprachen ein unentbehrliches Übel,
und also beinahe ein wirkliches Glück.

§2

Wie wenig Fortschritte würden wir getan haben, wenn jede Nation in die enge Sphäre ihrer Sprache eingeschlossen, für die Gelehrsamkeit allein arbeitete? Ein Newton unseres Landes würde   80
sich mit einer Entdeckung martern, die dem englischen Newton
lange ein entsiegeltes Geheimnis war. Er würde höchstens eine

Bahn durchlaufen, die jener schon zurückgelegt; und tausend
Fußstapfen würden ihm fehlen, seine ermüdeten Schritte aufzu-
muntern. —Jetzt aber, welch ein Schatz von Entdeckungen ist   85
jede Sprache der Gelehrsamkeit! Geheimnisse, die die mitter-
nächtliche Lampe der Alten erfand, siehet jetzt die Sonne des
Mittages. Schätze, die der Schweiß einer fremden Nation aus
den Adern der Tiefe grub; teilt ihre Sprache unter andre Völker
als Beuten aus. So sproßten die Samen, die im Morgenlande   90
keimten, unter den Egyptern: Griechenlands Sonne entfaltete
völlig ihre Knospen: und Rom reifte die griechische Blüte zur
Frucht. Es erhob sie durch seine Kolonien zu einem Baum, unter
dessen Schatten die Nationen ihre Samenkörner der Literatur
pflanzten. Eben so können die Neuern auf den Grundstein der   95
Alten bauen, bis endlich eine glücklichere Nachwelt das Gebäude so vieler Hände mit dem Kranz der Vollkommenheit
krönet.

§3

Und wie? gemeinschaftlich sollen sie bauen, ohne daß sie sich
verstehen, so daß jede Sprache der andern eine Sammlung leerer   100
Töne bleibt? —So arbeiteten sie ja so fruchtlos als jene an dem
babylonischen Turmbau in ihrer Verwirrung. —

§4

Aber ein Einwurf, und seine Widerlegung wird unsere Gründe
für mehrere Sprachen noch mehr stützen! —"Es sei, sagt man,
daß jede Sprache ein Schlüssel zu vielen Schatzkammern ist: daß   105
der Tempel der Wissenschaften in England voll tiefsinniger Beo-
bachter der Natur, voll Bacons und Lockens und Newtone sei:
daß Frankreich eine reiche Ernte von schönen Geistern, von Fon-
tenellen und St. Mards liefere, daß Italien mit Statuen und ihren
Bildhauern, mit Tonkünstlern und Mahlern prange —es sei alles   110
dies: sagt man; ist nicht der Weg der Übersetzungen kürzer, als
jedes dieser Werke in seiner Muttersprache zu lesen? Können
nicht einige diese Bürde auf sich nehmen, um tausend davon zu
befreien?"

§5

Allerdings ist der Weg kürzer; aber leider unsicher; er ist zu kurz, 115
um hinreichend zu sein. Es gibt immer Schönheiten, die durch
den Schleier der Sprache mit doppelten Reizen durchscheinen;
man reiße den Schleier weg, und sie zerstäuben. Es gibt Rosen-
knospen, die mit Dornen verwebt sind: Blüten, die man zerstört,
wenn man sie entfaltet. Jene heilige Reliquien der Dichtkunst 120
und der Beredsamkeit unter den Römern, den Griechen, und
insonderheit unserer Offenbarung, verlieren ihren Kern der
Stärke, das Kolorit, den Glanz der Einfalt, den klingenden
Rhythmus; alles verlieren diese Grazien von Blumen, wenn ich
sie wider ihre Natur verpflanze. Und verdient es nicht jener mäo- 125
nische Sänger, daß man ihn selbst höre, ohne bloß zerstückte
Glieder von ihm zu lesen! Hat er allein für seinen elenden Markt
gesungen; Pindar für sein Jahrhundert allein die olympischen
Kronen unter die Sterne verpflanzet; soll August allein das könig-
liche Vergnügen genießen, Horaze und Virgils zu hören? —Nein 130
o Kaiser! du wecktest sie durch deinen Mäcen auf; ich genieße
sie! Du o Ludwig, schufest durch deinen Kolbert das güldne
Jahrhundert der Wissenschaften; ich verpflanze mich darin; zwei
oder drei Sprachen darf ich lernen; und ich höre jeden großen
Geist mit seiner eignen Zunge reden. —   135

§6

Alsdenn erhebe ich mich zu ihm, und gebe meiner Seele die Aus-
dehnung jedes Klimas. So ward Cicero an Demosthenes Schriften ein Redner: so weinte Alexander am Grabe Achills nach dem
Ruhm des Überwinders; an Alexanders Bilde schuf sich Cäsar
zum Helden, und Peter an der Säule des Richelieu zum Schöpfer 140
von Rußland. Eben so, sagt Plato, so wie der Magnet durch die
Berührung seine eigne Kraft unzähligen Körpern auf einmal
mitteilt; so begeistern Genies, neue Genies mit fortgehenden
Wundern. Mit dem deutschen Fleiß, suche ich die gründliche
englische Laune, den Witz der Franzosen, und das schimmernde 145
Italiens zu verbinden. Ich sammle den Geist jedes Volkes in
meine Seele! —Belohnungen, wie ich denke, gnug, um unsern
Fleiß zu vielen Sprachen aufzuwecken.

Part III, §1

Aber welch ein grenzenloses Meer sehe ich hier vor mir, wohin
ich mich ohne einen Palinur zu haben, nicht wagen kann —ein 150
Labyrinth von Sprachen, wo ich mich ohne Leitfaden verirre!
Wohl! und dieser Leitfaden ist meine Muttersprache, der ich also
meine Erstlinge des Fleißes opfern muß. So wie uns gemeiniglich
die Liebe zu unserm Vaterlande mit innigen Banden fesselt: so
hat auch die Sprache unserer Väter Reize, die in unserm Auge 155
alle andere übertreffen. Sie druckten sich uns zuerst ein, und
bildeten sich gleichsam mit den feinsten Fugen unserer Empfind-
lichkeit zugleich. Oder unsre Muttersprache hat wirklich die zu-
sammenstimmendste Harmonie mit unsern feinsten Organen
und zartesten Wendungen. So wie nun ein Kind alle Bilder mit 160
dem ersten Eindruck vergleicht: so passet unser Geist insgeheim
alle Mundarten zu unserer Muttersprache, und wie nützlich
kann dieses sein? Dadurch bekommt die große Mannigfaltigkeit
der Sprachen Einheit: unsre Schritte in fremden Gegenden werden kürzer und gewisser, wenn das Ziel unseres Vaterlandes uns 165
stets in die Augen blickt: unser Fleiß wird durch sie erleichtert:
ich schwimme mit einer Rinde, die mich trägt.

§2

Wenn wir unsre Muttersprache auf der Zunge behalten: so werden wir desto tiefer in den Unterschied jeder Sprache ein-
dringen. Hier werden wir Lücken, dort Überfluß — hier Reich- 170
tum, dort eine Wüste erblicken: und die Armut der einen mit den
Schätzen der andern bereichern können. Denn in welchem ge-
nauen Bande steht Sprache und Denkungsart? Wer den Umfang
einer Sprache übersieht: überschauet ein Feld voll Gedanken,
und wer sie genau ausdrücken lernt: sammlet sich eben hiemit 175
einen Schatz bestimmter Begriffe. Die ersten Wörter, die wir lallen, sind die Grundsteine unserer Erkenntnis, und die Wärterin-
nen unsre erste Lehrer der Logik. —

§3

Und wozu kann unsre Muttersprache unentbehrlicher sein, als
zur Dichtkunst und Beredsamkeit; da mit den toten Sprachen die 180

größten Donner ihrer Stärke, die leuchtendsten Schönheiten ihrer Wendungen ausgestorben sind. Die Homere, die Ciceronen, die Voltäre, die Popens — waren sie es in erlernten Sprachen? Man nehme unter den Alten einen Terenz, und unter uns ein paar andre Schriftsteller aus; so verwarf niemand seine eigne 185 Mundart. Nur jene mittlere Zeiten, da man sich aus der Barbarei los wand, um bloß ein Nachahmer der Alten zu werden: da die Skaligers, die Buchners, die Rapins dichteten; nur diese Zeiten beteten die römische Sprache, als die einzige Monarchin an, und ließen die Muttersprache in Schlacken — wie gut ists aber, daß 190 diese Zeit nicht mehr ist!

§4

Noch immer rede ich über den gelehrten Nutzen der Muttersprache, und vergesse ihn im Gesichtspunkt der Menschheit. Der Gelehrte in fremden Sprachen, der in seiner eignen ein Barbar bleibt, der Massoret des Priscians, den jede Zeile eines deut- 195 schen Briefes lächerlich macht, der die Versarten des Horaz zählt, die Prosodie Anakreons und Lukrez verbessert, und dennoch — solch ein Gelehrter ist er — dennoch kaum die Dichter seiner Sprache versteht; o vor tausend Jahren wäre er ein Apostel der Weisheit unter Barbaren gewesen; jetzt ist er ein lächerlicher 200 Allwisser. —

§5

Unsre Gelehrsamkeit muß beiderlei Sprachen bauen, beide zum Bande der Wissenschaften verknüpfen. Oft müssen wir, wenn wir uns unserer Heimat entziehen, den Bienen nachahmen,

— — — — — die in zerstreueten Heeren   205
die Luft durchsäuseln, und fallen auf Klee und
    blühende Stauden,
und denn heimkehren zur Zelle, mit süßer Beute
    beladen
und liefern uns Honig der Weisheit — — —   210

Notes

Epigraph

1. *Hegel: Texts and Commentary,* trans. Walter Kaufmann, pp. 28–30.
2. *Augustins Soliloquien,* p. 190. This same passage was used by Lessing as the epigraph for his *Education of the Human Race.*
3. *Archilochos,* p. 94.

Introduction

1. *The Encyclopedia of Philosophy,* III, 487.
2. Cited in Reisiger, *Johann Gottfried Herder: Sein Leben in Selbstzeugnissen, Briefen und Bericht,* p. 350.
3. *Volk und Geschichte im Denken Herders,* p. 6. Cited by Wulf Koepke in his Introduction to *Johann Gottfried Herder: Innovator Through the Ages* (cited hereafter as *JGH*), p. 1.
4. *Herder,* p. 114.
5. Ibid., p. 114.
6. *Deutsche Literaturgeschichte,* pp. 225–26.
7. *Herder,* p. 114. For a number of other examples of essentially the same viewpoint, see my "Herder and the Possibility of Literature: Rationalism and Poetry in Eighteenth-Century Germany," *JGH,* p. 60.
8. See Clark, pp. 42 and 441 (n. 5), and Wulf Koepke, *Johann Gottfried Herder,* p. 8.
9. *Werke,* IX, 409.
10. Haym, I, 24–25.
11. Gaier, ed., *Frühe Schriften 1764–1772,* p. 870.

12. Clark, p. 51.

13. It is, to put it mildly, regrettable that the first new edition of Herder's works since 1877 to include *On Diligence* should have chosen the wrong text of the essay. I will not burden the analysis here with the results of the word-by-word comparison that I have made of the two versions. That would, in effect, call for a variorum edition of *On Diligence*, which may be more than even I think it merits. The comparison is, in any case, one that, in view of the essay's modest length, any interested reader can easily undertake for him- or herself. And I have no doubt that any reader to do so will agree that it is only in the revised and published version that Herder achieves the breakthrough to his distinctive mode of both thought and expression.

14. *Lebensbild,* I, 2, pp. 151–62.

15. *Sämtliche Werke,* XXX, 7–14. By the time of the publication of volume thirty, Suphan had died, and editorship of the project had passed to Carl Redlich.

16. *Sämtliche Werke,* I, 1–7. For ease of reference, I include the text of this version in the appendix to this study. I have at a few points modernized the spelling, where it seemed that the older forms might simply prove needlessly distracting, and for the same reason have substituted *für* for *vor* where Herder (in accordance with common eighteenth-century practice—see Adelung, II, 361–63, and IV, 1249) uses the latter in the sense now expressed exclusively by the former. All other references here to works of Herder are by volume and page number of the Suphan edition. All translations, from Herder as well as from other authors cited, unless otherwise indicated, are my own. The division of the text into parts, I should perhaps add to avoid any possible confusion, is not Herder's but rather reflects my understanding of the essay's structure. The numbering of the paragraphs is intended both to assist the reader in following the exposition and to make it easier to check my interpretation against Herder's own words.

17. *Herder,* p. 27.

18. Ibid., p. 30.

19. Ibid., p. 30.

20. Ibid., p. 32.

21. Ibid., p. 85.

22. Ibid., p. 27. Similarly, in connection with the essays on Ossian and Shakespeare in *On German Character and Art (Von deutscher Art und Kunst)*: "[Herder's] thoughts are tumbled out in overwhelming profusion, without any regard for formal effect" (p. 39); and, still later: " . . . logic and clarity were never his strong points . . ." (p. 53).

23. Ibid., p. 27.

24. Ibid., p. 37.

25. Ibid., p. 44.

26. Ibid., p. 27.

27. *Metaphorical Organicism in Herder's Early Works,* p. 33.

28. Ibid., p. 33. See appendix, 11.29–30.

29. Ibid., p. 33.

30. Ibid., p. 18.

31. Ibid., p. 18. See Eric Blackall, "The Imprint of Herder's Linguistic Theory on His Prose Style," pp. 512–18.

32. Ibid., p. 19.

33. *Herder*, p. 67.

34. Ibid., p. 92.

35. *Metaphorical Organicism*, p. 21.

36. Ibid., p. 21. See Markwardt, *Herders Kritische Wälder*, p. 308.

37. *The Psychological Basis of Herder's Aesthetics*, p. 82. Fugate cites the earlier *Schulrede* version of *On Diligence*. Cf. appendix, 11.32–37.

38. Ibid., p. 281.

39. *Herder and the Beginnings of Comparative Literature*, p. 10.

40. Ibid., p. 10.

41. *Herder: His Life and Thought*, p. 54.

42. Ibid., p. 54.

43. Ibid., pp. 54 and 131. Clark evidently bases his view of the matter entirely on a 1917 dissertation by Wilhelm Sturm, *Herders Sprachphilosophie in ihrem Entwicklungsgang und ihrer historischen Stellung;* see pp. 442 (n. 27) and 444 (n. 21).

44. Haym, I, 25.

45. Ibid., I, 25.

46. Ibid., I, 409.

47. There is an interesting parallel here to Thomas Sowell's distinction between "constrained" and "unconstrained" visions of human nature and social reality. See *A Conflict of Visions*, pp. 18–39, passim.

48. *Vico and Herder*, pp. 209–10, passim.

49. "Herder and the Enlightenment Philosophy of History," p. 167.

50. Ibid., p. 181.

51. See, for example, Copleston, *A History of Philosophy*, I, 2, pp. 230–32.

52. See Robert Joda, "Nicholas of Cusa: Precursor of Humanism," pp. 33–49; also Copleston, III, 2, pp. 37–54.

53. See Charles H. Kahn's *The Art and Thought of Heraclitus* as well as M. F. Burnyeat's review in *The New York Review of Books*.

54. Burnyeat, pp. 45–46.

55. Ibid., p. 46.

56. S/Z, p. 15.

Chapter 1

1. Haym, I, 26.

2. In his second prize essay, the *Discourse on the Origin of Inequality*, and in *The Social Contract*, Rousseau does develop a position similar to the one that, as we shall see here, is Herder's from the outset. In these later works Rousseau

moves beyond the negative assessment of culture and civilization that dominates the first *Discourse*. Like Herder, he comes to envisage a triadic pattern of development, from a condition of initial harmony, through disruption of that state, to an eventual reintegration of human beings, both within themselves and each with all the others. In a manner strikingly similar to what we shall see to be Herder's way of dealing with the twin notions of national language and national character, Rousseau interprets the development from the original state of nature to the proper form of human society as involving a transformation, but precisely thereby also the fulfillment, of the concept of nature itself. Ronald Grimsley describes this progression as follows:

> Man's nature is not fully mature until it becomes social. However, the natural man in the state of nature and the natural man in the social state cannot be identical. . . . If by "nature" is meant the merely primordial responses of the presocial man, then it is true to say that "good institutions denature man" inasmuch as they raise him up from the absolute self-sufficiency of the isolated primitive state to the level of a moral, relative existence based on an awareness of the common good and the need to live in harmonious relationship with his fellow men. . . . If "nature" intended man for a moral existence, then it also intended him for social life; indeed, only through the individual's participation in the "common unity" can full personal maturity become possible. "Nature" is still the norm, but one that has to be re-created, as it were, at a higher level, conferring on man a new rational unity which replaces the purely instinctive unity of the primitive state. (*Encyclopedia of Philosophy*, VII, 221–22)

The development of the race proceeds inexorably forward:

> In a corrupt society the recovery of a full human existence can never take the form of a mere return to nature, for the nature of man cannot be equated with the primordial state of nature. Although Rousseau was often nostalgically drawn to the innocence and simplicity of early times, he also treated nature as a dynamic, forward-looking concept. Starting from man as he is, the movement toward nature must be constantly sustained by the vision of what man might be. The achievement of this goal requires a radical transformation of human existence, the rediscovery and re-creation of a new nature. (*Ibid.*, p. 224)

That transformation, moreover, the envisaged rebirth and regeneration of humanity, must in some way, however paradoxically, emerge precisely out of the degeneration for which society in its current form is responsible. As Ernst Cassirer, summing up this aspect of Rousseau's thought, puts it, "Society heretofore has inflicted the deepest wounds on mankind; yet it is society too which through a transformation and reformation can and should heal those wounds" (*The Philosophy of the Enlightenment*, trans. F. C. A. Koelln and J. P. Pettegrove, p. 158).

A measure of the importance of both Rousseau and Herder in this regard for the development of German thought generally in the eighteenth century can be seen in the fact that the formulation Cassirer employs to characterize Rousseau's position, and which could equally well be applied to Herder, is also, in effect, Schiller's way of expressing the matter in his *Aesthetic Education* of 1795:

It was civilization itself which inflicted this wound upon modern man. Once the increase of empirical knowledge, and more exact modes of thought, made sharper divisions between the sciences inevitable, and once the increasingly complex machinery of State necessitated a more rigorous separation of ranks and occupations, then the inner unity of human nature was severed too, and a disastrous conflict set its harmonious powers at variance. . . . I will readily concede that, little as individuals might benefit from this fragmentation of their being, there was no other way in which the species as a whole could have progressed. . . . If the manifold potentialities in man were ever to be developed, there was no other way but to pit them against one another. This antagonism of faculties and functions is the great instrument of civilization—but it is only the instrument. . . . One-sidedness in the exercise of powers must, it is true, inevitably lead the individual into error; but the species as a whole to truth. . . . But can Man really be destined to miss himself for the sake of any purpose whatsoever? Should Nature, for the sake of her own purposes, be able to rob us of a completeness which Reason, for the sake of hers, enjoins upon us? It must, therefore, be wrong if the cultivation of individual powers involves the sacrifice of wholeness. Or rather, however much the law of Nature tends in that direction, it must be open to us to restore by means of a higher Art the totality of our nature which the arts themselves have destroyed. (*On the Aesthetic Education of Man,* trans. Wilkinson and Willoughby, pp. 33–43)

3. This apparent paradox anticipates a further aspect of the form of idealism that will later provide the philosophical foundation for much of German Romanticism. In this connection, see M. H. Abrams, *Natural Supernaturalism,* pp. 235–36.

4. Both 'palingenesis' and its German counterpart *Palingenese* (or *Palingenesie*) can refer either to this biological relationship between individual and species or to the spiritual doctrine of reincarnation. On the role in Herder's thought of a version of the concept of palingenesis in this latter sense, see Karl J. Fink, "Herder's Theory of Origins: From Poly- to Palingenesis," *JGH,* pp. 85–101.

5. See also the first section of *Another Philosophy of History for the Cultivation of the Human Race* (V, 480–501). It is important to note, however, that there is more than one side to Herder's use of this sort of genetic model. While it is frequently the case that, in the course of developing a given argument, he finds it an entirely apt and cogenial image, it can also happen that at a later stage in the same argument he will find it a hindrance and accordingly attempt to modify it. Such a shift occurs in the *Fragments* (see "Herder and the Possibility of Literature," pp. 43–45). The *Fragments,* in turn, are anticipated in this respect as well, as we shall see, by *On Diligence.*

6. In the eighteenth century, the meaning of *einfältig* is in transition. Adelung indicates that its basic connotations are still the neutral ones (with respect to evaluation) of simplicity and naturalness, as opposed to complication and ar-

tificiality. He also suggests, however, that the pejorative connotations of ignorance and simple-mindedness are gradually becoming the dominant ones (as
they have since done entirely), and he accordingly counsels the use of *einfach* to
express the older senses so as to avoid confusion (*Grammatisch-kritisches
Wörterbuch der Hochdeutschen Mundart,* I, 1697). Herder takes advantage of
this state of semantic flux in order to express with the term *einfältig* a simultaneously positive and negative notion.

7. See, for example, section V of the *Ode on Intimations of Immortality:*
"Our birth is but a sleep and a forgetting . . ." (v. 59ff.); also in this connection,
Shelley, *Ode to the West Wind,* in particular sections IV and V.

8. The idea that environment plays a major role in determining the character of society enters the stream of eighteenth-century thought principally, of
course, in the work of Montesquieu, with his *Spirit of the Laws* of 1748. Herder
never attempts to conceal the importance of Montesquieu for the formation of
his own ideas. At the same time, however, he is no less reluctant to criticize what
he regards as Montesquieu's reductionism, that is, his tendency to slight the
concrete particulars of phenomena for the sake of a uniform system of, in Cassirer's words, "ideal types" (*Philosophy of the Enlightenment,* p. 210). See, for
example, among the reflections noted down in connection with the *Travel Journal from the Year 1769 (Journal meiner Reise im Jahr 1769),* "Thoughts While
Reading Montesquieu" ("Gedanken bei Lesung Montesquieus"), IV, 464–67;
also *Another Philosophy of History,* V, 536–37. In this respect as well as others,
Montesquieu is, as Cassirer also notes, "a man of his time, a genuine thinker of
the Enlightenment" (Ibid., p. 214). Much of the tension in Herder's thought, in
contrast, stems precisely from the fact that, while part of him remains bound to
the Enlightenment, another part subjects it to critical examination and seeks to
move beyond it.

9. For a fuller discussion of the point, see "Herder and the Possibility of
Literature," pp. 45–48. A version of negative causation in this sense appears as
well in the *Ideas,* in the emphasis placed there on the importance for the development of human nature of the fact that we are able to stand and walk *upright.*
By thus having our hands freed from constant engagement elsewhere,
we acquire, in a literal sense, a free space, one undetermined in advance by
purely natural exigencies, in which we are then able to develop our distinctively
human capacities (XIII, 110 ff.).

10. Herder, *Briefe,* II, 209. See also Herder to Nicolai, July 2, 1772 (Ibid., p.
188).

11. *Herder,* p. 158.

12. The translation of *Faust* cited here is that of Walter Arndt. The manifold
links between Herder and Goethe's magnum opus are too obvious not to have
been noted repeatedly by scholars. Doubtless the most vigorously maintained as
well as the most ambitious statement of this sort is Günther Jacoby's *Herder als
Faust.*

13. See in this connection in particular Pindar's fourth Isthmian ode and his
fourteenth Olympian (*The Odes of Pindar,* pp. 138 and 42 respectively).

14. Cf. Gadamer, Nachwort, *Auch eine Philosophie der Geschichte:* "Even [the] loveliest youth of humanity is subject to the law of history. Every bit of progress is at the same time a loss" (p. 160).

15. The technique of developing a line of argument in such a way that the reader is inclined to suppose that it will continue in force without marked variation, and then abruptly changing direction—as with the "because, however" (*weil aber*) here—is an especially characteristic feature of Herder's style. He finds it particularly well-suited to establishing the sort of sustained tension between contrary poles that is throughout the goal of his writings. Precisely the same move occurs, for example, at a decisive point in the argument of the *Treatise on the Origin of Language* (see "Herder and the Possibility of Literature," pp. 47–48).

16. An echo of this theme, as well as a corresponding sense for the difficulties inherent in it, is apparent in Schiller's discussion of the "idyll" in *On Naive and Sentimental Poetry:*

. . . for the man who has once left the simplicity of nature and been given over to the dangerous guidance of his reason, it is of infinite importance that he be able again to view a pure instance of the legislation of nature and, in that true mirror, to purify himself again from the corruptions of culture (*Kunst*). There is, however, one consideration that greatly reduces the aesthetic value of such poetic works. Set *before the beginning of culture,* they exclude with its disadvantages at the same time all its advantages and find themselves by their very essence necessarily in conflict with it. They thus lead us *theoretically* backwards at the same time that they lead us *practically* forward and improve us. They unfortunately place *behind* us the goal *toward* which they should be leading us, and can therefore infuse in us only the sad feeling of loss, not, however, a cheerful one of hope. (*Sämtliche Werke,* V, 747)

Chapter 2

1. In his final speech (vv. 11559–86) Faust does, of course, evoke the prospect of a kind of synthesis of contentment on the one hand and continual change and development on the other. That synthesis, however, in the nature of the case, exists not actually but rather, in the sense of the term especially characteristic of the German tradition, *ideally,* that is, in the form of an endless project, and hence an infinite approach to the goal. As we shall see, the conclusion of *On Diligence* contemplates something not unlike this final Faustian vision.

2. French culture is surely the principal object of these animadversions. Especially for the young Herder, there is hardly a more characteristic feature of French society than the double entendre and the ulterior motive. See, for example, from the *Travel Journal:* "And, truly, in this character were to be seen the real hallmarks of the French, which are nothing but hypocrisy and debility" (IV, 440).

3. In this connection, we might also note the difference in grammatical voice

between "to determine" (*bestimmen*) in the transition paragraph and "enclosed" (*eingeschlossen*) at the beginning of part two.

4. The meaning of *vertauschen* was, moreover, in transition in Herder's time, and thus led to a situation analogous to the one seen earlier in connection with *einfältig*, with a corresponding possibility for multiple expression by means of a single term. The Grimms' *Deutsches Wörterbuch* says:

> The root-words *tausch, tauschen* . . . contain originally the concept of deceptive exchange and commerce; however, the oldest lexical as well as literary records of *vertauschen* . . . do not include the connotation of deceit. The sources indicate that this begins to appear only around 1700, at the same time as the sense of 'to make an exchange erroneously and unintentionally,' the sense that predominates in contemporary usage, while the former uses of the term have been replaced by *austauschen, eintauschen,* and *wechseln* (XII, 1. Abtl., p. 1867)

Among the examples given of the various uses of *vertauschen*, there is, interestingly enough, one from Herder (from a text of 1798), which seems to me to combine, in a way similar to *On Diligence,* more than one sense of the term: "We are what we are. Under certain circumstances, our character can decline; we can, however, never exchange (*vertauschen*) our nature" (XX, 343).

5. *Philosophisches Wörterbuch,* p. 45.

6. *Encyclopedia of Philosophy,* III, 436.

7. Fundamentally the same practice that we see here in connection with Herder's use of *vertauschen* and Hegel's of *aufheben* is also, of course, a technique favored by lyric poets in all generations, and not least by those of the Romantic period in Germany. We might consider in this regard (to mention but two examples) the different senses of *wandeln* in the first four strophes of Schiller's *Das Ideal und das Leben,* or the manifold connotations of the single word *Schauer* in Eichendorff's *Der Abend.*

8. The argument at this point, insofar as it identifies economic considerations as critical factors in the particular shape taken by a society's culture and institutions, is of a sort that is today often identified with Marxism. In noting a degree of anticipation of Marx by Herder in this respect, however, it may also be worth recalling that, in offering this sort of analysis, Herder, like Marx, is in turn carrying forward and developing a way of looking at man and society that can be traced back both to Montesquieu and, earlier still, to Vico.

9. We note that the text does not say that the rise of the "bond of learning" supplants the "chain" binding peoples together. The latter remains—Herder is under no illusions regarding the facts of political life in Europe (and its colonies) in the eighteenth century—and is, in fact, echoed in a secondary meaning of *Band* (in the expression *Band der Gelehrsamkeit*), namely *Fessel.* At the same time, however, the balance is preserved, for a secondary meaning of *Kette* (in *Kette der Völker*) in turn anticipates the more positive primary meaning of *Band.*

10. Lessing, in *Nathan der Weise,* enunciates a similar conception of the truth

as something that not so much *is* as it *becomes*. See Karl Guthke, *Gotthold Ephraim Lessing*, p. 70.

11. The passage from "colonies" to "nations" contains a very understated reminder that the Roman "tree" must in the meantime have fallen. Similarly, if we consider all the implications of the organic image as it has been constructed here, we see the same point made, in correspondingly subtle fashion, from another direction. The "shade" of that tree, in which the "seeds" in question were first planted, while initially a source of protection, would in time inevitably stunt the growth of new plants; hence the old tree must go. At the beginning of the second section of *Another Philosophy of History*, drawing on the same imagery as here in *On Diligence*, explicit reference is made to the Roman "tree" having been cut down (V, 514).

12. In these several respects, the image of the "wreath" combines important elements of two images that a generation later will be particularly favored by the German Romantics—the "tapestry" (*Teppich*) and the "garden."

13. This is, of course, a view with contemporary adherents as well. See, for example, the review of Robert Alter's 1985 study *The Art of Biblical Poetry* in *The Wilson Quarterly* (Spring 1986). Particularly apposite to a reading of Herder is the reviewer's comment that "Alter's underlying argument [is that] poetry is no mere ornamental aspect of the Bible; it is by poetry, and poetry alone, that the Bible's authors were able to 'realize' their mysterious, ever-compelling meaning" (p. 145).

14. Cf. Goethe's notion of *Weltliteratur*, as expressed, for example, in his *Einleitung* to Carlyle's biography of Schiller (XII, 364).

15. See Hans Dietrich Irmscher, Nachwort, *Abhandlung über den Ursprung der Sprache*, pp. 138–39.

16. It is worth noting that this proposal is, for the members of any given linguistic community, equivalent to a universal language scheme. Were the proposal to be carried out, the language of those individuals would become for them the sole medium of expression for the activities of all peoples at all times. We have, however, already seen something of why Herder rejects any such program, noting at the time that his reasons for that rejection would also become clearer still in the subsequent course of the exposition.

17. Essentially the same point, though somewhat clouded by the atmosphere of the gothic novels being discussed, is noted by Marshall Brown in "A Philosophical View of the Gothic Novel," p. 281.

18. Ludwig Wittgenstein, *Tractatus Logico-Philosophicus*, trans. D. F. Pears and B. F. McGuinness, 6.341. Interestingly, Wittgenstein's text shares with Herder's not only the image of a linguistic grid but also that of the "edifice" (*Gebäude*) it produces.

19. The expression "brilliance of their simplicity" (*Glanz der Einfalt*) combines, and so transforms, elements from parts one and two of the essay—the "simple contentment" (*einfältige Zufriedenheit*) of the Golden Age, from the opening paragraph, and the "glittering needs" (*glänzende Bedürfnisse*) of

the present age, referred to in the first paragraph of part two—and in so doing also imparts to the notion of *Glanz* the new evaluation that, as noted earlier, it would subsequently receive.

20. For his view of the "faculty psychology" of the eighteenth century, see, for example, the *Origin of Language*, V, 28–30.

21. The reference is to Homer, who is sometimes known as Maeonidēs "either because Maeonia was an ancient name for Lydia . . . where Homer was supposed to have been born, or because he was said to be the son of one Maeōn" (*The Oxford Companion to Classical Literature*, p. 256).

22. Herder's choice of verb to evoke the power of Pindar's Olympian odes— *verpflanzen*—has, of course, gestural significance for the argument. Coming immediately on the heels of a reference to transplantation in a negative sense— "these flowers of gracefulness lose everything when I transplant them against their nature"—it anticipates the way in which he will presently transform that notion into a positive one. This is, in fact, the second time in the essay that a reference to Pindar—arguably, perhaps, Herder's favorite poet, and certainly among those most frequently mentioned in his writings, always in terms of highest praise—has figured in such a movement from negative to positive (cf., part one, in connection with the Tower of Babel and the rise of Greek civilization).

23. If Herder can anywhere be accused of trying to represent the program for which he is arguing in *On Diligence* as easier to carry out than it really is, this is surely the place. Knowledge of "two or three languages" can obviously scarcely suffice to gain us access to all the myriad nations and cultures of the earth, past and present. One possible explanation for the discrepancy—though it is, to be sure, reaching a bit—would have him thinking here, in accordance with the title of the essay, only of the three "learned languages" of his time, Greek, Latin, and Hebrew (cf. his earlier reference to the "holy reliques of poetry and eloquence among the Romans, the Greeks, and especially in Scripture"). In that case, however, the allusion to French culture ("You, Louis, created through your Colbert . . .") immediately before the mention of "two or three languages" was not a particularly apt move. There seems, in the end, little alternative to regarding this passage as simply an instance of rhetorical exaggeration on Herder's part.

24. We noted earlier that *On Diligence* was originally composed and presented as a speech, only later being reworked for publication.

25. Interestingly, expressly on the "writings" of Demosthenes. Obviously, in view of the respective historical positions of the two, it could not have been otherwise. Still, the reference to writing in connection specifically with the influence of one orator on another is striking. In addition to reinforcing the overall theme of the present section regarding the need to "transplant" oneself—Cicero was, of course, able to read Demosthenes in the original—it makes a specific point similar to one seen in a passage from the *Fragments* cited earlier, that it is in principle possible to convey in writing essential qualities of at least one form of "the language of tone and gesture," namely oratory.

26. *Oxford Companion to Classical Literature*, p. 141.

27. Ibid., p. 101.

28. "Johann Gottfried Herder," *Deutsche Dichter des 18. Jahrhunderts,* p. 526 (cited hereafter as 'Irmscher').

29. Perhaps it is not too far-fetched to see even in the variations in spelling here—*goldne,* in the expression "Golden Age" in part one, appears now in the reference to "the golden century" as *güldne* (just as *Clima* ["environment"] in part one recurs as *Klima* in the final paragraph of part two)—a point of gestural significance for the argument, reinforcing the idea that the later stage, while analogous to the earlier, is nevertheless also something unique in its own right. These are, in any case, not inadvertent variations and so cannot be accounted for simply by the far-from-standardized orthography of German in Herder's time. A comparison of the original version of *On Diligence* with the published text reveals not only that *Clima* appears in the earlier version unchanged in both positions but also that the expressions *diese goldne Zeit* and *das güldne Jahrhundert* do not occur at all, in any form, in the *Schulrede.* Herder introduces them in precisely this form as part of his reworking of the text for publication at the same time that he changes *Clima* in part two to *Klima.* This seems to me to be somewhat more than coincidence ought to be called on to explain.

30. *Oxford Companion to Classical Literature,* p. 21.

31. That advance, however, had its price. The same source also notes:

As a result of [Alexander's] conquests the character of [Greek] civilization itself was changed. Greece sank into a secondary position; her city-states lost their independence, and with it the special atmosphere in which their literary masterpieces had been produced. (*Oxford Companion,* p. 21).

An acute awareness of the inevitable costs of progress is, as noted earlier, an especially important, and, for his time, especially distinguishing, mark of Herder's theory of historical development. The paragraph now under discussion contains in fact an implicit reminder of that point, in the form of a secondary resonance of the juxtaposition of Demosthenes and Cicero on the one hand and Alexander and Caesar on the other. The parallels between these figures are such that there can not only be constructed in overt terms the proportion:

Demosthenes : Cicero :   : Alexander : Caesar

It is at the same time possible to evoke, implicitly, a sense for another proportion, in which the parallel is not between relationships of influence and inspiration, but rather between similar forms of opposition:

Demosthenes : Alexander :   : Cicero : Caesar

Both Demosthenes and Cicero fought ultimately losing battles against a new order of things, the principal agents of which were, respectively, Alexander and Caesar. And, in fact, not only the institutions defended by the two orator-statesmen, but in the end their lives as well, were part of the price exacted by history for change, with Demosthenes committing suicide to avoid capture by his enemies and Cicero being assassinated.

32. That Caesar was, in addition, himself an author of distinction adds that much more to the image of the individual able to assume a leading role in both the political and the cultural sphere.

33. *Oxford Companion to Classical Literature*, p. 19.

34. Herder frequently uses *Säule* (or *Bildsäule*) when referring to statues of individuals. Cf. *Plastik*, VIII, 11–12, passim.

35. *Ion*, 533d–e.

36. Cf. Goethe, *Torquato Tasso*, I, iii, 549–51.

37. *Werke*, IX, 351–53. Cf. I, 436–37, on the poem *Mahomets-Gesang*.

38. Thus, two thirds of the way through the essay, Herder begins to tell us for the first time what its title actually means. As we have already had more than one occasion to note, in order for the essay to accomplish all that he intends that it should, its meaning—extending even to what is to be understood by individual terms—rather than being present in whole form from the beginning, must itself come into being in stages as the exposition unfolds. There will be more to say about this aspect of the essay's structure in the next chapter.

Chapter 3

1. In the preface to his monograph, Gillies describes Herder as "the fountain-head of German Romanticism" (p. v), and he later asserts flatly that "the whole of the Romantic movement in Germany is Herder's intellectual legacy" (p. 116). He also cites with approval Wilhelm Scherer's description of the Romantics as "'that group of German writers which developed and made the most of Herder's suggestions'" (p. 120). Gadamer maintains that "German Romanticism would not be conceivable without Herder; it is simply that his influence worked more covertly, beneath the surface" (Nachwort, *Auch eine Philosophie der Geschichte*, p. 176).

2. Cf. Lessing, *The Education of the Human Race*, §91: "Take your imperceptible course, eternal Providence! Only let me not doubt you on account of this imperceptibility.—Let me not doubt you, even if your course should seem to me to be going backward!—It is not true that the shortest line is always the straight one" (*Sämtliche Schriften*, XIII, 434).

3. The negative aspect of this point was anticipated at the beginning of part two. There, we recall, the interpretation of *Grenzen* as national borders was quickly seen to be an inadequate way in which to resolve the problem of determining the proper *Grenzen* of our efforts with respect to native and foreign languages. Again, however, the later stage of the exposition does not merely grow out of the earlier one. Precisely in so doing, it also, in reciprocal fashion, illuminates the full sense of that earlier stage. For it is only now, in light of the opening lines of part three, with their implicit recasting of the notion of *Grenzen* in accordance with the idea of mental activity, that we are able to see what specifically was wrong with the earlier geographical understanding of that notion.

4. See, for example, Brooks Otis's introduction to the work, pp. xii–xxi.

5. Cf. the conclusion of chapter 2, where we saw this subject-object duality anticipated.

6. Irmscher, p. 531.

7. Herder's position between Leibniz and Hegel is of considerable importance for the intellectual history of the eighteenth and early nineteenth centuries generally, and we shall have more to say about it in chapter 4.

8. The passage from the third collection of *Fragments* cited above (p. 103) continues:

> ... just as ... all our conceptions of beauty can be traced back to the first powerful impression, to which afterward the soul at once refers every image that it perceives ... so our native language is also ... for us an image of beauty. Just as a child compares all images and new concepts with what it already knows, so our mind automatically matches all languages and dialects to our native language. By cultivating that language in active use, the mind is subsequently able to penetrate all the more deeply into the uniqueness of different languages. By keeping that language constantly in view, when it discovers in foreign languages, here gaps and deserts, there riches and abundance, it grows fonder of the riches of its own, and, where possible, enriches the poverty of its own with foreign treasures. The native language is the guide without which, in the labyrinth of many foreign languages, it must go astray. It is the support that, on the vast ocean of foreign tongues, preserves it from sinking. It imparts to the otherwise confusing manifold of languages unity. (I, 400–01)

Much of what Herder here expresses in a passage from 1767, he had already worked out, as we have seen, in 1764 for the composition of *On Diligence,* and what we have not already seen of this, we will encounter as we continue to make our way through part three of the essay. (There is, in fact, still more from the *Fragments* that might be cited in this connection. The same section of that text to which we have twice had reference now also incorporates with almost no change the closing words of *On Diligence,* including the passage from Ewald von Kleist's poem *Der Frühling* of 1749, with which the essay concludes.)

In the immediately foregoing passage, we note, Herder clearly finds nothing amiss in passing without special comment from a consideration of aesthetic perception in particular to the way in which the mind apprehends other languages. He is able to do so because of the fundamental link that in his view obtains between language acquisition and use and the operations of the mind generally. The passage thus recalls a further point from *On Diligence,* seen earlier in part two, that for him there is no ultimate separation in human experience between its aesthetic and cognitive dimensions.

9. See, for example, Kantzenbach: "Kant's epistemological reflections were for Herder, in accordance with his talents and inclinations, hardly accessible. . . . He remained throughout his life a 'pre-critical' Kantian" (*Herder in Selbstzeugnissen und Bilddokumenten,* pp. 19–20).

10. *Critique of Pure Reason,* trans. Norman Kemp Smith, A 105. See also Robert Paul Wolff, *Kant's Theory of Mental Activity* (cited hereafter as 'Wolff'), pp. 120–34, especially p. 128. Among other things, Wolff speaks of the Kantian theory of the synthesizing activity of the mind as resolving "the paradox of a multiplicity which has unity without losing its diversity—the problem which the

ancients called the one and the many . . ." (p. 123; see also p. 126). In this light, the extent to which Herder anticipates Kant appears, of course, greater still.

11. Cf. the discussion in chapter 4 of Herder's notion of *Sichhineinfühlen,* from *Another Philosophy of History.*

In the preface to his translation of *Faust,* Bayard Taylor cites Goethe on the question of "alternative modes of translation":

> There are two maxims of translation . . . : the one requires that the author, of a foreign nation, be brought to us in such a manner that we may regard him as our own; the other, on the contrary, demands of us that we transport our-selves over to him, and adopt his situation, his mode of speaking, and his peculiarities. The advantages of both are sufficiently known to all instructed persons, from masterly examples. (pp. vi–vii)

Taylor goes on to ask, "Is it necessary, however, that there should always be this alternative? . . . [M]ay not both these 'maxims' be observed in the same trans-lation?" (p. vii). Taylor is speaking specifically of translation from German to English, and he regards that ideal as capable of realization in this case in virtue of the extremely close relationship between those two languages. For Herder, no such qualification is necessary. The twofold movement indicated here represents for him the ideal of linguistic assimilation in all cases.

12. Here, as elsewhere, Wilhelm von Humboldt draws directly on ideas intro-duced by Herder for the development of his own theories. For a striking illustra-tion of the extent of this influence, see the passages from Humboldt's "Über Religion," "Latium und Hellas," and *Über die Verschiedenheit des menschlichen Sprachbaues* cited by Marshall Brown in *The Shape of German Romanticism,* pp. 61–63.

13. Cf. Irmscher, p. 532, as well as the discussion in chapter 4 of Herder's conception of a "negative philosophy," as formulated in the second edition of the *Fragments.*

14. Cited in Frenzel, I, 203.

15. References this arcane are not ordinarily the stuff of Herder's style (as they are, for example, of Hamann's). He is, however, not entirely above an oc-casional flourish of this sort (cf. his earlier reference to "that Maeonic singer"). In the case at hand, I am unable to determine to my own satisfaction whether he means to parody a certain type of hypertrophic scholarship at the same time that he describes and criticizes it or has merely lapsed into a more or less gratui-tous display of erudition. However that may be, for the record, a "Masorete" is a scribe or scholar whose work concerns the Masora, a collection of notes and commentaries on the Hebrew Old Testament (and thus, by extension, anyone preoccupied with ancient and esoteric lore). "Priscian" (Priscianus Caesariensis, fl. ca. A.D. 500) was the author of an extensive Latin grammar, in which he drew heavily on classical authors for illustrations and which was widely known and consulted during the Middle Ages (see *Oxford Companion to Classical Litera-ture,* p. 345).

16. The passage, which Herder cites somewhat freely (cf. appendix, 11.205–

10), is, as mentioned earlier, from the poem *Der Frühling* by Ewald von Kleist. The corresponding section in Kleist's text runs as follows:

Zerstreute Heeren von Bienen
Durchsäuseln die Lüfte, sie fallen auf Klee und blühende Stauden
Und hängen glänzend daran wie Tau, vom Mondschein vergüldet;
Dann eilen sie wieder zur Stadt, die ihnen im Winkel des Angers
Der Landsmann aus Körben erbaut,—rechtschaffner Weltweisen Bildnis,
Die sich der Heimat entziehen, der Menschheit Gefilde durchsuchen
Und dann heimkehren zur Zelle, mit süßer Beute beladen,
Und liefern uns Honig der Weisheit.

(*Deutsche Dichtung im 18. Jahrhundert*, pp. 91–92)

17. For Dante, as Mark Musa notes, "the particular goal of mankind as a whole is to realize to the fullest all the potentialities of intellect (to have all the intellectual knowledge it is capable of having)" (Introduction, *Inferno*, p. 39).

18. *Hegel: Texts and Commentary*, p. 26.

19. Irmscher, p. 530.

20. Ibid., p. 540.

21. Ibid., p. 540.

22. Ibid., pp. 540–41. But see also *Letters for the Advancement of Humanity* (123d Letter, 1797), XVIII, 299–300.

23. Novalis, *Schriften*, I, 325.

Chapter 4

1. An important exception to this tendency is Thomas Seebohm's excellent "Der systematische Ort der Herderschen Metakritik," pp. 59–73.

2. A philosophical "turn," in this sense, is thus similar to what Thomas Kuhn, in his influential study *The Structure of Scientific Revolutions*, calls a "paradigm shift."

3. Wolff, pp. 320–21.

4. Ibid., p. 322.

5. Ibid., p. 62. Indeed, Wolff adds:

the argument which links the Table of Judgments . . . with the Table of Categories . . . is arbitrary in the extreme. No proof is given for the key statement that "[t]he same function which gives unity to the various representations *in a judgment* also gives unity to the mere synthesis of various representations *in an intuition* . . . " [B 104–5]. . . . This is probably the weakest link in the entire argument of the Analytic. (p. 77)

6. Richard Rorty, *The Linguistic Turn*, p. 3.

7. Nietzsche's fragment *On Truth and Falsehood* in an *Extra-Moral Sense* represents an important early stage in the development of one aspect of the direction of thought under consideration here.

8. See, in particular, the posthumously edited collection *On Certainty,* § 93–95, passim.

9. See, for example, "Vorbereitende Bemerkungen zu einer Theorie der kommunikativen Kompetenz" in Jürgen Habermas and Niklas Luhmann, *Theorie der Gesellschaft oder Sozialtechnologie,* pp. 101–41.

10. Irmscher, p. 532. In fact, again, as seen, the roots of this idea extend back at least to 1764, the year of *On Diligence.*

11. See, for example, *Grundzüge der Literatur- und Sprachwissenschaft,* I, 489; also *Princeton Encyclopedia of Poetry and Poetics,* p. 980.

12. Charles Morris, *Signs, Language, and Behavior,* pp. 217–18. Morris includes in the appendix to his study a useful section on "The History of Semiotic" (pp. 285–87). See also *Encyclopedia of Philosophy,* I, 32; V, 74; and VII, 348.

13. Franz von Kutschera, *Sprachphilosophie,* p. 31. In this connection, see also *Essential Works of Stoicism,* pp. 14–25, as well as the sections on Zeno and Chrysippus in Diogenes Laertius's *Lives of the Philosophers.*

14. Ibid., p. 343. Book III of Locke's *Essay Concerning Human Understanding* is devoted to language, and in the conclusion of the work he calls for a comprehensive study of "the science of signs" (see Copleston, V, 1, p. 114).

15. The bridge from the medical to the philosophical sphere here was conceivably provided by Locke himself, who was, of course, trained as a physician.

16. The passage is from a 1793 translation of Lavater's *Physiognomische Fragmente* (1775–78), iii, 27: "I shall now proceed to consider Medicinal Semeiotics, or the signs of Health and Sickness."

17. See, for example, Wellbery, *Lessing's Laocoon,* p. 4.

18. Lambert's conception of "Semiotic," for example, as described in the preface to his *Neues Organon,* exhibits nothing of either the range or the depth that Herder imparts to the notion.

19. Irmscher, p. 532.

20. Isaiah Berlin, *Vico and Herder,* pp. xviii–xix. See also Patrick H. Hutton, "The *New Science* of Giambattista Vico: Historicism in Its Relation to Poetics," pp. 359–67. The parallels between Vico's thought and Herder's are, in places, so striking that the question of possible influence could hardly be avoided even if one wanted to. That question remains, however, essentially an open one. There seems to be no positive evidence that Herder read the *New Science* itself before 1797, well after he had formulated his own views and written almost all his works. On the other hand, there are a number of indirect connections through which he could perhaps have acquired some knowledge of Vico's work earlier than this. For a discussion of the issue, see *Vico and Herder,* pp. 91, 147–48, and 193–94.

21. Ibid., p. xix.

22. See, for example, *Philosophical Investigations,* § 23.

23. Irmscher, p. 536.

24. See, for example, *Schriften zur Literatur,* pp. 8, 26–27, 45, 47–48, passim.

25. *Eine Duplik, Sämtliche Schriften,* XIII, 24.

26. See also *God, Several Conversations:* "The exploration of the truth has the greater allure; its possession may perhaps leave one sated and sluggish. . . . It is just this that gives value to a man's life" (XVI, 560). Cf. his apothegmatic dictum from the draft materials for the planned continuation of the *Ideas:* "Inertia is the original sin of mankind" (XIV, 567).

27. Irmscher, p. 536.

28. This is to be understood, of course, not as a distinct part of our being, but rather as "the entire arrangement of all human powers" (V, 28). As noted earlier, Herder categorically rejects the Cartesian dualism of mind and body.

29. The conception of the symbol alluded to here is common, in one form or another, to virtually all the Romantics. As a key element in his theory of "mediation," it assumes an especially prominent place in the poetry and philosophy of Novalis. In his essay *On Lessing,* Friedrich Schlegel writes, "The essence of higher art consists in the relationship to the whole. . . . through that whereby the appearance of the finite is everywhere brought into contact with the truth of the eternal and so dissolved into it: . . . through symbols . . ." (*Schriften zur Literatur,* p. 247). See also Goethe's famous definitions of symbol and allegory, in his *Maximen und Reflexionen* (XII, 471).

Bibliography

The best recent bibliography of literature on Herder is the one in Wulf Koepke's monograph. Other particularly useful sources are Robert Clark's study and the Günther-Volgina-Seifert bibliography compiled under the auspices of the *Nationale Forschungs- und Gedenkstätten der klassischen deutschen Literatur* in Weimar.

Abrams, M. H. *The Mirror and the Lamp: Romantic Theory and the Critical Tradition*. Oxford: University Press, 1953.

———. *Natural Supernaturalism: Tradition and Revolution in Romantic Literature*. N.Y.: Norton, 1971.

Adelung, Johann Christoph. *Grammatisch-kritisches Wörterbuch der Hochdeutschen Mundart*. 2d ed. Leipzig: Breitkopf und Compagnie, 1793. Hildesheim and N.Y.: 1970.

Archilochos. Ed. Max Treu. Munich: Ernst Heimeran Verlag, 1959.

Review of *The Art of Biblical Poetry*, by Robert Alter. *The Wilson Quarterly* 10 (1986): 144–45.

Augustins Soliloquien. With introduction and commentary by Hanspeter Müller. Bern: Benteli, 1954.

Barthes, Roland. *S/Z*. Trans. Richard Miller. N.Y.: Hill and Wang, 1974.

Berlin, Isaiah. *Vico and Herder: Two Studies in the History of Ideas*. London: Hogarth Press, 1976.

Blackall, Eric. "The Imprint of Herder's Linguistic Theory on His Early Prose Style." *PMLA* 76 (1961): 512–18.

Brown, Marshall. "A Philosophical View of the Gothic Novel." *Studies in Romanticism* 26 (1987): 275–301.

———. *The Shape of German Romanticism*. Ithaca and London: Cornell University Press, 1979.

Burnyeat, M. F. Review of *The Art and Thought of Heraclitus*, by Charles H.

Kahn. *The New York Review of Books* 29 (13 May 1982): 45–47.

Cassirer, Ernst. *Language and Myth*. Trans. Susan K. Langer. N.Y.: Dover, 1953.

———. *The Philosophy of the Enlightenment*. Trans. F. C. A. Koelln and J. P. Pettegrove. Princeton: University Press, 1951.

———. *The Philosophy of Symbolic Forms, Vol. I: Language*. Trans. Ralph Mannheim. New Haven and London: Yale University Press, 1955.

Clark, Robert T. *Herder: His Life and Thought*. Berkeley and Los Angeles: University of California Press, 1955.

Copleston, Frederick, S. J. *A History of Philosophy*. 9 vols. Garden City, N.Y.: Doubleday Image, 1962–77.

Culler, Jonathan. *On Deconstruction: Theory and Criticism after Structuralism*. Ithaca: Cornell University Press, 1982.

———. *The Pursuit of Signs: Semiotics, Literature, Deconstruction*. Ithaca: Cornell University Press, 1981.

Deutsche Dichtung im 18. Jahrhundert. Ed. Adalbert Elschenbroich. Munich: Hanser, 1960.

Diogenes Laertius. *Lives of the Philosophers*. Trans. and ed. A. Robert Caponigri. Chicago: Henry Regnery, 1969.

Dobbek, Wilhelm. "Die coincidentia oppositorum als Prinzip der Weltdeutung bei J. G. Herder wie in seiner Zeit." *Herder-Studien*. Ed. Walter Wiora. Würzburg: Holzner-Verlag, 1960. 16–47.

Eagleton, Terry. *Literary Theory: An Introduction*. Oxford: Blackwell, 1983.

Ellis, John M. *The Theory of Literary Criticism: A Logical Analysis*. Berkeley: University of California Press, 1974.

The Encyclopedia of Philosophy. Ed. Paul Edwards et al. 8 vols. New York: Macmillan and The Free Press; London: Collier Macmillan, 1967.

Essential Works of Stoicism. Ed. Moses Hadas. N.Y.: Bantam, 1961.

Frenzel, Herbert A. and Elisabeth. *Daten deutscher Dichtung: Chronologischer Abriß der deutschen Literaturgeschichte*. 9th ed. 2 vols. Munich: Deutscher Taschenbuch Verlag, 1973.

Fugate, Joe K. *The Psychological Basis of Herder's Aesthetics*. The Hague: Mouton, 1966.

Gadamer, Hans-Georg. Nachwort. *Auch eine Philosophie der Geschichte zur Bildung der Menschheit*. Frankfurt: Suhrkamp, 1967.

———. *Volk und Geschichte im Denken Herders*. Frankfurt: Klostermann, 1942.

Gillies, Alexander. *Herder*. Oxford: Blackwell, 1945.

Goethe, Johann Wolfgang von. *Faust*. Trans. Walter Arndt. Ed. Cyrus Hamlin. N.Y.: Norton, 1976.

———. *Werke*. Ed. Erich Trunz. 14 vols. Hamburg: Wegner Verlag, 1955.

Grimm, Jacob and Wilhelm. *Deutsches Wörterbuch*. Leipzig: S. Hirzel, 1854ff.

Grundzüge der Literatur- und Sprachwissenschaft. Ed. H. L. Arnold and Volker Sinemus. 4th ed. Munich: Deutscher Taschenbuch Verlag, 1976.

Guthke, Karl S. *Gotthold Ephraim Lessing.* 3d ed. Stuttgart: Metzler, 1979.
Habermas, Jürgen, and Niklas Luhmann. *Theorie der Gesellschaft oder Sozial-technologie.* Frankfurt: Suhrkamp, 1971.
Haym, Rudolf. *Herder, nach seinem Leben und seinen Werken dargestellt.* 2 vols. Berlin: Weidmannsche Buchhandlung, 1880 and 1885.
Hegel: Texts and Commentary. Trans. and ed. Walter Kaufmann. Garden City, N.Y.: Doubleday Anchor, 1966.
Heidegger, Martin. *Being and Time.* Trans. John Macquarrie and Edward Robinson. N.Y.: Harper and Row, 1962.
———. *An Introduction to Metaphysics.* Trans. Ralph Mannheim. Garden City, N.Y.: Doubleday Anchor, 1961.
———. *Poetry, Language, Thought.* Trans. and intro. Albert Hofstadter. N.Y.: Harper and Row, 1971.
Heintel, Erich. Introduction. *Johann Gottfried Herder: Sprachphilosophische Schriften.* Hamburg: Felix Meiner, 1960.
Herder-Bibliographie. Eds. Gottfried Günther, Albina A. Volgina, and Siegfried Seifert. Berlin and Weimar: Aufbau-Verlag, 1978.
Herder, Johann Gottfried. *Briefe: Gesamtausgabe 1763–1803.* Ed. W. Dobbek and G. Arnold. Weimar: Hermann Böhlaus Nachfolger, 1977.
———. *Frühe Schriften 1764–1772.* Ed. Ulrich Gaier. Frankfurt: Deutscher Klassiker Verlag, 1985.
———. *Sämtliche Werke.* Ed. Bernhard Suphan. 33 vols. Berlin: Weidmannsche Buchhandlung, 1877–1913. Hildesheim: Georg Olms Verlagsbuchhandlung, 1967.
———. *Werke.* Ed. Wolfgang Pross. 2 vols. Munich: Hanser, 1984 and 1987.
Herder-Kolloquium 1978: Referate und Diskussionsbeiträge. Ed. Walter Dietze. Weimar: Hermann Böhlaus Nachfolger, 1980.
Hutton, Patrick H. "The *New Science* of Giambattista Vico: Historicism in Its Relation to Poetics." *The Journal of Aesthetics and Art Criticism* 30 (1972): 359–67.
Irmscher, Hans Dietrich. "Beobachtungen zur Funktion der Analogie im Denken Herders." *Deutsche Vierteljahrsschrift für Literaturwissenschaft und Geistesgeschichte* 55 (1981): 64–97.
———. "Grundzüge der Hermeneutik Herders." *Bückeburger Gespräche über Johann Gottfried Herder 1971.* Ed. Johann Gottfried Maltusch. Bückeburg: Schaumburger Studien, 1973. 17–57.
———. "Herder über das Verhältnis des Autors zum Publikum." *Bückeburger Gespräche über Johann Gottfried Herder 1975.* Ed. Johann Gottfried Maltusch. Rinteln: C. Bösendahl, 1976. 99–138.
———. "Johann Gottfried Herder." *Deutsche Dichter des 18. Jahrhunderts.* Ed. Benno von Wiese. Berlin: Erich Schmidt, 1977. 524–50.
———. Nachwort. *Abhandlung über den Ursprung der Sprache.* Stuttgart: Reclam, 1966.
Jacoby, Günther. *Herder als Faust.* Leipzig: Felix Meiner, 1911.

Joda, Robert, S. J. "Nicholas of Cusa: Precursor of Humanism." *The Renaissance and Reformation in Germany: An Introduction*. Ed. Gerhart Hoffmeister. N.Y.: Frederick Ungar, 1977. 33–49.

Johann Gottfried Herder: Innovator Through the Ages. Ed. Wulf Koepke. Bonn: Bouvier Verlag, 1982.

Johann Gottfried von Herder's Lebensbild. Ed. Emil Gottfried von Herder. Erlangen: Verlag von Theodor Bläsing, 1846.

Kahn, Charles H. *The Art and Thought of Heraclitus: An Edition of the Fragments with Translation and Commentary*. Cambridge: Cambridge University Press, 1979.

Kant, Immanuel. *Critique of Pure Reason*. Trans. Norman Kemp Smith. N.Y.: St. Martin's Press; Toronto: Macmillan, 1965.

Kantzenbach, Friedrich Wilhelm. *Johann Gottfried Herder in Selbstzeugnissen und Bilddokumenten*. Reinbek: Rowohlt, 1970.

Koepke, Wulf. *Johann Gottfried Herder*. Boston: Twayne, 1987.

Kuhn, Thomas. *The Structure of Scientific Revolutions*. Chicago and London: University of Chicago Press, 1962.

Kutschera, Franz von. *Sprachphilosophie*. Munich: W. Fink, 1971.

Lambert, J. H. *Philosophische Schriften*. Ed. Hans-Werner Arndt. Hildesheim: Georg Olms Verlagsbuchhandlung, 1965.

Lessing, G. E. *Sämtliche Schriften*. Ed. Karl Lachmann and Franz Muncker. 3d ed. Stuttgart: G. J. Göschen'sche Verlagshandlung, 1886–95. Leipzig: 1897–1902.

Lévi-Strauss, Claude. *The Savage Mind*. Chicago: University of Chicago Press, 1966.

Lovejoy, Arthur O. "Herder and the Enlightenment Philosophy of History." *Essays in the History of Ideas*. Baltimore: Johns Hopkins University Press, 1948. 166–82.

Markwardt, Bruno. *Herders Kritische Wälder*. Leipzig: Quelle und Meyer, 1925.

Martini, Fritz. *Deutsche Literaturgeschichte: Von den Anfängen bis zur Gegenwart*. 17th ed. Stuttgart: Kröner, 1977.

Mayo, Robert S. *Herder and the Beginnings of Comparative Literature*. Chapel Hill: University of North Carolina Press, 1969.

Morris, Charles. *Signs, Language, and Behavior*. N.Y.: Prentice-Hall, 1946.

Musa, Mark. Introduction. *The Divine Comedy, Vol. I: Inferno*. Harmondsworth: Penguin, 1984.

Nietzsche, Friedrich. "Über Warheit und Lüge im außermoralischen Sinn." *Werke*. Ed. Karl Schlechta. 3 vols. Munich: Hanser, 1956. III, 309–22.

Novalis. *Schriften*. Ed. Paul Kluckhohn and Richard Samuel. 2d ed. Stuttgart: Kohlhammer, 1960.

Otis, Brooks. Introduction. *The Aeneid*. Indianapolis: Bobbs-Merrill, 1965.

The Oxford Companion to Classical Literature. Ed. Sir Paul Harvey. Oxford: Clarendon, 1966.

Philosophisches Wörterbuch. Ed. Georgi Schischkoff. 19th ed. Stuttgart: Kröner, 1974.

The Odes of Pindar. Trans. Richmond Lattimore. Chicago: University of Chicago Press, 1947. Chicago: Phoenix Books, 1959.

The Collected Dialogues of Plato. Ed. Edith Hamilton and Huntington Cairns. Princeton: University Press, 1961.

Princeton Encyclopedia of Poetry and Poetics. Ed. Alex Preminger. Princeton: University Press, 1974.

The Quest for the New Science: Language and Thought in Eighteenth-Century Science. Ed. Karl J. Fink and James W. Marchand. Carbondale and Edwardsville: Southern Illinois University Press; London and Amsterdam: Feffer and Simons, Inc., 1979.

Reisiger, Hans. *Johann Gottfried Herder: Sein Leben in Selbstzeugnissen, Briefen und Bericht.* Berlin: Propyläen-Verlag, 1942.

Rorty, Richard, ed. Introduction. *The Linguistic Turn: Recent Essays in Philosophical Method.* Chicago and London: University of Chicago Press, 1967.

Rousseau, Jean Jacques. *The Social Contract and Discourses.* Trans. and intro. G. D. H. Cole. N.Y.: E. P. Dutton; London: J. M. Dent, 1950.

Ruprecht, Erich. "Vernunft und Sprache: Zum Grundproblem der Sprachphilosophie Johann Gottfried Herders." *Bückeburger Gespräche über Johann Gottfried Herder 1975.* Ed. Johann Gottfried Maltusch. Rinteln: C. Bösendahl, 1976. 58–84.

Sanner, Rolf. *Der Prosastil in den Jugendschriften Herders als Ausdruck seiner Geistesart.* Triltsch: Zentral-Verlag für Dissertationen, 1960.

Sapir, Edward. "Herder's 'Ursprung der Sprache.'" *Modern Philology* 5 (1907): 109–42.

Schick, Edgar B. *Metaphorical Organicism in Herder's Early Works: A Study of the Relationship of Herder's Literary Idiom to His World-View.* The Hague: Mouton, 1971.

Schiller, Friedrich. *On the Aesthetic Education of Man, in a Series of Letters.* Trans. and ed. E. M. Wilkinson and L. A. Willoughby. Oxford: Clarendon, 1967.

———. *Sämtliche Werke.* Ed. G. Fricke and H. G. Göpfert. Munich: Hanser, 1959.

Schlegel, Friedrich. *Schriften zur Literatur.* Ed. Wolfdietrich Rasch. Munich: Deutscher Taschenbuch Verlag, 1972.

Schnebli-Schwegler, Brigitte. *Johann Gottfried Herders Abhandlung über den Ursprung der Sprache und die Goethe-Zeit.* Winterthur: P. G. Keller, 1965.

Seebohm, Thomas M. "Der systematische Ort der Herderschen Metakritik." *Kant-Studien* 63 (1972): 59–73.

Sowell, Thomas. *A Conflict of Visions: Ideological Origins of Political Struggles.* N.Y.: William Morrow, 1987.

Staiger, Emil. "Der neue Geist in Herders Frühwerk." *Jahrbuch der deutschen Schillergesellschaft* 6 (1962): 66–106.

Steiner, George. *After Babel: Aspects of Language and Translation.* N.Y. and London: Oxford University Press, 1975.

Taylor, Bayard, trans. Preface. *Faust.* N.Y.: Modern Library, 1930.

Walzel, Oskar. *German Romanticism.* Trans. Alina Elise Lursky. N.Y.: G. P. Putnam's Sons, 1932. N.Y.: Capricorn Books, 1966.

Wellbery, David. *Lessing's Laocoon: Semiotics and Aesthetics in the Age of Reason.* Cambridge: University Press, 1984.

Whorf, Benjamin Lee. *Language, Thought, and Reality: Selected Writings of Benjamin Lee Whorf.* Ed. John B. Carroll. Cambridge: MIT Press, 1956.

Williams, T. C. "Herder's 'Essay on Language' as the Cameo Model of the 'Critique of Pure Reason.'" *Proceedings of the Ottawa Congress on Kant in the Anglo-American and Continental Traditions 1974.* Ed. P. Laberge et al. Ottawa: University of Ottawa Press, 1976. 199–212.

Winckelmann, Johann Joachim. *Sämtliche Werke.* 12 vols. Osnabrück: Otto Zeller, 1965.

Wittgenstein, Ludwig. *The Blue and Brown Books.* N.Y.: Harper and Row, 1958.

———. *Philosophical Investigations.* Trans. G. E. M. Anscombe, 3d ed. N.Y.: Macmillan, 1968.

———. *Tractatus Logico-Philosophicus.* Trans. D. F. Pears and B. F. McGuinness. London: Routledge and Kegan Paul; N.Y.: The Humanities Press, 1972.

———. *Über Gewißheit / On Certainty.* Ed. G. E. M. Anscombe and G. H. von Wright. N.Y.: Harper and Row, 1972.

Wolff, Robert Paul. *Kant's Theory of Mental Activity: A Commentary on the Transcendental Analytic of the* Critique of Pure Reason. Gloucester, Mass.: Peter Smith, 1973.

Index